FAITH
TO LIVE BY

A PRACTICAL GUIDE

FAITH
TO LIVE BY

A PRACTICAL GUIDE

PAUL BARKER

EVERY NATION
R E S O U R C E S

This book is dedicated to my wife Aleta. Her love and encouragement have been my constant inspiration for forty amazing years.

FAITH TO LIVE BY

A Practical Guide
Copyright © 2012–2019 by Paul Barker
All rights reserved

Published By Every Nation Resources
P.O. Box 1787
Brentwood, TN 37024-1787 USA

ISBN: 9781073321773

Printed in the Unites States of America

Contents

Preface

What Is Different about This Book?

There are at least five answers to the question: "What is different about this book?"

First, it is comprehensive. I have attempted to examine the essential issues as thoroughly as possible. No doubt I have missed some topics and overemphasized or underemphasized others. But I have done my best to make this series as complete as possible.

Second, it is sequential. I have attempted to cover all the related topics in the order that will best help you understand and grow in your faith.

Third, it is rooted in history. I am a fervent student of Church history, and I am passionate that we draw from the collective resources of two thousand years of men and women who walked with God and learned from him. I believe that any topic as vast as faith should be understood in the light of what the Church has said about it throughout her long history.

Fourth, it is a composite of different perspectives. My views on faith have been shaped by a diversity of ministries. I don't necessarily agree with everything each one of them says, but I have learned something about faith from all of them. One piece of a 1,000-piece jigsaw puzzle can never represent the whole picture. Even a section of the puzzle cannot. But when you put all the pieces together, you see the picture clearly.

Fifth, it is an interactive study for individual or small group ministry. Each chapter has a memory verse, discussion questions (designed especially for small groups), and suggested assignments. There is also a wealth of varied material in the appendices.

My objective in writing this series was to create a definitive workbook that would provide you with everything you needed to develop a dynamic life of faith. May God bless you as you read and study his word. As Charles Spurgeon said,

> Faith is the mightiest of the mighty. It is the monarch of the realms of the mind. There is no being superior to its strength, no creature that will not bow to its divine prowess. The lack of faith makes a person despicable; it shrivels him up so small that he might live in a nutshell. Give him faith, and he is a leviathan that can dive into the depths of the sea, a giant who takes nations and crumbles them in his hand, vanquishing hosts with his sword and gathering up all the crowns as his own. There is nothing like faith. Give us faith and we can do all things.[1]

---

[1]   Charles H. Spurgeon, *The Triumph of Faith in a Believer's Life* (Lynnwood, WA: Emerald Books, 1994), 128.

01

The Life of Faith

Building Foundations That Will Last

Introduction

Faith did not come easy for me. I do not know why it took me so long to understand what I now see are very simple concepts, but it did. And if it weren't for God's mercy and grace, I would still be confused.

I don't think I am alone. I am not sure of all the reasons, but faith seems to be a challenging concept to comprehend for many people. Maybe because it goes against our natural mind, or maybe because the enemy fights so hard to keep it from us—but for whatever reasons, it is a difficult concept for many of us to grasp.

In this chapter, I want to share with you my journey of faith. Hopefully it will encourage you, and it may even shed light on your own journey. It will certainly give you a context for everything else I say in this book.

My Journey of Faith

I was born and raised in metro St. Louis, Missouri, the home of the St. Louis Cardinals, Ted Drewes Frozen Custard, and Imo's Pizza—all St. Louis institutions. My parents were devout Roman Catholics. They worked hard to make sure I received a good Catholic education, and I am very grateful for the foundation it laid in my life. Even when I tried desperately to escape from God during my agnostic college years, I knew deep within that there was a God. I knew I could never escape from him, no matter how hard I tried. C. S. Lewis once said in reference to his conversion:

> You must picture me alone in that room in Magdalen College, night after night, feeling the steady, unrelenting approach of Him whom I so earnestly desired not to meet.[2]

I felt a lot like that.

I went to university at Southeast Missouri State in Cape Girardeau. My hobby was attending dorm Bible studies and disrupting them with pseudo-intellectual questions (heavy emphasis on the word "pseudo"). I usually left triumphant because, unfortunately, I knew my stuff better than most of the Christians did.

But there was one guy on my dorm floor who refused to argue with me. His name was Mike, and he was from a small farming community about an hour north of the university. He was a sincere and unpretentious fellow, and I don't think he felt qualified to engage me at an intellectual level. Whenever I would present my latest argument (usually something I learned that day in psychology or biology class), he would listen patiently to my rant. When I finished, he would look me in the eyes and say, "I don't know how to answer your questions. But I do know that Jesus loves you, and he wants to change your life."

How I hated when he said that! I could deal with intellectual rebuttals—I welcomed them—but I had no answer to that response.

Eventually, as my personal life deteriorated, God's love broke through my hardened exterior and I surrendered my life to him. That day was Sunday, July 11, 1976.

Soon after my conversion, I became aware that God was calling me to serve him in vocational ministry. Three years later, I graduated from university and married my wife, the former Aleta Mueller. Two days after our honeymoon, we started our life in ministry together.

Within a few months, we received a call from a pastor in Knoxville, Tennessee, who led a small campus church at the University of Tennessee. He was in need of an associate pastor and wanted us to work with him. So on Thursday, October 25, 1979, we packed everything we owned into our 1974 Audi Fox and drove to Knoxville. Fifteen months later, the pastor

---

[2] C. S. Lewis, *Surprised by Joy: The Shape of My Early Life* (United Kingdom: Geoffrey Bles, 1955), Chap. XIV.

left to start a new campus church in Arizona. He left me in charge. I was twenty-four years old and clueless.

I did the best I could leading that small church, but it was an uphill climb. I did not really know what I was doing, so I tried every new thing that came my way. But month after month, our membership declined. I was losing the battle, and I was not even sure why.

Every two months, I attended meetings with the other leaders in the organization of campus churches I belonged to, and each time, I heard testimonies of successful activities that had worked in other locations. So every two months, I instituted a new program. Still, nothing ever worked out very well.

But in the fall of 1981 while attending one of these meetings, I heard what I was sure must be the key to my success. A pastor talked about conducting a full month of outreach meetings at his campus. Many were saved, he testified, and great things had happened. Certainly this was the answer to my dilemma.

That November, I staged a full month of outreach activities. We had special speakers, music groups, evangelistic films, street preaching, and everything else you could imagine. But after one month of daily meetings, I had very little to show for my labor. The church members were tired and disgruntled. The budget was in disarray. And there were no salvations. (Two people did raise their hands at the end of one meeting, but as soon as we dismissed the service they ran from the building as fast as they could. I did not feel that it was right to count them among the converted.)

That was it for me. I had done everything I knew and nothing had worked. I seriously considered resigning from the ministry. Maybe I could drive a truck, sell shoes, or do something that was actually helping someone. I was sure that what I was doing in ministry was not helping anyone.

I did not know it at the time, but I later realized that God was orchestrating the details of my life to get my attention. My circumstances had put me in a listening frame of mind. I was desperate and open to anything God had to say. Solomon said, "One who is full loathes honey, but to one who is hungry everything bitter is sweet" (Proverbs 27:7). I was very hungry and ready for anything God had for me.

About this time, someone gave me a set of audio tapes by a well-known preacher. I had heard this man speak before, and frankly, I was not impressed. He was a businessman who had built a successful faith-teaching ministry.

His message was simple and straightforward, but his delivery style was one of a kind. I had a university degree in English, and he did things to the English language that I don't think had ever been done before. I found it difficult to listen to him and even harder to believe God was speaking to me through him.

But though his grammar was questionable, his faith was not. I listened continuously to these tapes for weeks. Gradually, I noticed a change taking place. Not on the outside—people were still staying away from our church in crowds—but on the inside. Something was changing in me. I was beginning to think differently. A new image was growing on the inside. I started to see that I could experience success and fruitfulness because of God's Word and his promises.

In the first week of January 1982, I read the following verse from Luke's Gospel:

> And when he had finished speaking, he said to Simon, "Put out into the deep and let down your nets for a catch." And Simon answered, "Master, we toiled all night and took nothing! But at your word I will let down the nets." LUKE 5:4–5

Like the disciples, I had toiled hard at fishing, and like them, I had caught nothing. But Jesus was asking me to put my nets out again. So I scheduled another outreach meeting. This time, I was not as ambitious as before (three days instead of a month), and this time I was acting on his Word—not on someone else's good idea. I saturated the event with prayer and strong faith confessions and waited expectantly to see what God would do.

When the meetings were over, seventy-five students had given their lives to Christ. I know that is not a large amount when compared with big campaigns, but considering my situation, it was a landslide! Through this experience, I began to understand many of the essential biblical concepts of how faith works. And the truth I learned became part of the foundations I would continue to build my life on.

Having the right foundations is crucial to a successful Christian life. Before we begin an examination of what faith is and how it works, let's look at some principles related to foundations.

Foundations

The Merriam-Webster dictionary defines a foundation as the "basis upon which something stands or is supported." A foundation bears the weight of what is built upon it. Foundations are the core principles our lives are built upon. The Bible has a lot to say about foundations and their importance in our lives.

If we do not get our foundations right at the beginning, the repair costs can be very high at the end.

It took nearly two hundred years to construct the 190-foot freestanding bell tower next to the cathedral in Pisa, Italy. But because of a weak foundation, the tower began leaning even before construction finished in 1372. By 1988, the tower was leaning fifteen feet off-center. They closed it to tourists for fear that it would topple. However, after ten years and $27 million in repairs, workers finally succeeded in anchoring the tower with a permanent 13.5-foot lean. (No tourist would pay to see the "Straight Tower of Pisa!")

Anything built on faulty foundations will collapse in time. If we do not build a proper foundation of faith, we will look like the Leaning Tower of Pisa, and it will take a huge investment and a lot of time to set things right. That is why the Psalmist said:

If the foundations are destroyed, what can the righteous do? PSALM 11:3

The higher we want our lives to go, the deeper we have to build our foundations.

The main building on the campus of Philippine Christian College in Cabanatuan City, Philippines, was built in 1964 with three stories. The foundation the builders laid was sufficient for a building of that size. But a few years later, the school added three additional stories without making any changes to the foundation. In 1990, a 7.8 earthquake hit the region, killing 1,600 people. All of the three-story buildings in Cabanatuan City were untouched. The only building to collapse was the six-story school building, killing over 100 students and staff. The earthquake proved that the foundation was strong enough for three floors, but inadequate for six.

What dreams and aspirations do you have for your life? The larger the dream, the deeper the foundations must be.

Coach Mike Krzyzewski of the Duke University Blue Devils is widely recognized as one of the most successful college basketball coaches in the history of the NCAA. In thirty-nine years at Duke, he won five NCAA Championships, twelve ACC Championships, eleven National Coach of the Year honors, two Hall of Fame awards, and five Olympic gold medals. Perhaps the most impressive statistic of all is that only two of his athletes have failed to graduate. Coach K said recently about his accomplishments: "It has been my goal to give Duke a program that will last." Enduring programs require deep foundations, and so do enduring lives.

Building strong foundations is hard work.

I learned this the hard way several years ago when I decided that the deck in our backyard had to go. It was old, small, and beginning to rot. I am not very handy when it comes to home projects, so I hired a friend of mine who taught industrial education at one of the local high schools. His job was to design and oversee the project and mine was to provide the labor, with the help of my two teenage sons. The first task he assigned us was to destroy the old deck. That was demanding work because it was the middle of the summer with temperatures near 100°F every day. But since there is something deeply satisfying about swinging a sledge hammer and destroying stuff, I almost enjoyed it. However, I was not prepared for what was to come.

The next task was to dig foundations for the new structure. Because my plans called for a much larger deck than before (it would seat around thirty-five people), I had to dig four deep holes to support it. That was excruciatingly painful. (I kept thinking about that fellow in Luke 16 who was too ashamed to beg and too weak to dig. I could identify with him completely.)

After the holes were finally dug, we made an appointment with the city building inspector. If the holes met the proper standards, he would issue me a permit, and I could proceed with the project. If not, I would have to try again until I got it right. I prayed for a merciful inspector, but instead I got "Legalistic Larry." He measured the holes with care and then delivered the bad news: "Unacceptable." I would have to keep digging.

I did get the holes right the second time. We poured the foundations and finally started the interesting work of constructing the deck. But I learned a valuable lesson in the process: laying foundations is hard work. That is why many people start the work of laying strong faith foundations, but do not finish. The work is too demanding and the pressure is too great. In the end, they take the path of least resistance.

The challenges of life reveal how strong our foundations are.

> When the whirlwind passes, the wicked is no more, but the righteous has an everlasting foundation. **PROVERBS 10:25 NASB**

Storms happen to everyone, and some get swept away by them, but those with a strong foundation are unmoved. Jesus never promised us storm-free lives. Storms will come; we cannot avoid them. However, we can storm-proof our lives by building them upon a solid foundation of obedience to God's Word.

> Everyone then who hears these words of mine and does them will be like a wise man who built his house on the rock. And the rain fell, and the floods came, and the winds blew and beat on that house, but it did not fall, because it had been founded on the rock. And everyone who hears these words of mine and does not do them will be like a foolish man who built his house on the sand. And the rain fell, and the floods came, and the winds blew and beat against that house, and it fell, and great was the fall of it. **MATTHEW 7:24–27**

Paul confirmed these words of Jesus when he told the Corinthians, "the fire will test what sort of work each one has done" (1 Corinthians 3:13).

At 6:34 p.m. local time on Sunday, August 8, 1993, an 8.1 earthquake shook the island of Guam. It lasted for a full minute. Buildings swayed, vehicles moved, and the ground opened up in places. The quake damaged structures and lifelines throughout the island. However, not a single building collapsed, and injuries were generally minor. Why was there such minimal damage? Because nearly all the buildings in Guam were built with a solid foundation of reinforced concrete. Construction in Guam is governed by the Uniform Building Code,[3] the same standard used in most seismically active regions of North America. The officials in Guam knew an earthquake was coming, they just did not know when it would come or how big it would be. But they were prepared with stringent building codes to endure earthquakes of any size.

---

[3] In 2000, the Uniform Building Code was replaced by the upgraded International Building Code.

No one likes strict codes during the building phase. They are expensive and time-consuming. But everyone likes strict building codes when their structures are still standing after a severe earthquake. In the same way, we generally do not like building our personal lives according to strict codes—especially when there are so many shortcuts available and so many people who seem to be taking them. But when the earthquakes and the storms of life sweep by with no damage, we are glad we built our lives upon the solid foundation of faith in God!

And we can be sure that difficult days are coming. As Paul told Timothy, "But understand this, that in the last days there will come times of difficulty" (2 Timothy 3:1).

Timothy must have thought that difficult times had already begun! Paul had left him with the "wild beasts" and false teachers in Ephesus,[4] and he was obviously struggling under the pressure. Timothy was not always a confident man (1 Corinthians 16:10). He seemed to have struggled with fear and intimidation (2 Timothy 1:7–8). Paul regularly urged him to be strong (2 Timothy 2:1, 3) because he knew Timothy had strong foundations.

> But as for you, continue in what you have learned and have firmly believed, knowing from whom you learned it and how from childhood you have been acquainted with the sacred writings, which are able to make you wise for salvation through faith in Christ Jesus.
> **2 TIMOTHY 3:14–15**

Strong foundations were first laid in Timothy's life by his mother and grandmother. Jewish boys began their formal study of the Scriptures at age five.[5] Timothy's mother and grandmother had no doubt begun teaching him at an even earlier age because the Greek word Paul used, *brephos*, refers to a newborn child or an infant.[6]

Paul then reinforced those foundations and built upon them when he began to disciple Timothy.

---

[4]   1 Corinthians 15:32; 1 Timothy 1:3

[5]   Don Closson, "Hermeneutics: Accurately Interpreting Bible Teaching," Probe For Answers, Updated May 27, 1994 https://probe.org/hermeneutics. Copyright 2019 Probe Ministries.

[6]   It can also refer to an unborn child still in the womb. It is possible that Lois and Eunice started speaking the Word to Timothy before he was even born.

Now you followed my teaching, conduct, purpose, faith, patience, love, perseverance. **2 TIMOTHY 3:10 NASB**

Conclusion

Timothy survived and even conquered in difficult times because of the strong foundations in his life. The author of Hebrews tells us that faith towards God is one of the essential qualities necessary to a strong foundation.

> Therefore let us leave the elementary doctrine of Christ and go on to maturity, not laying again a foundation of repentance from dead works and of faith toward God. **HEBREWS 6:1**

One of the primary goals of this series is to help you build those strong foundations of faith.

In this chapter, we have examined the importance of laying strong foundations of faith in our lives. But why, exactly, is faith so important? We will examine that question in the next chapters.

Application

Discuss

1. What are the main challenges you have with the message of faith? Why? What can you do to face these challenges and begin to overcome them?

2. How strong is the foundation of faith in your life? Has there ever been a time in your life when it was stronger? If so, what has changed, and what can you do to get back to the place where you were?

3. How big are your dreams, and is your current foundation of faith strong enough to sustain them? If not, what areas need the most work, and what should you do about them?

_____

_____

_____

4. When was the last time you received bad news? How did you respond? What did God show you about the foundations of your faith through that response? What is the key to a proper response the next time bad news comes?

_____

_____

_____

Act

Do a personal inventory of your foundations. Take thirty minutes and ask the Holy Spirit to reveal to you what areas of your foundations need the most work. Ask him for a plan to strengthen your foundations.

Meditate

If the foundations are destroyed, what can the righteous do? PSALM 11:3

02

The Importance of Faith: Why We Need It

Part One

Introduction

One of the first words my children learned to say when they were growing up was "why." There were periods during their early development when it seemed like that was the most important word in their vocabulary.

"Why is ice slippery?"

"Why don't cats cry?"

"Why is broccoli green?"

Answering all the "why" questions was often exasperating. But it helped me greatly when I finally realized that my children were only responding to the desire that God had put in them to understand and know the reasons and causes behind the things around them. God has put this same desire to understand and know "why" in all our hearts. It is a part of the image of God in man—what theologians call the *Imago Dei*.[7]

So it seems like a good idea to start this book on the life of faith by asking and answering the all-important "why" questions: Why do I need faith? Why is faith so important?

In this chapter and the next, we will look at eight reasons we need faith.

---

[7] *Imago Dei* is Latin for "The Image of God."

We need faith to please God.

When I fell in love with my wife many years ago, I was determined to find out all the things that pleased her. As I discovered them, I set about making it my life's ambition to practice them with all my heart. I haven't always succeeded in our forty years together, but I am still pursuing that course.

In the same way, when a man loves God, he should make it his ambition to find out all the things that please him. When he discovers those things, he should make it his life's purpose to practice them with all his heart. The New Testament concurs with this sentiment and states several things about pleasing God:

- Ephesians 5:10 exhorts us to *try to discern what is pleasing to the Lord*.
- 2 Corinthians 5:9 exhorts us to *make it our aim to please him*.
- 1 Thessalonians 2:4 exhorts us to not *please man but God, who tests our hearts*.
- Colossians 1:10 exhorts us to live that we may be *fully pleasing to him*.

But of all the things it tells us about pleasing the Lord, the one thing that stands out the most is *how* we please him.

And without faith it is impossible to please him, for whoever would draw near to God must believe that he exists and that he rewards those who seek him. **HEBREWS 11:6**

Marvin Vincent, in his book, *Word Studies of the Epistles*, explains that the word "please" is used in the aorist tense in this verse. The aorist tense provides an emphasis that is lost in the English translations. The emphasis is that you cannot please God *at all or in any way* without faith. Vincent also says that this word is stated in such a way as to be a universal proposition without reference to any particular time frame. In other words, faith has always been the only way to please God in ages past, and it will always be the only way to please God in the ages to come.[8]

There are many benefits to a life of faith: health, prosperity, peace, victory over sin, etc., and we will discuss each of these as this book progresses. However, the one benefit that seems to be talked about the least is in fact the most important: faith is how we please God. Much of the discussion about faith centers on our individual needs and what is in it for us. That

[8]   Marvin R. Vincent, *Vincent's Word Studies* (Hendrickson Pub, 1985), Vol. 4.

is the human side of faith, and it certainly is valid. But the primary focus of faith should be on God and what it means to him. This should be the central focus of our lives. As Martin Luther said in his commentary on the book of Galatians:

In my heart reigns this one article, faith in my dear Lord Christ, the beginning, middle, and end of whatever spiritual and divine thoughts I may have, whether by day or by night.[9]

If pleasing God is our goal and life's ambition, then it is futile to do things we *think* please him but in reality do not.

When I was eleven, I gave my dad a book for his birthday, and it was called *The True Story of Bonnie and Clyde*. There was one problem, however: he did not want the book—I did. To this day, I can still remember the look on his face when I gave it to him. He obviously had no interest in the book and was not especially pleased with my present. He was polite and appreciative, but he knew I had bought it for him because I wanted to read it myself. I had not taken the time to discover what would please him. I simply did what I thought would please him—primarily because I knew it would please me.

Fortunately, God is very clear about what pleases him; there is no mystery. Faith is what pleases God. Bible reading, prayer, giving, evangelism—these are all important things, but they do not please God, at least not without faith. Therefore, since it is *impossible* to please God without faith, we should make the pursuit of faith our number one goal.

The author of Hebrews uses the word "impossible" in two other places. In 6:18, he tells us it is impossible for God to lie. In 10:4, he tells us it is impossible for the blood of bulls to take away sin. We can conclude from his other uses of the word "impossible" that it is just as likely to please God without faith as it is for the blood of bulls to take away sin or for God to lie. In other words, it is not going to happen.

The author uses another form of the word "please" later in the text:

But my righteous one shall live by faith, and if he shrinks back, my soul has no pleasure in him. But we are not of those who shrink back and are destroyed, but of those who have faith and preserve their souls. **HEBREWS 10:38-39**

---

[9]   Martin Luther, *Commentary on Galatians* (CreateSpace Independent Publishing Platform, 2012).

God has no pleasure in those who shrink from faith into fear or cowardice. Adam Clarke said in his commentary on this passage:

> The word *hupostellein* [the Greek word translated "shrinks back"] signifies, not only to draw back, but to slink away and hide through fear. As cowards are hated by all men, so those that slink away from Christ and His cause, for fear of persecution or secular loss, in them God cannot delight.[10]

There are serious consequences to not living by faith and this is a sobering reality. The writer of Hebrews states clearly that if we will not live by faith, the only other option is to shrink back—not just to some neutral state—but to destruction. The Greek word translated "destruction" here is *apoleia*, which means ruin or loss, either physically, spiritually, or eternally. This same word is also used in other sobering passages in the New Testament.

> Enter by the narrow gate. For the gate is wide and the way is easy that leads to destruction [*apoleia*], and those who enter by it are many. MATTHEW 7:13

> But those who desire to be rich fall into temptation, into a snare, into many senseless and harmful desires that plunge people into ruin and destruction. [*apoleia*]. 1 TIMOTHY 6:9

> As he does in all his letters when he speaks in them of these matters. There are some things in them that are hard to understand, which the ignorant and unstable twist to their own destruction [*apoleia*]. 2 PETER 3:16

Clearly, destruction is not a very appealing option. Therefore, just as we are determined to please God with our faith, we should be determined not to displease him through our unbelief.

We need to live by faith.

Faith is not something we do occasionally. It is how we live every moment of every day. Every activity of life, from the most mundane to the most

---

[10] Clarke, Adam. "Commentary on Hebrews 10: The Adam Clarke Commentary." https://www.studylight.org/commentaries/acc/hebrews-10.html. 1832.

sublime, should be done by faith. This is the sentiment reflected in one of the most quoted Old Testament verses by the apostolic writers:

The righteous shall live by faith. ROMANS 1:17

I once heard someone say that many believers have a "spare tire faith." The spare tire is that thing you hope you never have to use, and, in case of emergency, you hope you remember how to use it.

I am not mechanically inclined. I know very little about cars and how they work, but I do know how to change a flat tire. At least I thought I did. A few years ago, I had a tire blowout on the interstate. I was forced to the median strip and had to change my tire while hundreds of cars flew by me at great speeds. I suppose I must have choked under the pressure because after changing the tire, I found that the car would not move. Exasperated, I called a friend to help me. When he arrived, he gave me the embarrassing news that I had put the tire on backwards.

Faith in the New Testament is not a spare tire. We don't just use it during emergencies. The Scriptures exhort us to live by faith—not to occasionally dabble in faith. That means that we do everything by faith—not just spiritual things like prayer and Bible reading—but everything! We wake up by faith, we brush our teeth by faith, we drive to work by faith, and we get parking spaces by faith. We do everything by faith!

For example, my son used to play basketball. Several years ago as a high school freshman, he struggled with his free-throw shooting. His percentage was around 55 percent—not bad for a freshman—but he knew he could do better. I once commented after a game during the middle of his season that his free-throw shooting had improved noticeably in his last six games. When we calculated his percentage during those games, it was almost 85 percent. He said, "Dad, before I shoot, I quote the Bible verse: 'I am more than a conqueror through Christ who makes me strong.'" I said, "Son, I don't think that is one verse, but actually two verses stuck together." He responded, "I don't care, Dad; it's working."

The moral of the story is: faith works in the everyday experiences of life.

Often the message of faith is associated exclusively with healing and prosperity. Healing and prosperity are important (especially when you are sick and broke!) and both require faith; but faith is for much more than that. It is for every area of life.

To understand healing and prosperity, let's look at it as part of the preseason. In the preseason, a team prepares for the regular season, and as part of this preparation, they play preseason games. These games are real contests played against real opponents. But the main purpose of the contest is to prepare the athletes for the more difficult upcoming games and to help them discover their weaknesses and strengths. Then, when the regular season begins, they will be more effective.

I don't want to minimize the importance of healing and prosperity because a significant part of this book is dedicated to these two topics. But learning how to believe God in these areas can help train us on how faith works. We can then use those lessons to live by faith in every area of life.

If you read through the list of men and women of faith in Hebrews 11, you will see that faith for them was a lot more than just healing and prosperity—they did everything by faith. Here is a partial list of the things they did by faith and the things we should do by faith:

- By faith we understand. (v. 3)
- By faith we give. (v. 4)
- By faith we prepare. (v. 7)
- By faith we obey. (v. 8)
- By faith we receive. (v. 11)
- By faith we sacrifice. (v. 17)
- By faith we refuse. (v. 24)
- By faith we leave. (v. 27)
- By faith we conquer. (v. 33)
- By faith we obtain. (v. 33)

This is also reflected in Paul's statement: "For we walk by faith, not by sight" (2 Corinthians 5:7). The original Greek word translated "walk" in this verse is *peripateo*. It is a word that referred to both the physical act of walking and to a person's general conduct or behavior. When Paul said "we walk by faith and not by sight," he meant that we should conduct our lives by the information received from the Word of God and not from our five physical senses. This does not mean we ignore the physical world, but that we reference a higher source of information for decisions. We conduct every aspect of our lives by faith.

What does it mean to live by faith? It means that we are continually aware of the promises of God and how they affect our current situation.

We need faith to do God's work.

The Apostle John records a time when the crowds followed Jesus to Capernaum. They asked him,

> Then they said to him, "What must we do, to be doing the works of God?" Jesus answered them, "This is the work of God, that you believe in him whom he has sent." JOHN 6:28-29

What is the work God requires? What is the mandate he has given us? To *go and make disciples of all nations* (Matthew 28:19). We need to understand that Jesus did not say, "Go and make disciples *in* all nations;" rather, he said, "Go and make disciples *of* all nations." This is the Great Commission, and in order to accomplish it, we must first make disciples in a nation, and then proceed to make the whole nation a disciple. Or, to say it another way, evangelism and discipleship is followed by the transformation of society. Therefore, God's work includes world evangelism *and* world transformation. These are not just difficult tasks—they are impossible. But what is impossible with men is possible with God (Luke 18:27). The Great Commission is going to take faith.

When my children were young, they used to watch a cartoon called *Pinky and the Brain*. The show featured the antics of two mice, a smart one (the Brain) and a dumb one (Pinky). Every episode began the same way. Pinky would ask the Brain, "Gee, Brain, what do you want to do tonight?" And the Brain would always reply, "The same thing we do every night, Pinky—try to take over the world." This is the Great Commission in cartoon version. Our job description is to try to take over the world every day, one disciple at a time. This mandate can only be accomplished through pursuing a life of faith.

Another reason we need faith to do God's work is because every time we increase our effectiveness in accomplishing the Great Commission, we should anticipate a new attack from our enemy. As someone once said, "For every new level, there is a new devil." The resistance increases as we set about to engage the enemy and take ground for the kingdom of God. There are many well-meaning believers that have set out on this path and ended up shipwrecked.

> This charge I entrust to you, Timothy, my child, in accordance with the prophecies previously made about you, that by them you may wage the good warfare, holding faith and a good conscience. By rejecting this, some have made shipwreck of their faith. 1 TIMOTHY 1:18-19

What did these shipwrecked believers reject? They rejected the good fight of faith. They rejected the need to hold on to faith. They rejected a good conscience. As a result, the enemy overwhelmed them and they ended up shipwrecked.

There is not much demonic pressure on people who are only looking to do the "Minimum Daily Requirement" of the Christian life. Those who are just looking to get by and not cause too much difficulty for the enemy are rarely troubled by intense demonic pressure. But the minute they decide to do something for God, they can anticipate that the enemy will attack them like a roaring lion.

I am sure there must be a special battalion of demons assigned to Christians who are determined to do their part in fulfilling the Great Commission. Because of this, our faith must be strong when we set about to do God's work, and we must continue to increase it or we may end up shipwrecked.

We can only do God's work with God's power, and faith allows us to access the power God has made available to us. Charles Spurgeon said:

> Many grand deeds have also been born of faith, for faith works wonders. Faith in its natural form is an all-prevailing force.[11]

When asked to explain where the power came from to heal a man crippled from birth who was now walking and jumping and praising God, Peter said:

> And his name—by faith in his name—has made this man strong whom you see and know, and the faith that is through Jesus has given the man this perfect health in the presence of you all. ACTS 3:16

How much power is available to us by faith? Paul tells us in Ephesians 1:19 when he talks about:

... his ***incomparably great power*** for us who believe. NIV

... the ***exceeding greatness of His power*** toward us who believe. NKJV

... the ***surpassing greatness of His power*** toward us who believe. NASB

... the ***incredible greatness of God's power*** for us who believe him. NLT

... the ***immeasurable greatness of his power*** in us who believe. RSV

... the ***unlimited greatness of his power*** ... GOD'S WORD

This power, Paul said, is "according to the working of ***His*** mighty power which He worked in Christ when He raised Him from the dead" (Ephesians

---

[11] Charles H.Spurgeon, *The Triumph of Faith in a Believer's Life* (Lynnwood, WA: Emerald Books, 1994), 36.

1:19–20 NASB). The phrase "according to" is a preposition that means "as determined by." Think of it as a credit limit. If you own a credit card and your credit limit is $1,000, then your spending power is according to, or determined by, that limit. Once you reach your limit, you have no more spending power. Paul is stating that the credit limit on the power available to us is the amount of power released in the resurrection of Christ. How much power is that? Lawrence Richards said concerning this passage:

> Paul piled up synonyms to emphasize the overwhelming nature of that divine power which had its fullest demonstration in the raising of Christ from the dead. The words Paul used include *dynamis* (intrinsic capability), *energeia* (effective power in action), *kratos* (power exerted to control and overcome resistance), and ischys (the vital power inherent in life).[12]

Paul says it another way later in the same letter:

> Now to him who is able to do far more abundantly than all that we ask or think, according to the power at work within us . . . **EPHESIANS 3:20**

Again, Paul piled on synonyms to express the immensity of this power that is available to us by faith. Paul started with the root word, *perissos*, which means "superabundant in quantity, excessive, and beyond measure." It is the same word Luke used to describe the twelve leftover baskets after Jesus multiplied the loaves and fishes. It is a word that means more than enough of whatever you need. For example, if you needed $20,000 to buy a car and you had $21,000, you would have *perissos*—more than enough.

Paul then added the prefix, *huper*, which means "over, beyond, and above." (We get our word *hyper* from this word.) When you add this prefix, the word now means "way beyond; superabundant in quantity." Continuing our example, you now have $100,000 to buy that $20,000 car.

But Paul is not finished. He tacked on the prefix, *ek*, which intensifies whatever word it goes with. Then, for good measure, he threw in an extra *huper* just in case we didn't get his meaning! Using our metaphor, we now have all the money in the world to buy our $20,000 car.

The exciting thing about this power is where it is located. It is within us. Colossians 1:29 says:

---

[12]   Lawrence O. Richards, *The Victor Bible Background Commentary* (Wheaton, IL: Victor Books, 1994).

To this end I strenuously contend with all the energy Christ so *powerfully works in me*. NIV

For this purpose also I labor, striving according to his power, which *mightily works within me*. NASB

That's why I work and struggle so hard, depending on *Christ's mighty power that works within me*. NLT

For which also I labour, striving according to *his working that is working in me* in power. YLT

For this I toil, striving with all *the energy* which *He mightily inspires within me*. RSV

This is my work, and I can do it only because *Christ's mighty energy is at work within me*. TLB

To do this, I work and struggle, using *Christ's great strength that works so powerfully in me*. NCV

The evangelist Smith Wigglesworth[13] said, "The life that is in me is a thousand times bigger than I am outside."[14] God's great power working in us by faith enables us to accomplish his work.

Conclusion

In this chapter, we have begun to examine why faith is so important. In the next chapter, we will continue to look at other reasons we need faith.

---

[13] Smith Wigglesworth was an English preacher who was very influential in the early history of Pentecostalism. He is sometimes referred to as the "Apostle of Faith."

[14] Smith Wigglesworth, *Every Increasing Faith*, (Whitaker House, 2001), 95.

Application

Discuss

1. Why should you understand the reasons you need faith? What practical difference will it make in your life?

   _____

   _____

   _____

2. Give an example from a recent experience where you saw one of these three reasons why you need faith working in your life. What did you learn through that experience?

   _____

   _____

   _____

3. Which of the three reasons discussed in this chapter stood out to you as needing the most attention in your life? Why? What action step can you take to apply what you have understood?

   _____

   _____

   _____

4. Do you have a spare tire mentality about faith? If so, why? What can you do to change your attitude and adopt the biblical attitude to live by faith?

   _____

   _____

   _____

5. Have you ever been guilty of trying to do God's work in your own natural strength? Why was it difficult to have faith in God's power in that situation? What did you learn about yourself through that situation, and what can you do to make sure it doesn't happen again?

_____

_____

_____

Act

Read Paul's letter to the Galatians and look for every reference to the words *faith*, *believe*, and *believing*. (There are more than twenty.) Record the thoughts and insights God will give you.

Meditate

And without faith it is impossible to please him, for whoever would draw near to God must believe that he exists and that he rewards those who seek him. HEBREWS 11:6

The Importance of Faith: Why We Need It

Part Two

Introduction

In the last chapter, we said that faith was important because we need it to please God, we need it to live by, and we need it to do God's work. In this chapter, we will conclude with five more reasons we need faith.

We need faith to experience God's righteousness.

One of the most startling revelations of the New Testament is that God has made us righteous. This righteousness is found in Christ and is appropriated by faith.

> . . . the righteousness of God through faith in Jesus Christ for all who believe. **ROMANS 3:22**

Righteousness is the result of the judicial act of God, by which he pardons the sins of all those who believe in Christ, and accounts us as righteous in the eyes of the law. The law is not relaxed or set aside, but declared fulfilled in the strictest and most complete sense.[15] This is the act of a judge and not of a sovereign. A sovereign can set aside the law, but a judge cannot.

---

[15] Adapted from: M.G. Eaton, *The Illustrated Bible Dictionary* (Wheaton, IL: Tyndale House, 1980), 401.

This is an important idea to understand. Righteousness is not God acting as a sovereign and setting aside the law to arbitrarily pardon guilty sinners. Righteousness is God acting like a judge and declaring that in Christ we have perfectly fulfilled all the requirements of the divine law.

A ruler may sovereignly declare a guilty man innocent, but a judge cannot. For example, before leaving office, former American president Bill Clinton exercised the sovereign right of his office and granted a presidential pardon to Marc Rich, a billionaire commodities trader who had fled to Switzerland to avoid prosecution for income tax evasion and racketeering. The presidential pardon was not based on the merit or righteousness of Marc Rich. He was still guilty, but the law was set aside. This was the act of a sovereign, not a judge.

By contrast, the doctrine of righteousness declares that the law of God was fulfilled completely and totally in Christ. Therefore, the benefits God confers upon us are now based on our perfect obedience to the law—an obedience fulfilled in Christ and not in ourselves. God treats us as if we have perfectly obeyed every detail of his law—because we have—in Christ. Righteousness is not forgiveness. It is a declaration that we have perfectly satisfied the law forever.

This righteousness is the righteousness of Christ, and it is received by faith. This was the official doctrine of the Protestant Reformation. Martin Luther said:

> Jesus Christ died for our sins and was raised again for our justification. He alone is the Lamb of God who takes away the sins of the world. All have sinned and are justified freely, without their own works and merits, by His grace, through the redemption that is in Christ Jesus, in His blood. It is clear and certain that this faith alone justifies us.[16]

Not only was this the official doctrine of the Reformation, but it has also been the informed view of the Church throughout history. Here are the words of some of the early Fathers of the Church:

---

[16]   Martin Luther, *The Smalcald Articles* (Dodo Press, 2009), Part Two, Article One.

Justin Martyr: "O unexpected benefit [. . .] that the righteousness of One should justify many transgressors."[17]

John Chrysostom: "He made a righteous Person to be sin, in order that he might make sinners righteous [. . .] it is the righteousness of God, when we are justified, not by works [. . .] but by grace, where all sin is made to vanish away."[18]

Augustine of Hippo: "We conclude that a man is not justified by the precepts of a holy life, but by faith in Jesus Christ."[19]

The person who is made righteous is entitled to all the advantages and rewards arising from perfect obedience to the law.

I look to the Old Testament and I see certain blessings attached to the Covenant of Works and I say to myself by faith, "Those blessings are mine, for I have kept the Covenant of Works in the Person of my Covenant Head and Surety. Every blessing which is promised to perfect obedience belongs to me, since I present to God a perfect obedience in the Person of my great Representative, the Lord Jesus Christ."[20]

The sole condition for this righteousness is faith. Faith is called a condition because it is the instrument by which the soul appropriates Christ and his righteousness. Therefore, faith does not earn righteousness, it receives it.[21]

Paul spent a good part of his ministry combating men who insisted that faith in Christ was insufficient and that adherence to the Mosaic Law was required for right standing with God. These men followed after Paul's ministry and tried to force his converts to receive circumcision. There was

---

[17] Reprinted from *Ante-Nicene Fathers, Vol. 1, The Epistle of Mathetes to Diognetus*. Translated by Alexander Roberts and James Donaldson. Edited by Alexander Roberts, James Donaldson, and A. Cleveland Coxe. (Buffalo, NY: Christian Literature Publishing Co., 1885), Revised and edited for New Advent by Kevin Knight. http://www.newadvent.org/fathers/0101.htm.

[18] Paul Tarazi, *The Chrysostom Bible—2 Corinthians: A Commentary* (OCABS Press, 2013), 57–63.

[19] St. Augustine, *On the Spirit and the Letter* (Beloved Publishing, LLC, 2014), Chapter XXII.

[20] Charles Spurgeon, *The Tenderness of Jesus* (June 8, 1890), Sermon #2148.

[21] See Note 12.

no other group that incited Paul to anger like these people. He warned the Galatians and the Philippians:

> But even if we or an angel from heaven should preach to you a gospel contrary to the one we preached to you, let him be accursed. As we have said before, so now I say again: If anyone is preaching to you a gospel contrary to the one you received, let him be accursed.[22]
> GALATIANS 1:8–9

> Look out for the dogs, look out for the evildoers, look out for those who mutilate the flesh. PHILIPPIANS 3:2

Those people stirred righteous indignation so fervently in Paul because they vilified the work of Christ through their assertion that righteousness came through human effort. Paul knew that if anyone could qualify for righteousness based on works and not on faith, it was certainly himself. He had an impressive religious resumé.

Though I myself have reason for confidence in the flesh also. If anyone else thinks he has reason for confidence in the flesh, I have more: circumcised on the eighth day, of the people of Israel, of the tribe of Benjamin, a Hebrew of Hebrews; as to the law, a Pharisee; as to zeal, a persecutor of the church; as to righteousness under the law, blameless (Philippians 3:4–6).

Paul makes an astonishing statement when he says he was blameless by the standards of legalistic righteousness. Who else could make such a claim? But was Paul's righteousness enough? Hardly.

> Indeed, I count everything as loss because of the surpassing worth of knowing Christ Jesus my Lord. For his sake I have suffered the loss of all things and count them as rubbish, in order that I may gain Christ and be found in him, not having a righteousness of my own that comes from the law, but that which comes through faith in Christ, the righteousness from God that depends on faith.
> PHILIPPIANS 3:8–9

Paul uses an interesting Greek word in this passage, one that is sanitized considerably by most English translators: *skubalon*. The NIV translates it as

---

[22] "Paul knows that he has just made what some will consider an extreme statement [in verse 8]. But it is a deliberate one and not mere excitement. He will stand by it to the end. He calls down a curse on any one who proclaims a gospel to them contrary to that which they had received from him" (Word Pictures in the New Testament).

"rubbish," but the literal translation should be "the excrement of dogs." This is a fitting description of all our attempts to achieve the righteousness of God through our own efforts!

This same spiritual force that energized Paul's enemies to seek righteousness through human effort is still with us today. It effectively seduced many of the Galatians. Paul wrote:

> You unthinking and foolish Galatians! Who has put the evil eye on you? Have you taken leave of your senses? For it's obvious that you no longer have the crucified Jesus in clear focus. His sacrifice on the cross was certainly set before you clearly enough. Let me ask you this one question: How did your new life begin? Was it by working your heads off to please God? Or was it by hearing and believing God's Message? Are you going to continue this insanity? For only crazy people would think they could complete by their own efforts what was begun by God. If you weren't smart enough or strong enough or good enough to start it, how do you suppose you could finish it? GALATIANS 3:1-3[23]

It has also seduced many throughout the history of the Church. Why is this tendency to establish our own righteousness so strong within us? Because it feeds our ego. If righteousness is a free gift and there's nothing we can do to earn it, then we are more flawed than we would like to believe. And as long as we still have a human ego, we will have to fight this force.

The following example may help illustrate my point. Imagine these two different scenarios:

John Q. Christian's alarm clock goes off at 4:30 on a Saturday morning, and he immediately rises to start his devotions. After two hours of prayer and two more hours of Bible reading, he rushes off to the local shopping mall for a day of witnessing. By 10:30 that evening, he has led three people to Christ. He finally arrives home about midnight and falls immediately into bed.

Jim Q. Christian's alarm clock goes off at around noon on Saturday. Instead of rousing from his slumber, he hits the snooze button seventeen consecutive times—aiming for a world record! He finally forces himself from the bed to his couch, snagging the television remote in the process.

---

[23] This passage is a conflation of several versions.

He spends the rest of the day in mindless channel surfing, interspersed with large quantities of pizza, ice cream, and soda. About midnight, as his friend John is returning from his labors at the mall, Jim crawls back to his room and falls immediately to sleep.

Which one of these scenarios reflects a biblical righteousness?

The answer is, of course, we do not know. Righteousness is not based on works, it is based on faith, and we do not know which of these men was exercising faith. It is possible to do all the things John did for the express purpose of gaining God's favor. It is also possible to do all the things Jim did by faith. This usually comes as a great shock to the average Christian, but it is true.

Certainly God wants us to live right and walk in holiness—but holiness should be the fruit of a life of faith and not the motivation for God's favor. This is often difficult to grasp because so much of our lives are oriented around performance. Do well at work and you receive a performance bonus. Do well in school and you get high grades. Do well on the team and you get the trophies. This seems normal, reasonable, and fair. But it is not the way of the kingdom of God.

However, God does not want sloppiness or our second best. He is a God of excellence. Everything he does is always first-class, and we should reflect that in every area of our lives. But it should come out of a heart of gratitude and faith and a desire to honor God—not because we feel we can gain his approval if we do.

We need faith to give glory to God.

> No unbelief made him waver concerning the promise of God, but he grew strong in his faith as *he gave glory* to God, fully convinced that God was able to do what he had promised. ROMANS 4:20–21

Abraham's strong faith gave glory to God. John Piper, describing this passage, said:

Giving glory to God does not mean adding to God's glory. It does not mean improving upon God's gloriousness. It *does* mean calling attention to God's glory, showing it to be what it really is. Giving glory to God is making Him look real good.[24]

I remember being at the public swimming pool as a small boy many years ago in my hometown of Collinsville, Illinois. My family and friends were there and everyone seemed to be having a great time. But I was hesitant to enter the water, since it looked so cold, scary, and a little too deep. My father, standing in water barely up to his waist, beckoned me to jump. He stood a little back from the edge and promised to catch me.

At that moment, I had the opportunity to make my dad look really good. If I immediately and unhesitantly jumped in, all those around us would see that he was a trustworthy father. My faith in him would make him look good. It would, in a very small way, give glory to him. But if I hesitated, balked, or demonstrated excessive reluctance, it might have the opposite effect. It might make him look bad. My unwillingness to believe him would reflect one of three possible reasons:[25]

Possibility #1: I thought he was unable to catch me; he wasn't strong enough.

Possibility #2: I thought he was untrustworthy and wouldn't catch me; he didn't love me enough.

Possibility #3: I thought he had a bad plan that wouldn't work; he wasn't smart enough.

When we demonstrate strong faith in God, we make him look powerful. We declare to the world that he is strong enough to do what he said he would do. When we demonstrate strong faith in God, we make him look loving. We declare to the world that he cares enough to meet our every need. When we demonstrate strong faith in God, we make him look wise. We declare to the world that his plans are always the best plans.

---

[24] John Piper, "In Hope Against Hope for the Glory of God," Desiring God, updated September 26, 1999, https://www.desiringgod.org/messages/faith-in-hope-against-hope-for-the-glory-of-god.

[25] This story really happened to me, but the application of it was inspired by John Piper's sermon. For those who care, I did eventually jump.

The more impossible the promise of God looks, the better he looks when it finally comes to pass. When Abraham chose to believe God in the midst of impossible circumstances, he made God look very good. That is what it means to give glory to God.

We need faith for answered prayers.

Jesus has given us some magnificent and astonishing promises concerning prayer. All effective prayer is based on a strong confidence in these promises.

And *whatever* you ask in prayer, you will receive, if you have faith. MATTHEW 21:22

Whatever you ask in my name, this I will do, that the Father may be glorified in the Son. If you ask me *anything* in my name, I will do it. JOHN 14:13–14

I say to you, *whatever* you ask of the Father in my name, he will give it to you [. . .] Ask and *you will receive*, that your joy may be full. JOHN 16:23–24

And this is the confidence that we have toward him, that if we ask *anything* according to his will he hears us. And if we know that he hears us in *whatever* we ask, we know that we have the requests that we have asked of him. 1 JOHN 5:14–15[26]

All things for which you pray and ask, believe that you have received them, and they shall be granted you. MARK 11:24 NASB[27]

These verses make it plain that faith is an essential prerequisite for answered prayer.

---

[26] Sometimes people get hung up over this question, "But how do we know his will?" The answer is simple: Whatever is recorded in Scripture is his will. "For no matter how many promises God has made, they are 'Yes' in Christ" (2 Corinthians 1:20). To have the confidence John is referring to, find Bible verses that address the thing that you want. Meditate on them until you are convinced that they are for you.

[27] *The New Commentary on the Whole Bible* says about this verse, "The verb for receive in the Greek is an aorist tense, which is always used to describe an accomplished past action. The Christian whose faith is of that quality that he believes he has 'already received it' when he asks, will discover that he actually has it. This verse sets out how far a person's faith can reach."

George Müller[28] recounted an incident he experienced while crossing the Atlantic on an ocean liner to an engagement in Quebec, Canada. During the voyage, the ship encountered a severe fog that threatened to delay its arrival. Müller found the captain and said, "I must be in Quebec on Saturday." When the captain told him his request was impossible, Müller responded, "I have never missed an engagement in fifty-seven years; let us go to the chart room and pray." Once in the chart room, the incredulous captain said, "Mr. Müller, do you know how dense the fog is?" "No," Müller said, "my eye is not on the fog, but on God who controls every circumstance of my life." He then knelt and said a simple, faith-filled prayer. When he finished, the captain knelt and began to pray also. Müller stopped him, saying, "As you do not believe, there is no need for you to pray. Get up, Captain, open the door and you will find the fog has lifted." The captain did as he was instructed only to see that the fog had lifted. George Müller made his engagement in Quebec on time.

Another example from George Müller's diary shows the importance of persistent faith in prayer.

> In November 1844, I began to pray for the conversion of five individuals. I prayed every day without a single intermission, whether sick or in health, on the land, on the sea, and whatever the pressure of my engagements might be. Eighteen months elapsed before the first of the five was converted. I thanked God and prayed on for the others. Five years elapsed, and then the second was converted. I thanked God for the second, and prayed on for the other three. Day by day, I continued to pray for them, and six years passed before the third was converted. I thanked God for the three, and went on praying for the other two.

These two remained unconverted. Thirty-six years later, he wrote that although the other two were still not converted, "I hope in God, I pray on, and look for the answer. They are not converted yet, but they will be." In

---

[28] George Müller (1805–1898) was a minister who cared for orphans in Bristol, England. He never made requests for financial support and never went into debt, but he cared for over ten thousand orphans during his lifetime.

1897, fifty-two years after he began to pray, these two men were finally converted—after Müller died.[29]

We need faith to receive the promises of God.

God's Word is filled with promises, but they generally will not come to us unless we actively believe. The writer of Hebrews confirmed this when he wrote:

> So that you may not be sluggish, but imitators of those who through faith and patience inherit the promises. **HEBREWS 6:12**

Notice that we do not inherit the promises just because they are ours. We have to supply faith and patience in order to inherit them. Paul wrote to Timothy:

> Take hold of the eternal life to which you were called. **1 TIMOTHY 6:12**

Our English phrase "take hold" is translated from the Greek word *epilambanomai*, which means "to seize, lay hold of, or take possession of." It comes from a metaphor drawn from the act of seizing someone with both hands to rescue him from peril.[30] It is a very active and aggressive word, and it clearly implies that if we want to experience God's promises, we must take hold of them with a violent and aggressive faith.

On September 4, 1987, Henry Dempsey was flying a commuter jet about four thousand feet above the Atlantic Ocean from Maine to Boston. He heard a rattling sound toward the rear of the plane, and leaving the controls to his co-pilot, he went to investigate. As he approached the tail section, the plane hit turbulence and he was thrown forward against the rear door.

The door was hinged at the bottom but not latched properly. When Dempsey crashed against the door, it opened and sucked him out of the plane. The co-pilot saw the 'door ajar' indicator flash on and immediately requested an emergency landing at the nearest airport. He radioed the Coast Guard and asked for a search and rescue operation for a pilot who had fallen out of the plane.

But the rescue was not needed. The moment Dempsey had tumbled out of the plane, he seized the outdoor ladder railings. He held on for ten

---

[29] Ben Patterson, *Deepening Your Conversation with God* (Bethany House Publishers, 2001), 105–106.

[30] Joseph Thayer and James Strong, *Thayer's Greek-English Lexicon of the New Testament: Coded with Strong's Concordance Numbers* (Hendrickson Publishers: Reissue, 1995).

minutes upside down with only his feet inside the plane. When they landed, his head was twelve inches from the ground.

When the rescue workers arrived, he could not let go of the rail. He had seized it so tightly that it took more than fifteen minutes for the workers to pry his hands free. Henry Dempsey's amazing rescue vividly portrays the essence of *epilambanomai*. He seized the ladder railings the way we must seize the promises of God.

We need faith to resist the devil.[31]

We have a real enemy, and he is playing for keeps.

> Your adversary the devil prowls around like a roaring lion, seeking someone to devour. Resist him, firm in your faith. **1 PETER 5:8–9**

We will not be able to resist the devil apart from a strong, assertive faith.

Smith Wigglesworth was once at a bus stop with several others waiting for a bus. The door of a nearby house opened, and out stepped a very proper elderly woman. As she approached the bus stop, she became aware that her little dog had left the house and was following her. She immediately implored her dog in the sweetest tones to return home. After much cajoling, the dog finally acquiesced. However, as soon as she turned toward the bus stop, the dog began following her again. The woman entreated her puppy as sweetly as possible, and once again he consented. But as soon as she turned her back, the dog began following her again. Finally, after several more rounds with the dog, the woman stomped her foot with authority and shouted, "Scat!" The dog tucked his tail between his legs, scurried home, and was not seen again. Without a moment's hesitation, Wigglesworth bellowed, "That's how you have to talk to the devil!"[32]

Martin Luther would talk to the devil just like that. He once said,

> By faith in Christ a person may gain such sure and sound comfort, that he need not fear the devil, sin, death, or any evil. "Sir Devil," he may say, "I am not afraid of you. I have a Friend whose name is Jesus Christ, in whom I believe. He has abolished the Law,

---

[31] We will examine this topic in great depth later.

[32] Andrew Strom, "Great Healing Revivalists—How God's Power Came: Smith Wigglesworth," Smith Wigglesworth (1859–1947), February 24, 2003, http://www.evangelo.org/risvegli.asp?operazione=visualizza&id=18&ln=eng.

condemned sin, vanquished death, and destroyed hell for me. He is bigger than you, Satan. He has licked you, and holds you down. You cannot hurt me." This is the faith that overcomes the devil.[33]

Everything of value in God's kingdom comes at a great cost.[34] Part of that cost is the opposition from our spiritual enemy who will do everything possible to stop us from experiencing God's best. Faith is of great value. Therefore, we should expect that it will come at a great cost and that it will require a great fight. In order to remain in that fight and persevere in the quest for faith, we must be aware of the benefits and value of faith. We need to know why we need faith if we are to pursue it diligently—and to hold on to it in the midst of opposition and pressure.

Conclusion

We have examined the eight reasons we need faith. In the next chapter, we will look at what faith is.

Application

Discuss

1. Is biblical righteousness the result of God acting as a sovereign or as a judge? Why does it matter? What difference will it make in your life?

_____

_____

_____

---

[33] Martin Luther, *Commentary on Galatians* (CreateSpace Independent Publishing Platform, 2012).

[34] Cost is measured by value. There is a great cost obtaining anything in God's kingdom, but the value is so great, the cost seems small in comparison. "The kingdom of heaven is like a merchant looking for fine pearls. When he found one of great value, he went away and sold everything he had and bought it" (Matthew 13:45, 46). The pearl was costly, but in comparison to its value, it was the deal of a lifetime.

2. Many Christians find it difficult to experience God's righteousness. They know it is the truth and that it is an important doctrine of the Church, but it just doesn't seem real to them. Why do you think that is? Have you felt that way at times in your life? Why? What can you do about it?

_____

_____

_____

3. How strong is the faith component of your prayer life? Why? What can you do to make it stronger?

_____

_____

_____

4. Faith takes an aggressive attitude towards God's promises. How do you rank on the passive/aggressive scale? Are you as aggressive in laying hold of God's promises as you should be? Why? What can you do to increase your aggressiveness?

_____

_____

_____

Act

Read the account of Jesus' dealings with the devil in Matthew 4:1–11 and Luke 4:1–13. Record all the principles and insights concerning faith you can find in this event.

Meditate

No unbelief made him waver concerning the promise of God, but he grew strong in his faith as he gave glory to God, fully convinced that God was able to do what he had promised. ROMANS 4:20–21

What Is Faith?

Part One

Introduction

In these next few chapters we will try to understand what faith is. In order to help us comprehend the essence of faith, looking at what faith is not will be helpful. We will examine three common substitutes for faith: hope, knowledge, and presumption.

Hope

In order to understand what the Bible teaches about hope, we must first understand that we use the word differently. Sometimes we use it to refer to wishful thinking or strong desire. For example, someone might ask, "Are you going to get that raise?" You might respond, "I sure hope so." Your response is just another way of saying, "I am not confident it will happen, but I sure want it to."

While this is a valid use of the word, the Bible does not use it that way. In fact, that is the exact opposite of how the Bible uses it. Biblical hope is a firm assurance about things that are unseen and still in the future.[35] It is the climate that faith works in. It is the dream, desire, or goal that we expect to receive. It is the confident expectation of good things to come.

---

[35] Robert Youngblood, *Nelson's Illustrated Bible Dictionary* (Thomas Nelson, Inc.: Revised, 2000).

Hope starts the process of faith by painting a vivid image of what could be. Then faith goes to work.

Hope is an important part of our life of faith, but it is not faith.

One of the most important distinctions between faith and hope is that hope always lives in the future tense.

> For in this hope we were saved. But hope that is seen is no hope at all. Who hopes for what they already have? But if we hope for what we do not yet have, we wait for it patiently. ROMANS 8:24–25

There are many benefits to a strong, Bible-based hope. Here are a few.[36]

Hope activates our faith.

> Against all hope, Abraham in hope believed and so became the father of many nations. ROMANS 4:18

The God's Word Bible translates this verse, "When there was nothing left to hope for, Abraham still hoped and believed." The Weymouth translation says, "Under utterly hopeless circumstances he hopefully believed." The New American Standard says, "In hope against hope he believed."[37]

Abraham kept a strong Bible-based hope long after all natural hope was gone. His confident expectation and firm assurance of God's promise stimulated and activated his faith. He saw the promise clearly, and would not waver when everything around him said there was no hope left.

Hope fuels our endurance.

> We remember before our God and Father [. . .] your endurance inspired by hope in our Lord Jesus Christ. 1 THESSALONIANS 1:3 NIV

In the early morning hours of July 4, 1952, Florence Chadwick dove into the Pacific Ocean off Catalina Island. She intended to swim the twenty-plus miles to the California coast. Chadwick was already an accomplished

---

[36] Throughout the New Testament, hope is closely tied to the return of Jesus Christ, and everything that means for us believers (Acts 23:6; 24:15; Romans 5:2; 8:20–23; Colossians 1:5, 27; 1 Thessalonians 5:8; Titus 1:2; 2:13; 3:7; 1 Peter 1:3–5, 13; 1 John 3:2, 3). Yet this eschatological hope does not eliminate intermediate hopes for lesser goods, even for material blessings (Britannica Ultimate Reference).

[37] The sentence structure in the NASB is unusual, but it closely follows the original Greek.

long-distance swimmer. Two years earlier, she had crossed the English Channel in both directions—the first woman to ever accomplish that feat.

But the conditions that day were not in her favor. The water was icy, the fog nearly impenetrable. She could barely see the boat she was supposed to follow. Several times, her team drove sharks away with rifle fire. After fifteen hours in the water, she gave out. Her trainer urged her on—they were so close. But all she could see was fog. She quit—one mile from her goal. She said later, "If I could have seen the land I might have made it."

Two months later in clear weather, Florence swam the channel successfully, setting a new speed record. There was no fog, and she could clearly see her goal. Because the land was in sight, she endured to the end.

That is what hope does for us.

The author of Hebrews reinforces this idea when he exhorts us to follow the example of Jesus, who endured the cross because of the joy that was set before him. If we fix our eyes on him, the author says, we will not grow weary and lose heart. This is a clear reference to the athletic competitions of Greece. The races were laid out on a straight track with the spectators on either side. The judge sat at the finish line holding the laurel wreath for the winner. From the start of the race to the finish, the competitors could see the prize. If they kept their eyes focused on it, they could find the strength to endure.

A clear and detailed hope enables us to endure obstacles and press on to the finish line.

Hope anchors our soul.

We have this as a sure and steadfast anchor of the soul, a hope that enters into the inner place behind the curtain. HEBREWS 6:19

Albert Barnes, commenting on this verse in his *Notes on the New Testament*, said:

Hope accomplishes for the soul the same thing an anchor does for a ship. It makes it secure. An anchor preserves a ship when the waves beat and the wind blows, and as long as the anchor holds, so long the ship is safe. So with the soul of the Christian. In the tempests and trials of life, his mind is calm as long as his hope is firm.[38]

---

[38] Albert Barnes, Notes on the New Testament (Kregel Classics; 8th Edition, 1962).

There are many more advantages that hope brings into our life. But as valuable as it is, hope is not faith. We should not get these two confused, or we may substitute hope for faith.

Knowledge

Knowledge is another important part of our faith life, but knowledge is not faith. Faith begins with knowledge—you have to know God's Word before you can believe it, but it does not end there. Knowledge is believing with the intellect; faith is believing with the heart. Knowledge that enters your mind must drop the all-important eighteen inches from your head to your heart.

For with the heart one believes and is justified. ROMANS 10:10

Knowledge is mentally agreeing with the truth of the Bible without personally appropriating it by faith. John Wesley once said, "The devil has given the Church a counterfeit to faith—mental assent." Mental assent is head knowledge. It is agreeing with the Word of God in the mind without believing it in the heart. Knowledge is the starting point of faith, but if knowledge is not appropriated, it remains mental assent. Mark 4 gives us a good picture of mental assent.

On that day, when evening had come, he said to them, "Let us go across to the other side." MARK 4:35

The Gospel writers do not always give us chronological information in their accounts, but when they do, we should take note because the information is an important clue to understanding what is happening in the scene. When Mark tells us that the event he is about to describe took place on "that day," he wants us to know that the prior events of that day have special significance concerning what is about to happen. We must then ask, "What was so special about that day?"

Jesus had spent that day teaching about the Word of God and the power it has in the life of a person who receives it by faith. The disciples had listened to Jesus speak the Word the entire day. They were saturated with the Word, and they were more than ready for the faith challenge that was to come that night. Jesus knew what was coming and so he prepared his disciples in advance. He had taught them that day that the devil comes immediately to steal the Word, and he knew that the storm they were about to experience was demonically inspired to steal the Word of God out of their hearts. He wanted them to be ready.

And leaving the crowd, they took him with them in the boat, just as he was. And other boats were with him. And a great windstorm arose, and the waves were breaking into the boat, so that the boat was already filling. MARK 4:36–37

All the disciples but one were from Galilee, and they knew about storms on that sea. The particular location of the Sea of Galilee makes it susceptible to sudden and fierce storms. The surface of the water is almost seven hundred feet below sea level, and the sea is surrounded on several sides by high hills. Cool air from these highlands rushes down the gorges and ravines and strikes the water with intense violence. Because the disciples had lived near its shores, it is very possible that they each knew someone who had drowned in a storm just like the one they were experiencing. Their terror was understandable.

But he was in the stern, asleep on the cushion. And they woke him and said to him, "Teacher, do you not care that we are perishing?" And he awoke and rebuked the wind and said to the sea, "Peace! Be still!" And the wind ceased, and there was a great calm. He said to them, "Why are you so afraid? Have you still no faith?" MARK 4:38–40

William Ewing, writing in the International Standard Bible Encyclopedia, *tells this story about his experience with the Sea of Galilee: "Twice in over five years the present writer witnessed such a hurricane. Once it burst from the South. In a few moments the air was thick with mist, through which one could hear the roar of the tortured waters. In about ten minutes the wind fell as suddenly as it had risen. The air cleared, and the wide welter of foam-crested waves attested the fury of the blast. On the second occasion the wind blew from the East, and the phenomena described above were practically repeated."[39]*

Faith can sleep in a storm, but unbelief is always troubled.

We see this truth illustrated in an incident that happened to John Wesley during a sea voyage to America. A huge storm buffeted the ship, and a wave broke over the deck and split the main sail in pieces. Wesley recorded in his diary, "A terrible screaming began among the English, but the German Moravians calmly sang on." Wesley was deeply impressed that

[39]   James Orr, *The International Standard Bible Encyclopedia* (Delmarva Publications Inc., 2014)

even the women and children manifested no fear but were perfectly calm. He concluded about himself, "I have a fair summer religion; I can talk well [. . .] and believe while no danger is near. But let death stare me in the face and my spirit is troubled."[40]

The disciples were like John Wesley that day. They forgot everything Jesus had preached and immediately reverted to fear and worry. They even challenged the character of God by accusing Jesus of not caring.[41]

If faith comes by hearing, you would expect that a full day of hearing Jesus preach the Word would produce a certain level of faith. That is why Jesus said to his disciples after he rebuked the storm, "Do you still have no faith?" How could the people who heard the Word all day end up with no faith? Martin Luther once said:

> If it were not for the example of the Galatian churches, I would never have thought it possible that anybody who had received the Word of God with such eagerness as they had could so quickly let go of it.[42]

The disciples certainly did. Jesus said they had no faith. There are a few adjectives Jesus used to describe the faith of people he encountered during his ministry. On two occasions, he used the adjective "great."

> Then Jesus answered her, "O woman, **great** is your faith! Be it done for you as you desire." And her daughter was healed instantly.
> MATTHEW 15:28

> When Jesus heard this, he was amazed at him [the Centurion], and turning to the crowd following him, he said, "I tell you, I have not found such **great** faith even in Israel." LUKE 7:9 NIV

Matthew used the Greek word *megas* to describe the Syrophoenician woman's faith. The word means "of considerable size, number, quantity, magnitude, or extent." Luke used the Greek word tosoutos to describe the centurion's faith. The word means "vast in quantity and amount; large;

---

[40] Reprinted from *The Journal of John Wesley* (Chicago: Moody Press, 1951), 29.

[41] Fear and worry is always an attack against the character of God.

[42] Martin Luther, *Commentary on Galatians* (CreateSpace Independent Publishing Platform, 2012).

notably above the average in size or magnitude." If Jesus ever describes your faith, you want him to use one of these words![43]

But there were several times when Jesus could not describe his disciples' faith with those words. In those cases, he used the adjective "little."

> Jesus immediately reached out his hand and took hold of him, saying to him, "O you of *little* faith, why did you doubt?" MATTHEW 14:31

> But if God so clothes the grass, which is alive in the field today, and tomorrow is thrown into the oven, how much more will he clothe you, O you of *little* faith! LUKE 12:28

Both Matthew and Luke used the Greek word *oligos*. The word means "puny in extent or degree; of inferior size, strength, or significance." It is definitely not as good as *great faith*—but at least it is some faith. That is much better than how Jesus described the disciples' faith on the day we are discussing: *no faith*. None. Nada. Zip. Nil. The disciples had listened to the Word all day and had received no faith. It was all head knowledge; it was all mental assent.

Mental assent is passive and superficial, and it produces no lasting change in us. It only fools us into thinking that we have real faith. But difficult times and challenging circumstances always reveal what we actually believe. And Jesus has a way of arranging difficulties and challenges to help us see what is really in our hearts. He does not do this to shame us, but to give us a chance to replace the mental assent with true Bible faith. The following is a good example of the difference between mental assent and real Bible faith.

Charles Blondin (1824–1897) was one of the greatest acrobats of all time. Raised in a circus family, he began his training at five years of age. Within six months, he was astonishing crowds as "the Little Wonder." Blondin performed many dangerous feats during his career, but the most outstanding were his exhibitions on a 1,100-foot-long tightrope stretched 160 feet above Niagara Falls. He crossed the Falls several times, always with different theatrical variations: blindfolded, on stilts, pushing a wheelbarrow. Once, he even sat on the tightrope and cooked an omelet!

---

[43] It is interesting that in the above cases, both people had faith for someone else and not themselves. Faith works by love (Galatians 5:6), and it is often the case that our moments of greatest faith are for someone that we love very much.

But his first crossing stands out above all the others. After successfully crossing Niagara, Blondin asked the gathered crowd, "Who believes I can cross back over the Falls?" The crowd roared together, "We believe!" "Then who," Blondin said, "is willing to get on my back while I cross?" The crowd was silent. Finally, one brave man stepped out of the crowd and said, "I will." He climbed on Blondin's shoulders, and they both walked successfully over Niagara Falls.

The crowd at Niagara Falls mentally assented to Blondin's ability to cross, but the brave man who climbed on his shoulders believed from his heart.

Presumption

Presumption is also not faith. However presumption is different from knowledge and hope because both knowledge and hope have a valid role in the life of faith, and presumption never does. Presumption is arrogant overconfidence. It is taking something for granted and supposing it is true without examination or proof. It is acting as if you know God's will when you have no scriptural evidence to support your supposition. The seven sons of Sceva provide us with a good example of presumption.

Extraordinary miracles were taking place in Ephesus. Many were being healed. Demons were coming out of people. Handkerchiefs that Paul had prayed over were even being placed on demonized people and the evil spirits were leaving. Sceva's boys presumed they could get in on the action.

> Then some of the itinerant Jewish exorcists undertook to invoke the name of the Lord Jesus over those who had evil spirits, saying, "I adjure you by the Jesus whom Paul proclaims." Seven sons of a Jewish high priest named Sceva were doing this. But the evil spirit answered them, "Jesus I know, and Paul I recognize, but who are you?" And the man in whom was the evil spirit leaped on them, mastered all of them and overpowered them, so that they fled out of that house naked and wounded. ACTS 19:13–16

Presumption can leave you naked and bleeding.

The Israelites also acted presumptuously when they were in the wilderness. In Numbers 14, the people believed the bad report the ten spies gave them about the Promised Land and threatened to stone Joshua and Caleb. They wanted to elect a new leader to take them back to Egypt. But God intervened, as we see in Numbers 14:11:

And the Lord said to Moses, "How long will this people despise me? And how long will they not believe in me, in spite of all the signs that I have done among them? NUMBERS 14:11

God relented from judging them because of Moses' intercession, but declared that because of their unbelief and disobedience:

None of the men who have seen my glory and my signs that I did in Egypt and in the wilderness, and yet have put me to the test these ten times and have not obeyed my voice, shall see the land that I swore to give to their fathers. And none of those who despised me shall see it. NUMBERS 14:22–23

The next day the people had a change of heart. Now they were ready to go. Now they were ready to obey. Now they were ready to believe. But what they thought was faith was really presumption. They were acting as if going to the Promised Land was God's will when they had no scriptural evidence to support their assumption. Actually, just the opposite was true, as they would soon discover.

And they rose early in the morning and went up to the heights of the hill country, saying, "Here we are. We will go up to the place that the Lord has promised, for we have sinned." But Moses said, "Why now are you transgressing the command of the Lord, when that will not succeed? Do not go up, for the Lord is not among you, lest you be struck down before your enemies. For there the Amalekites and the Canaanites are facing you, and you shall fall by the sword. Because you have turned back from following the Lord, the Lord will not be with you." NUMBERS 14:40–43

But the people did go in spite of Moses' word to them. The results were predictable.

But they **presumed** to go up to the heights of the hill country, although neither the ark of the covenant of the Lord nor Moses departed out of the camp. Then the Amalekites and the Canaanites who lived in that hill country came down and defeated them and pursued them, even to Hormah. NUMBERS 14:44–45

Presumption never ends well.

In the New Testament, James also warned us about acting presumptuously.

Come now, you who say, "Today or tomorrow we will go into such and such a town and spend a year there and trade and make a profit"—yet you do not know what tomorrow will bring. What is your life? For you are a mist that appears for a little time and then vanishes. Instead you ought to say, "If the Lord wills, we will live and do this or that." JAMES 4:13–15

Why is this presumption? Because the person who is making these assertions about what he will do has no scriptural evidence to support them. He has no promise from God about what will happen tomorrow. He thinks he has faith, but he is instead arrogant and overconfident. Faith begins when the will of God is known, and if we do not know his will, all our boasting is just presumption.

I knew a young man who had recently come to faith in Christ. After listening to a stirring message on faith, he determined he would receive healing for his eyes. He prayed what he thought was a mighty faith prayer, took off his glasses, and threw them in a nearby dumpster. He was healed, he declared, and he had the corresponding action to prove it. Three days later, this young man, myself, and several friends spent a fruitless hour rummaging in that trash bin searching for his discarded glasses. We never found them, and he had to purchase new ones. He made the mistake of confusing activity with faith. He assumed that all he had to do was show God he believed by tossing his glasses away and then God would be obligated to heal his eyes. He confused presumption for faith.

Conclusion

If faith is not hope, mental assent, or presumption, then what is it? In the next two chapters, we will try to answer that question.

Application

Discuss

1. Hope is a clear picture of what you want God to do in and through your life. The clearer the picture, the stronger your hope. How clear is your picture and how strong is your hope? What can you do to strengthen it?

_____

_____

_____

2. God uses situations to reveal to us that what we thought was faith was only mental assent. What situations have you been in this last year that showed you how much mental assent you had? What did God teach you through those situations? How can you ensure if a similar situation occurs that you will respond in true Bible faith and not with mere mental assent?

_____

_____

_____

3. Presumption is acting as if you know God's will when you have no scriptural evidence to support your supposition. Give a recent example of presumption in your life. What did God teach you through that event?

_____

_____

_____

Act

Using a concordance, Bible software, or online resource, look up ten verses from the New Testament concerning hope. Record your thoughts about each verse.

Meditate

We have this as a sure and steadfast anchor of the soul, a hope that enters into the inner place behind the curtain. HEBREWS 6:19

05

What Is Faith?

Part Two

Introduction

In the last chapter, we saw that faith is not hope, knowledge, or presumption. In this chapter and the next, we will examine what faith is.

Faith is a relationship with God.

First and foremost, faith is a relationship with God.

Because of centuries of church tradition, we tend to think of faith in a creed, in a doctrine, in a form of theology, but it isn't; it is a relationship with God.[44]

Faith is not a formula, set of rules, or prescription. Faith is how we interact with God. Paul wrote to the Ephesians:

In whom we have boldness and access with confidence through our faith in him. EPHESIANS 3:12

Through faith, we may approach God with confidence and with full assurance. The writer of Hebrews urges us to approach God confidently through faith in what Jesus has accomplished for us. He said:

Therefore, brothers, since we have **confidence** to enter the holy places by the blood of Jesus, by the new and living way that he opened for us through the curtain, that is, through his flesh, and

[44] Derek Prince, *Faith Relates Us to the Invisible* (Derek Prince Legacy Radio, Nov. 17, 2008).

since we have a great priest over the house of God, let us draw near with a true heart in full assurance of faith, with our hearts sprinkled clean from an evil conscience and our bodies washed with pure water. **HEBREWS 10:19–22**

Let us then with confidence draw near to the throne of grace, that we may receive mercy and find grace to help in time of need. **HEBREWS 4:16**

Our English word "confidence" is derived from the Latin word *fides*, which means *faith*, and the prefix *con* which means *with*. Someone who is confident is someone *with faith*. The fact that the word is used in both of these passages concerning our relationship with God underscores how important faith is in that relationship.

It is significant that the writer refers to the throne as of grace and not of judgment (although God will judge the living and the dead). He also did not call it the throne of truth (although God is true though every man be a liar), or the throne of righteousness (although God is a righteous judge who expresses his wrath every day). But he did call it the throne of grace, a throne where we draw near to receive mercy and grace to help in our time of need—which is every moment of every day. And this throne of grace is accessed by faith.

We also need to understand that faith is not a mere ticket to get us the things we want. Faith should not be seen as a ticket to get something but more as a treasure of value. A ticket only has value for what it represents. Once we exchange it for the thing we really want, we simply discard it. A treasure, however, has intrinsic and lasting value.

For example, in 2009, a friend of mine gave me four tickets to watch the St. Louis Cardinals play the Chicago Cubs at Busch Stadium over the Fourth of July weekend. To a lifetime Cardinal fan, things don't get much better than that, and I had great expectations about the game. First, because any chance to see my team play is always a treat. Second, because there has been a long-standing rivalry between the two teams (it is a requirement for all Cardinal fans to root against the Cubs). Third, because it was a holiday weekend, and the two clubs were locked in a feverish pennant race.

So those tickets were precious to me—but only for what they represented. Once they got me into the game (along with my dad and two sons), I discarded them. They no longer had any value.

But faith is not a ticket—an item to be discarded once you receive what you want. Faith is a relationship with God. And that is our treasure. As John Piper said:

> To put it positively, "belief" in Jesus is coming to Him to feed on Him; that is to get my satisfaction, to have my soul-thirst satisfied from Him.[45]

Faith is total trust in God's character.

The foundation of faith is the character of God. Because God is trustworthy, we can trust him and have faith in him.

> If we are faithless, he remains faithful—for he cannot deny himself.
> **2 TIMOTHY 2:13**

John Calvin declared that a right definition of faith must include the idea that it is a firm and certain knowledge of God's benevolence toward us. This certain knowledge of God's loving character is founded upon the truth of the freely given promise in Christ, both revealed to our minds and sealed upon our hearts through the Holy Spirit.[46]

The author of Hebrews tells us that:

> By faith even Sarah herself received ability to conceive, even beyond the proper time of life, since she considered Him faithful who had promised. **HEBREWS 11:11 NASB**[47]

---

[45] Quoted from Todd Shaffer, "Battling Unbelief: Series With John Piper." Faith By Hearing, Posted on May 28, 2007, http://faithbyhearing.wordpress.com.

[46] John Calvin, *Institutes of the Christian Religion* (Hendrickson Publishers, 2007), Book 3, Chapter 2, Section 8.

[47] There is some disagreement among translators concerning whether this verse refers to Abraham or Sarah. Both interpretations are possible because of the unique construction of the original Greek sentence. The New International Version, New Revised Standard, and New Century Version prefer Abraham. The New American Standard, King James, and New King James prefer Sarah. But whether it was Abraham or Sarah, they still "considered Him faithful." *The Bible Knowledge Commentary* says, "The writer here chose to introduce his first heroine of faith, one who was able to overlook the physical limitation of her own barrenness to become a fruitful mother. Her faith in fact, contributed to the startling multiplication of her husband's seed, when old Abraham was as good as dead."

The word translated "considered" could be defined this way: "to think about carefully and thoroughly so as to form a proper judgment." Sarah carefully and thoroughly thought about the faithfulness of God, and the result was faith—total confidence in God's character.

A television program preceding the 1988 Winter Olympics featured blind skiers being trained for slalom skiing. Paired with sighted skiers, the blind skiers were taught on the flats how to make right and left turns. When that was mastered, they were taken to the slalom slope, where their sighted partners skied beside them shouting, "Left!" and "Right!" at the appropriate times. As they trusted and obeyed the sighted skiers, they were able to navigate the course and cross the finish line. They depended solely on the sighted skiers' word. It was either complete trust or catastrophe.[48]

We are the blind skiers attempting to navigate the slippery slopes of life. But fortunately, we have a trustworthy guide whispering directions in our ears. If we trust him, we will finish the course. And we can trust him because he is perfect in integrity and worthy of our trust. Integrity is a rigid, unyielding, and steadfast adherence to the truth. Faith is impossible without it. Because God is perfect in integrity, we have a strong foundation for our confidence in God.

And also the Glory of Israel will not lie or have regret, for he is not a man, that he should have regret. 1 SAMUEL 15:29

Let God be true though every one were a liar. ROMANS 3:4

It is impossible for God to lie. HEBREWS 6:18

In my years in university ministry I would occasionally encounter a skeptic who posed this question to me, "Can God make a rock so big he cannot move it?" I never bothered to supply an intelligent answer to such a silly question, and I usually responded, "No, because that is dumb, and God doesn't do dumb things." I then quickly followed my retort with something along these lines: "But if you are wondering if there is anything God cannot do, if there is anything that is impossible for him, there is one thing he cannot do: he cannot lie—it is impossible for him." Then I would usually add, "And he says, 'Unless you repent, you will perish.' Since it is impossible for him to lie, I would take that statement very seriously if I were you."

---

48 Robert W. Sutton, "Trust," Sermon Illustrations, http://www.sermonillustrations.com/a-z/t/trust.htm.

John Paton (1824–1907) spent over forty-five years as a missionary to the New Hebrides in the South Pacific. When he was translating the New Testament into their native tongue, he struggled to find a comparable word in their language he could use for faith. The natives were cannibals that ate the flesh of their defeated foes. They practiced infanticide and widow sacrifice, killing the widows of deceased men so that they could serve their husbands in the next world. Their whole worship was one of slavish fear, and they had no idea of a God of mercy or grace.[49] One day a native ran up the stairs into Paton's house, rushed into his study, and flung himself on a chair. He said to the missionary, "It is good to rest my whole weight in this chair." Paton had found the word he would use for faith. Faith is resting your whole weight on God. Paton finished his translation shortly afterwards, and before he died testified that the entire island had been won to faith in Christ.

Because of God's absolute integrity, we can rest in total dependence upon what he has said he will do. When George Müller was asked what faith was, he replied:

> What is faith? In the simplest manner in which I am able to express it, I answer: Faith is the assurance that the thing which God has said in His Word is true, and that God will act according to what He has said in His Word.[50]

God's Word is surer than that of a trusted friend. Martin Luther said:

> Faith honors him whom it trusts with the most reverent and highest regard since it considers him truthful and trustworthy. There is no other honor equal to the estimate of truthfulness and righteousness with which we honor him whom we trust. [. . .] On the other hand, there is no way in which we can show greater contempt for a man than to regard him as false and wicked and to be suspicious of him, as we do when we do not trust him.[51]

---

[49] James Paton, John G. Paton: *Missionary to the New Hebrides, An Autobiography* (Banner of Truth, 1994), 69, 334.

[50] Copied for WholesomeWords.org from George Müller, *An Hour With George Müller: the Man of Faith to Whom God Gave Millions*, ed. by A. Sims (Grand Rapids, MI.: Zondervan Publishing House, 1939).

[51] Martin Luther and John Dillenberger, *Martin Luther: Selections from His Writings* (Anchor, 1958), 59.

That is why unbelief is a sin. It questions the character of God and challenges his integrity. It impugns his character and suggests that he is not dependable, and therefore, we cannot depend upon him.[52] But real faith rests confidently in God, knowing that he is trustworthy and that he will perform what he has spoken.

> Faith is the primary covenant requirement of God, precisely because it humbles us and amplifies the trustworthiness and all-sufficiency of God.[53]

Faith is complete confidence in God's written Word.

The author of Hebrews provides us with a succinct definition of what faith is:

> Now faith is the assurance of things hoped for, the conviction of things not seen. **HEBREWS 11:1 NASB**

The word "assurance" derives from the Greek word *hupostasis*, which means "that which stands under anything." It originally referred to the sediment or foundation under a building. Faith is the foundation, the root, the underlying substance of hope.[54] In the first century, it was used as a legal term referring to the transfer of property, and was commonly used in business documents as the basis or guarantee of transactions. It was essentially a title deed. So, Hebrews 11:1 could be reworded this way:

> Faith is the "title deed" of all the things we hope for.

A few illustrations from contemporary society may help clarify this concept.

If you make an offer on a piece of property and the owner accepts the offer, then you must wait while the proper legal documents are processed and the deal is closed before you can take possession of the property. While you are waiting for this process to conclude, someone might ask you, "Is that property yours?" You would have to say, "I hope so." You have a confident expectation that it will be yours soon, but it is not yours yet. But the day

---

[52] See Note 41.

[53] Quoted from "John Piper, Preaching as Worship : Meditations on Expository Exultation," in Bernard H. Rom Lectures, Trinity Evangelical Divinity School, Chicago, IL, November 2–3, 1994.

[54] George MacDonald, "Faith, the Proof of the Unseen," The Golden Key, updated 2015, www.george-macdonald.com.

the paperwork is completed and your name is recorded on the title deed, then you can boldly say, "The property is mine." When you have the title deed, you have the property. The title deed is the assurance of the thing you had hoped for.

If you are about to graduate from college and your father calls to say he has bought you a new car, you would enthusiastically tell your friends. But some might be doubtful. They might say, "I don't see any car," or, "How do you know he really bought you a car?" However, the next day a special delivery package arrives with the title deed to a brand new car—and it has your name on it. As you wave the title deed in front of your skeptical friends, they now have to agree that you certainly have the car. They still can't see it, but they know you have it. It may still take a while for the actual car to arrive, since it has to be shipped from another state. But that is all just logistics. You have the title deed, and it is just a matter of time before you will have the actual car.

Faith is the title deed, the assurance that what God has promised is yours—even if you cannot see it yet!

I received a bad report a number of years ago from a friend who had just come from the doctor's office. The physician had discovered a malignant tumor, and he was very concerned she would not live. I did not have sufficient time to prepare myself in prayer to respond to her situation, so I cast my care upon the Lord and planned a time when I could respond properly and in faith. The next day I set aside the necessary time for prayer. I began by building my faith through declaring every scriptural promise I knew that covered this case. I was determined not to pray for her until I had the title deed, the full assurance of what I was hoping for. I did not know how long it would take, but I knew that until I had the assurance, praying was pointless.

After an hour and a half of bold declaration and meditation, the assurance came. Describing this experience is difficult, but when the assurance comes, you know that you know that you have it. I like to picture the doorbell ringing and the FedEx man delivering a package. Inside is the title deed, and the thing for which I have hoped is at last mine.

After you have assurance, prayer is easy. I prayed a simple thirty-second prayer, and waited for the good report that I knew would come. Within days, my friend called and said that the situation had resolved itself. (She was not a believer and did not understand what had really happened.)[55]

Hebrews 11:1 also tells us that faith is the conviction of things not seen. The word "conviction" derives from the Greek word *elengchos*, a forensic term referring to a lawyer's presentation of irrefutable evidence in the courtroom. It was a word used in the criminal courts to describe the process by which a prosecutor would present evidence to prove to the jury that the criminal was guilty. The prosecutor would present the evidence so cogently and clearly that the jury would feel they had actually seen the crime, even though, of course, they had not. *Elengchos* is a word that means someone is so convinced about something, he acts as though he has seen it with his own eyes, when in fact he has not. It is evidential proof that produces an unshakeable confidence. As Charles Spurgeon said:

> If God has spoken to us in the Scriptures and revealed a truth that has no analogy in nature, that is not supported by the judgment of learned men, and to which our own experience seems to be in contradiction, still God must be believed. The fact that God has said it should weigh the scales of our understanding. Surely you are not going to set the evidence of your eyes against the declaration of God who cannot lie. I am determined that if my senses contradict God, I would rather deny every one of them than believe that God could lie.[56]

Faith is obedience to God.

The Bible makes a direct connection between obedience and faith. Paul said that God had given him grace and apostleship to call people from among all the Gentiles to the *obedience that comes from faith* (Romans 1:5 NIV). In the same letter he first told the Romans that their *faith was proclaimed in all the world* (Romans 1:8). Then he told them that *everyone has heard about*

---

[55] Don't get the idea that it is this easy or straightforward all the time. Faith is a fight, and we encounter great challenges when we decide to live by faith. Not every experience I have had in prayer has been this glorious or straightforward. But it does illustrate the principle that faith is complete confidence in God's Word.

[56] Charles Spurgeon, *The Triumph of Faith in a Believer's Life*, (Lynnwood, WA: Emerald Books, 1994), 80–81.

your obedience (Romans 16:19 NIV). Obviously, faith and obedience were synonymous to Paul.

The writer to the Hebrews also made the same connection between faith and obedience when he described what happened to the Israelites who followed Moses out of Egypt. He first states that the Israelites could not enter the Promised Land because of their disobedience.

> And to whom did he swear that they would not enter his rest, but to those who were disobedient? **HEBREWS 3:18**

Then, in the next verse, he states that they could not enter the Promised Land because of unbelief.

> So we see that they were unable to enter because of unbelief.
> **HEBREWS 3:19**

Apparently, the author saw unbelief and disobedience as synonymous concepts.

We see examples of this all through Scripture. When God told Samuel to go to Jesse's house to anoint a new king, he did not tell him who the king would be. Samuel obeyed God and went because he believed God would speak to him when he arrived. His faith motivated his obedience, and his obedience completed his faith.

We see faith and obedience working together when Jesus instructed his disciples to . . .

> Go to the village ahead of you, and just as you enter it, you will find a colt tied there, which no one has ever ridden. Untie it and bring it here. If anyone asks you, "Why are you doing this?" tell him, "The Lord needs it and will send it back here shortly." **MARK 11:2–3**

For the two disciples to complete this task, they had to take their commitment to obedience seriously. Maybe they played out different scenarios in their minds of all the bad things that could happen to them. (This would be like walking into a man's garage and driving away with his Lexus!) Or maybe they had seen Jesus provide for them so many times that they were assured this would turn out just like he said it would.

> And they went away and found a colt tied at a door outside in the street, and they untied it. And some of those standing there said to them, "What are you doing, untying the colt?" And they told them what Jesus had said, and they let them go. **MARK 11:4–6**

Faith should express itself in obedience. Faith that does not express itself in obedience is not Bible faith at all.

Faith is acting on the Word.

Real faith is expressed by acting on the Word.

> So also faith by itself, if it does not have works, is dead. But someone will say, "You have faith and I have works." Show me your faith apart from your works, and I will show you my faith by my works [. . .] For as the body apart from the spirit is dead, so also faith apart from works is dead. JAMES 2:17–18, 26

The obvious implication from this verse is that you cannot show a person your faith in any other way than by your actions. Therefore, if a person has no actions, he has no faith.

James continues his explanation of the relationship between faith and works by providing evidence that actions are the expression of faith. He reminds us that Abraham, because of his faith in God, offered up his son Isaac on the altar. His actions complemented his faith and made his faith complete.

> The doer is he who from the heart embraces God's word and **testifies by his life** that he really believes, according to the saying of Christ, "Blessed are they who hear God's word and keep it."[57]

William Carey was burdened as a young man by the desire to take the gospel to the world. The vast majority of church leaders, however, did not share his zeal. When he proposed to a meeting of ministers,

> The command given to the apostles to teach all nations was binding on all succeeding ministers to the end of the world,"[58]

he was greeted with this response:

---

[57] John Calvin, "Commentary on James 1: Calvin's Commentary on the Bible," Study Light, https://www.studylight.org/commentaries/cal/james-1.html, 1840–57.

[58] Dr. R. L. Hymers, Jr. "Missionary Lessons from Dr. Carey," Sermons for the World, https://www.rlhymersjr.com/Online_Sermons/2006/021906PM_MissionaryLessons.html.

Young man sit down! When God pleases to convert the heathen, he'll do it without consulting you or me![59]

But God was not converting the heathen without them. Carey was convinced that faith in the Great Commission should be expressed by the obedient action of going. So in 1793, with the backing of the mission society he established, he took it upon himself to obey the Great Commission and went to India.

The expected lifespan of an Englishman in rural India in the late 1700s was six months. But in spite of the humid, unsanitary conditions, Carey survived malaria, dysentery, cholera, tigers, and cobras, and ministered for forty-one years without a furlough. He preached for seven years before he baptized his first convert! Through intense hardships, his indefatigable spirit and strong confidence in God's call carried him through to victory. His often repeated motto was, "Expect great things from God; attempt great things for God."

Conclusion

In this chapter, we have seen that faith is a relationship with God, total trust in his character, complete confidence in his written Word, obedience to God, and acting on the Word. In the next chapter, we will examine four more definitions of faith.

Application

Discuss

1. Which of the characteristics of faith in this chapter is the easiest for you to believe? Which is the most difficult? Has this changed since you first came into relationship with God?

_____

_____

_____

---

[59] See Note 58.

2. Why do you think approaching faith as a formula is easier? Have you ever found yourself looking at faith as a formula rather than a relationship? If yes, why? What can you do to ensure that you will not fall in that trap again?

_____

_____

_____

3. Unbelief shows up in so many ways in our lives: worry, fear, doubt, anxiety. Why are all these forms of unbelief such an insult to God? What does it say about his character?

_____

_____

_____

4. Because faith is an action, it is revealed in how we respond when we receive bad news. Think back to the last time you received bad news. How did you respond? How should you have responded? What can you do to ensure that the next time you hear bad news you respond in faith?

_____

_____

_____

Act

Read Hebrews 11 and record your insights concerning what faith is.

Meditate

Now faith is the assurance of things hoped for, the conviction of things not seen. HEBREWS 11:1

What Is Faith?

Part Three

Introduction

In the last chapter, we began our examination of what faith is. We concluded that faith is . . .

> . . . a relationship with God.

> . . . total trust in God's character.

> . . . complete confidence in God's written Word.

> . . . obedience to God.

> . . . acting on the Word.

In this chapter, we will continue to look at what faith is.

Faith is agreeing with God's Word even when it is contrary to circumstances.

Paul gives us a graphic description of the faith of our father Abraham.

> He did not weaken in faith when he considered his own body, which was as good as dead (since he was about a hundred years old), or when he considered the barrenness of Sarah's womb. No unbelief

made him waver concerning the promise of God, but he grew strong in his faith as he gave glory to God, fully convinced that God was able to do what he had promised. ROMANS 4:19–21

Abraham's faith was not an uninformed faith; it was not a faith divorced from reality. He contemplated his own body. He faced the facts. He recognized how old he was. He knew how dead Sarah's womb was. He was aware, very aware, of the odds against him having a child, and he weighed the facts carefully. But in the midst of all his careful analysis, he did not become weak in faith. In the end, the promise of God carried more weight than his circumstances—as hopeless as they seemed. As F. F. Bruce said:

> Abraham did not shut his eyes to these unfavorable circumstances; he took them into careful consideration. But when he set them over against the promise of God, he found that the certainty of God's ability and will to fulfill His promise outweighed them all.[60]

In the late 1990s, I led a discipleship training program for the ministry organization that employed me. One particular year, the Lord directed me to believe for nineteen students. I then began the process of praying and declaring my faith. Three weeks prior to the start of the nine-month program, I had the desired nineteen students. But just before class began, I received a call from one student telling me he would not be able to attend. So I began the year with eighteen students. But I had prayed for nineteen, and I continued to believe God that I would have nineteen—even though it was contrary to my circumstances.

If someone would have asked me in the first weeks of the program, "How many students do you have?" I would have replied, "Eighteen," because that was how many I had, and I am a faith realist. I don't say things that aren't true. It is very possible at this point to be confused about the message of faith. People often make outlandish claims and statements that do not reflect the facts, and all the time they think that is what faith is. But we should learn a lesson from Abraham—the ultimate faith realist. He did not ignore the truth of his physical condition. He looked the facts squarely in the eyes. But he showed greater respect for God's promise and agreed with God's Word even when it was contrary to his circumstances. He put God's

---

[60] F. F. Bruce, *Romans: Tyndale New Testament Commentaries* (Eerdmans; Revised, Subsequent Edition, 1986), 109–110.

Word first, and when he did, his faith grew stronger—even as the situation grew more impossible.[61]

> The King James Version and the New King James are the only major Bible versions that translate Romans 4:19 "he considered not his own body." The KJV is based on the manuscript called the Textus Receptus (Latin for "received text"), compiled by the humanist (and later opponent of Martin Luther) Desiderius Erasmus at the beginning of the sixteenth century. Erasmus's work was a huge accomplishment for the times, especially considering the scarcity of manuscripts that were available (he only had five or six very late manuscripts dating from the tenth to the thirteenth century to work with). However, an explosion of discoveries and linguistic research in the nineteenth and twentieth century rendered the Textus Receptus relatively obsolete.
>
> The English word "not" used in the KJV is translated from a simple Greek particle of negation, transliterated as "ou." All of the more recently discovered manuscripts (dating from the early to mid-fourth century) do not have this particle. It is likely that the "ou" is a gloss that entered the text through a later copyist's error.
>
> The overwhelming majority of contemporary scholars accept the vast amount of evidence from the wealth of new discoveries. That is why all the versions of the last century translate Romans 4:19 something like "Abraham contemplated his own body." Here are a few examples:
>
> "Without weakening in his faith, he faced the fact that his body was as good as dead . . . " (NIV)
>
> "He did not weaken in faith when he considered his own body . . . " (NRSV)
>
> "Abraham didn't weaken. Through faith he regarded the facts . . . " (God's Word)
>
> "Abraham thought about all this, but his faith in God did not become weak." (NCV)
>
> "And Abraham's faith did not weaken, even though, at about 100 years of age, he figured his body was as good as dead. . ." (NLT)

After a few weeks of class, a pastor called and asked if one of his members could come sit in the class for a few days and see if it was the right thing for him to do. I said it was fine, and after the first day the young man told me he thought God wanted him to join the class. I told him I was sure God wanted him to—he was number nineteen.

---

[61] That is one way you can be sure you have real Bible faith. Mental assent weakens when the circumstances grow more bleak; Bible faith gets stronger.

Faith does not deny reality, it just acknowledges that there is something more real: the Word of God. This is not always easy, especially when our natural reason and our five physical senses are being bombarded with contrary circumstances. But it is how faith works. As Martin Luther said:

> It is a quality of faith, that it wrings the neck of reason and strangles the beast, which else the whole world, with all creatures, could not strangle. But how? It holds to God's Word, and lets it be right and true, no matter how foolish and impossible it sounds. So did Abraham take his reason captive and slay it, inasmuch as he believed God's Word, wherein was promised him that from his unfruitful and as it were dead wife, Sarah, God would give him seed.[62]

Faith is seeing the unseen.

People commonly use the expression, "Seeing is believing."[63] The phrase usually refers to a person with a skeptical point of view, someone who requires tangible evidence before he will believe. I know something about this attitude. My home state is Missouri, commonly called the "Show-Me State." In 1899, Missouri congressman Willard Vandiver popularized the phrase when he said in a speech, "I come from a state that raises corn and cotton and cockleburs and Democrats, and frothy eloquence neither convinces nor satisfies me. I am from Missouri. You have got to show me."[64]

Jesus' disciple Thomas knew something about this attitude also, and it got him in a lot of trouble. His first mistake was to miss the evening meeting on Resurrection Sunday (John 20:24). We don't know why Thomas wasn't there—perhaps he had a prior engagement, an urgent errand, or maybe he was just worn out from all the recent activity. But I am certain he regretted it later because the meeting turned out to be hugely important. It started when Jesus walked through the locked door—an impressive way to start any meeting! Jesus showed the disciples his pierced hands and his wounded

---

[62] Martin Luther, quoted in: Philip Schaff, *History of the Christian Church, Volume 7* (Hendrickson, 1996), Chap. 1.

[63] The humorist James Thurber once said, "Seeing is deceiving." That may be a more accurate idiom.

[64] *Official Manual of the State of Missouri 1979–1980,* (Missouri Secretary of State Office, 1980), 1486.

side. Then he breathed on them and said, "As the Father has sent me, even so I am sending you [. . .] Receive the Holy Spirit. If you forgive the sins of any, they are forgiven them" (John 20:19–23).

When the other disciples saw Thomas later, they told him, "We have seen the Lord!" But Thomas was unconvinced. He said, "Unless I see the nail marks in his hands and put my finger where the nails were, and put my hand into his side, I will not believe it." He wanted evidence, tangible proof. He wanted to see it before he would believe it. (Thomas would have made a good Missourian.)

A week later, Thomas got his chance. He must have known he was in trouble when Jesus walked through the locked door again. "Put your finger here," Jesus said. "Stop doubting and believe." Thomas was smitten. All he could say was, "My Lord and my God!" Jesus responded, "Because you have seen me, you have believed; blessed are those who have not seen and yet have believed" (John 20:27–29 NIV).

Faith is not moved by what natural sight reveals.

Now faith is the assurance of things hoped for, the conviction of things *not seen*. HEBREWS 11:1

Faith sees something that the natural eyes cannot see.

By faith he [Moses] left Egypt, not being afraid of the anger of the king, for he endured as *seeing him* who is invisible. HEBREWS 11:27

Seeing is not believing in the traditional sense of the phrase and the way Thomas understood it. But seeing is believing when you see through the eyes of faith. This theme is everywhere in the book of Hebrews.

By faith Moses [. . .] considered the reproach of Christ greater wealth than the treasures of Egypt, for he was *looking* to the reward. HEBREWS 11:24, 26

Now in putting everything in subjection to him, he left nothing outside his control. At present, we do not yet see everything in subjection to him. But we see him who for a little while was made lower than the angels, namely Jesus, crowned with glory and honor because of the suffering of death, so that by the grace of God he might taste death for everyone. HEBREWS 2:8–9

These all died in faith, not having received the things promised, but **having seen** them and greeted them from afar, and having acknowledged that they were strangers and exiles on the earth.
HEBREWS 11:13

Looking to Jesus [. . .] for the joy that was set before him endured the cross, despising the shame, and is seated at the right hand of the throne of God. **HEBREWS 12:2**

So, "Seeing is believing"—when you are seeing what is unseen.

As we look not to the things that are seen but to the things that are unseen. For the things that are seen are transient, but the things that are unseen are eternal. **2 CORINTHIANS 4:18**

What is seen with our natural senses is temporary, fleeting, momentary—lasting only for a short time. It is subject to change, and **will** change in this transient world. But what is unseen (by our natural senses, perhaps, but perceived by the eye of faith) is eternal, unchanging, permanent—lasting forever. For heaven and earth will pass away, but God's Word stands forever (Matthew 24:35). Augustine said:

Faith is to believe what you do not see; the reward of this faith is to see what you believe.

Several years ago, we had a recent college graduate living in our home. David was on his way to the University of Arkansas as a full-time campus minister. But he had a problem: he did not own a car. If he was going to have a chance to be successful in campus ministry, he was going to need reliable transportation.

While David was reading the testimony of the Korean pastor Dr. Yonggi Cho, he was struck by how the Lord taught Cho the importance of praying specific prayers. Cho needed transportation for his ministry to the poor and needy in Seoul, and so he asked the Lord for a bicycle. He prayed in faith, but after six months, he still did not have a bicycle. When he spoke to the Lord about it, the Lord said, "I do not know what kind of bicycle you want." Cho then described to the Lord a precise picture of the bicycle he wanted, and in a short time he had it.

God stirred David's heart at that moment to believe for the car he needed. He decided (after careful deliberation) to ask for a powder blue, Volkswagen Rabbit with a diesel engine (gasoline had reached the unimaginable price of $1.38 per gallon and this car got 55 miles per gallon). He also wanted a high-end Blaupunkt stereo system. Searching through several magazines, David found a picture of the car he wanted and hung it on his wall. Every day he would look at the picture, meditate on the promises of God, and thank God for his powder blue, Volkswagen Rabbit diesel with a Blaupunkt stereo.

A few months later, I received a call from a minister friend who had heard David was in need of a car. He said, "A member of my church has a car he wants to give to someone starting out in ministry, and he wondered if David was the person he should give it to."

I said, "That depends. What kind of car is it?"

"It is a Volkswagen Rabbit," he replied.

"Is it a diesel?" I asked.

After a moment's hesitation he said, "Yes, I think it is."

"What color is it?"

"Light blue," he said.

"Could you call that powder blue?"

"Yes, I suppose you could," replied my friend. He continued, "And he just installed a very expensive German stereo that I think is called Blaupunkt or something like that."

"David will take the car!"

And he did! David saw the unseen, and it became more real to him than the physical world.[65] As Dr. J. Oswald Sanders said:

Faith enables the believing soul to treat the future as present and the invisible as seen.

Faith is giving a good report.

Then Caleb silenced the people before Moses and said, "We should go up and take possession of the land, for we can certainly do it." But the men who had gone up with him said, "We can't attack those people; they are stronger than we are." And they spread among the

---

[65] This story is not a license to claim any kind of car or other material possession and start visualizing its existence. It is easy to become excessive at this point and start claiming anything you want. David clearly needed a car to obey God's will, and he prayed in line with God's purpose and not his own. The point of the story is simply that by faith we will often see the answer before we receive it.

Israelites a bad report about the land they had explored. They said, "The land we explored devours those living in it. All the people we saw there are of great size." **NUMBERS 13:30–32 NIV**

Twelve men went to spy out the land. They all had the same assignment: spy out the land and determine the best strategy for taking it. However, when they were going to report their findings, two distinct groups emerged. One group of ten saw the impossibility of the circumstances and gave a bad report: "We can't attack those people; they are stronger than we are." The other group of two saw the power and promises of God and gave a good report: "We should go up and take possession of the land, for we can certainly do it."

The first group was telling the truth: there were real giants in the land. But they could not see beyond the obstacles in their way, and so their report was filled with doubt and fear. The second group was also telling the truth: God was a lot bigger than any giant, and so were his covenant promises. They could see beyond the obstacles in their way, and so their report was filled with faith and courage.

Both groups saw the same things, but they processed what they saw through an entirely different filter. The people who gave the bad report saw only the physical reality in front of them. The people who gave the good report saw the same physical reality, but through the filter of God's Word.

A good report, then, is a faith-filled declaration of God's perspective of reality.

I read a story years ago that provides a natural example of what a good report looks like. It concerns the American war hero Lieutenant General Lewis "Chesty" Puller. Puller was the most decorated Marine in history with over fifty-two medals.[66] Even though he retired from active duty in 1955 and died in 1971, it is still a common occurrence for Marines in boot camp to end the day with the chant, "Good night, Chesty Puller, wherever you are!"

Puller's confidence in battle was a constant encouragement to his men. One time, when his aggressive tactics had caused the enemy to completely surround his unit, he uttered the words he is most well-known for, "They're on our left, they're on our right, they're in front of us, they're behind us. They can't get away this time!"

That is the ultimate good report!

---

[66] He collected five Navy Crosses, three Air Medals, two Legion of Merits, a Distinguished Service Cross, Silver Star, Bronze Star, and Purple Heart, just to name a few.

Faith is a decision that never wavers.

James gives us a vivid metaphor of the instability of unbelief.

> But let him ask in faith, with no doubting, for the one who doubts is like a wave of the sea that is driven and tossed by the wind. For that person must not suppose that he will receive anything from the Lord; he is a double-minded man, unstable in all his ways. **JAMES 1:6–8**

The Greek word translated "doubt" in this passage presents a picture of a mind at war and divided against itself. Here is what three different commentators said about this passage:

> The man who is not thoroughly persuaded [. . .] resembles a wave of the sea; he is in a state of continual agitation; driven by the wind, and tossed: now rising by hope, then sinking by despair.[67]

> The wave of the sea has no stability. It is at the mercy of every wind, and seems to be driven and tossed every way. So he that comes to God with unsettled convictions, is liable to be driven about by every new feeling that may spring up in the mind. At one moment, hope and faith impel him to come to God; then the mind is at once filled with uncertainty and doubt, and the soul is as agitated and restless as the ocean.[68]

> The man who asks without faith is a walking contradiction. His answer will only be as firm as his request. James coined a new expression, "double minded," to describe this kind of man. He speaks of someone who maintains two entirely opposite mind-sets at the same time—first operating from one, then the other.[69]

There are many promises in God's Word, but this is not one you want to claim: "That man should not think he will receive anything from the Lord." This is not just a warning and a rebuke but it is also a promise—not the kind of promise we might see embroidered on a tapestry or ornately lettered on

---

[67] Adam Clark, *Adam Clarke's Commentary of the Bible* (Baker Book House, 1967).

[68] Albert Barnes, *Barnes' Notes on the Old and New Testament* (Baker Book House, 1957).

[69] James Douglas, *New Commentary on the Whole Bible: Old Testament Volume* (Tyndale House Publishers, 1991).

a poster—but a promise nonetheless. And God is always faithful to keep his promises. If you waver and doubt, you will receive **nothing** from the Lord.[70]

A double-minded man is one who will not make a quality decision. He is John Bunyan's character "Mr. Facing-both-ways" from *Pilgrim's Progress*. He is the man with two brains. He is unstable and fickle, staggering and reeling like a drunken man. And he is always looking for reasons life has not worked out for him the way he planned.

The converse is true for a man who holds steadfast to God's Word without wavering.

> If we find a man who takes hold of the promises of God with firmness; who feels the deepest assurance when he prays that God will hear prayer; who always goes to Him without hesitation in his perplexities and trials, never wavering, we shall find one who is firm in his principles, steady in his integrity, settled in his determinations, and steadfast in his plans of life.[71]

> For the righteous will never be moved; he will be remembered forever. He is not afraid of bad news; his heart is firm, trusting in the Lord. His heart is steady; he will not be afraid, until he looks in triumph on his adversaries. **PSALM 112:6–8**

The man who looks in triumph on his foes is a man who made a quality decision. A quality decision is one that you do not go back on, and it's the opposite of a New Year's Resolution.

I overheard two trainers talking a few years ago at the health club I frequented. One had been there a long time and the other was fairly new. The new trainer said, "The club has been very crowded the last week." (It was early January.) The other trainer who had seen this many times replied, "Just wait a few weeks and they will all be gone!"

And they all were! Because they had never made a quality decision. When the challenge of change became too great, they opted for the easy way out.

---

[70] God is sovereign, and he does what he pleases at all times. Sometimes that means doing something when our faith is weak or nonexistent. This fact does not disprove this verse. It only means that the general rule is that God has chosen to respond to faith and that he expects us to believe and not to waver.

[71] See Note 68.

But that is not what Bible faith is—it begins with a quality decision to put the Word of God first, and it never looks back.

Luke presented an example of a quality decision from the life of Jesus:

> As the time approached for him to be taken up to heaven, Jesus resolutely set out for Jerusalem. **LUKE 9:51 NIV**

The word "resolute" describes something as firm and unwavering; characterized by determination and purpose; unyielding, steadfast, and tenacious. Jesus made a quality decision to resolutely head toward Jerusalem—even though he knew what was waiting for him there. And because we are new creations in Christ, we have the same ability to make quality decisions—not by might nor by power, but by his Spirit. This is not human willpower. It is the Spirit of him who raised Jesus from the dead living in us—giving life to our mortal bodies (Romans 8:11). It is the grace of God teaching us to live self-controlled, upright, and godly lives in this present age (Titus 2:11–14). It is the resurrection power of Jesus enabling us to live a new life (Romans 6:3–7).

Conclusion

In these chapters, we have examined the foundation of faith, why we need it, and what it is. In the following chapters, we will look at how faith grows, what it looks like in action, and how it is fueled by both the Word of God and God's covenant with us.

Application

Discuss

1. What was so remarkable about Abraham's faith as described by Paul in Romans 4:19–21? Why do you think that an informed and realistic faith is difficult for people to understand? Have you encountered the challenge of having to face facts squarely in the eye without losing faith? What did God teach you in those circumstances?

    _____

    _____

    _____

2. Why is the attitude of Thomas common among believers? When is the last time you displayed Thomas-like behavior when you were faced with a situation that required Abraham-like faith? Why did you find it difficult to make the right response? What did you learn from that experience that will help you the next time you encounter something similar?

    _____

    _____

    _____

3. Some people find it harder than others to give a good report, maybe because of their upbringing or their temperament or other factors, but they have a natural tendency to negativity. What is your tendency when faced with potentially negative circumstances? Are you more prone to a bad report? If so, why, and what can you do about it?

    _____

    _____

    _____

4. People of faith make quality decisions based on the Word of God. What situation are you facing right now that requires a quality decision? What are the obstacles hindering you from making the decision, and how will you overcome them?

_____

_____

_____

Act

Review the last three chapters on what faith is. Examine the current state of your faith and create an action plan to immediately begin to maximize the areas that you are strong in and improve the areas that you are weak in.

Meditate

But let him ask in faith, with no doubting, for the one who doubts is like a wave of the sea that is driven and tossed by the wind. For that person must not suppose that he will receive anything from the Lord; he is a double-minded man, unstable in all his ways. JAMES 1:6–8

07

How Does Faith Grow?

Part One

Introduction

Nearly everyone is conscious of our need for more faith. Meeting someone who would say "I have too much faith" is highly unlikely. Such people, if they exist at all, are extremely rare. Most people would say the opposite—"I do not have enough faith." So then, where do we get more faith? There are a number of answers to that question, but the starting point is this simple fact: if you are a Christian, you already have faith. Paul said to the Romans:

> God has allotted to each a measure of faith. ROMANS 12:3 NASB

God has given to each of us a measure or portion of faith. Think of it as our *Faith Starter Kit*. Everything we need to get started is already in the package. But there are some things we have to add to the *Kit* to make our faith grow. Think of these as *Faith Additives*. The word "additive" means something added to something else to improve or strengthen it.

So God gives us faith, and then, by his grace, we add to it. This causes our faith to grow. Simple enough? Then let's look at five *Faith Additives* for growing strong faith.

Faith grows by hearing the Word of God.

The clearest answer to the question of how faith grows is found in Paul's letter to the Romans.

> So faith comes from hearing, and hearing through the word of Christus. **ROMANS 10:17**

This familiar verse should not be lifted out of the chapter without any reference to its setting. The context of the verse is preaching, and the apostle emphasizes in the verses before and after this verse that it is the *preached Word* that produces faith in the hearer. Our private devotional interaction with the Word of God is certainly important and it does increase our faith, but hearing the Word preached under the anointing is the best and fastest way to cause our faith to grow. There is a good example of this in Luke's account of an incident that took place during Paul's preaching ministry in Lystra.

> And there they continued to preach the gospel. Now at Lystra there was a man sitting who could not use his feet. He was crippled from birth and had never walked. He listened to Paul speaking. And Paul, looking intently at him and seeing that he had faith to be made well, said in a loud voice, "Stand upright on your feet." And he sprang up and began walking. **ACTS 14:7-10**

Luke tells us that Paul saw that this man had the faith needed to be healed. Where did this man get the faith? God gave it to him as he heard the Word that Paul preached under the anointing. This is a clear example of the Romans 10:17 principle: faith comes by hearing the Word of God preached. In the same way, faith will come to us as we steadfastly listen to the preached Word.

Because faith comes from hearing God's Word, the best way to increase our faith is to increase the amount of time we spend listening to it. Martin Luther said:

> God creates faith in us through the Word. He increases, strengthens, and confirms faith in us through His Word. Therefore, the best service that anybody can render God is diligently to hear and read God's Word.[72]

But does hearing God's Word *automatically* increase our faith? Is it possible to hear God's Word without our faith growing at all? The writer of Hebrews says that this is possible when he reminds us of the Israelites who

---

[72] Martin Luther, *Commentary on Galatians* (CreateSpace Independent Publishing Platform, 2012).

fell in the wilderness even after they listened to God's Word. They heard the Word, but their faith did not increase.

> For we also have had the gospel preached to us, just as they did; but the message they heard was of no value to them, because those who heard did not **combine** it with faith. HEBREWS 4:2 NASB

The Greek word translated "combine" in this passage is *kerannumi*, which means, "a mixing of two things, so that they are blended and form a new compound."[73] There is a similar but different Greek word used in other places in the Scriptures for "combine." It is *mignumi*, which implies "a mixing together without such composition."[74]

> *The authorship of Hebrews is one of the great mysteries of the New Testament. The Church Father Origen claimed the thoughts were Paul's, but the words were Luke's or Clement's. Clement of Alexandria thought that Paul wrote it in Hebrew and that Luke translated it into Greek. The fourth century church historian Eusebius thought it was translated from the original Hebrew by Clement, but he was unsure who the original author was. Martin Luther thought Apollos wrote it. Others have suggested Barnabas, Philip, Silas, Stephen, Mark, and even Priscilla and Aquila! But perhaps Origen said it best: "Only God knows with certainty who wrote Hebrews."*

An experiment I did in high school chemistry class will help us understand the difference between the two words. The teacher started the experiment with a quantity of sodium, an element so highly reactive it explodes on contact with water. Then she added the poisonous gas chlorine. After combining these two dangerous elements together, she was able to eat the product. It was common table salt. This is what the word *kerannumi* means—mixing two things together to get something new.

However, *mignumi* is comparable to combining oil and vinegar in a container. If we shake the container vigorously, the two compounds will not form anything new. They may seem to combine briefly, but they will still retain their original characteristics. Before long, the oil will settle on the bottom and the vinegar at the top.

---

[73] W. E. Vine, *Expository Dictionary of New Testament Words* (Zondervan, 1982), Vol. III, 71–72.

[74] See Note 73.

This describes what the Israelites did. They heard the Word of God, but they never allowed it to do anything in their heart. They did not combine it (*kerannumi*) with a decision to believe. They heard the Word, but they retained their original characteristics (*mignumi*), and they were not transformed and changed.

So then, hearing is not enough—we must actively decide to believe the words we are hearing. Paul calls this "hearing with faith."

> I would like to learn just one thing from you: Did you receive the Spirit by the works of the law, or by **believing what you heard**? [. . .] So again I ask, does God give you his Spirit and work miracles among you by the works of the law, or by your **believing what you heard**? GALATIANS 3:2, 5 NIV

I once prayed with a college student who was distraught because she could not receive the Holy Spirit and speak in tongues. She told me, "I cannot speak in tongues. I do not know what my problem is. I try and try, but for some reason I cannot speak in tongues. I have had prayer several times, but I cannot speak in tongues!" After she calmed down a bit I said to her, "I can tell you what your problem is." She looked at me, and a glimmer of hope appeared on her countenance. "You can?" she said meekly.

I said, "You have just told me what you believe. You expressed what you really believe with the words you said. Three times you said, 'I cannot speak in tongues.' Now, let me ask you this question, what does the Bible say will happen when I lay my hands upon you?"

"I will be filled with the Holy Spirit and speak with tongues," she said.

"I am sorry," I said, "I did not hear you. Would you repeat that please?"

"I will be filled with the Holy Spirit and speak with tongues," she said a little louder.

"I am sorry, there must be something wrong with my hearing; could you say that again?"

"I will be filled with the Holy Spirit and speak with tongues," she said with greater force.

I said, "All you have done so far is undo the three negative faith declarations you made earlier. Now," I said, "tell me what you believe."

"I will be filled with the Holy Spirit and speak with tongues."

I then called three of her friends over and made her say it four times to them. By then she was ready. We laid our hands on her, she received the Holy Spirit, and spoke in tongues fluently.

She had heard the Word concerning the infilling of the Holy Spirit many times, but it had been of no value to her. But when she "heard with faith"—when she made a quality decision to believe what she heard—she received immediately.

The Israelites referred to in Hebrews 4:2 heard the Word of God but would not believe. The writer of the letter describes their unbelief and disobedience in great detail in this section as a warning to us. There is much we do not know about the letter to the Hebrews, but one thing we are sure of is that the recipients were a congregation in danger of drifting away from faith in Christ. The author continually exhorts them concerning the danger of unbelief.

So, as the Holy Spirit says: "Today, if you hear his voice, do not harden your hearts as you did in the rebellion, during the time of testing in the wilderness, where your ancestors tested and tried me, though for forty years they saw what I did." [. . .] See to it, brothers and sisters, that none of you has a sinful, unbelieving heart that turns away from the living God. HEBREWS 3:7–9, 12 NIV

Unbelief is called sinful in this passage. The author continues:

And with whom was he *angry* for forty years? Was it not with those who sinned, whose bodies perished in the wilderness? HEBREWS 3:17 NIV

Apparently, unbelief makes God angry. This is confirmed by an incident recorded by Mark concerning the unbelief of Jesus' disciples after his resurrection.

When Jesus rose early on the first day of the week, he appeared first to Mary Magdalene, out of whom he had driven seven demons. She went and told those who had been with him and who were mourning and weeping. When they heard that Jesus was alive and that she had seen him, they did not believe it. Afterward Jesus appeared in a different form to two of them while they were walking in the country. These returned and reported it to the rest; but they did not believe them either. Later Jesus appeared to the Eleven as they were eating; he *rebuked* them for their lack of faith and their *stubborn refusal to believe* those who had seen him after he had risen. MARK 16:9–14 NIV

The Greek word translated "rebuked" in this passage is a very strong word meaning "to reprimand or criticize angrily, vehemently, and at length." The only other time this word was used in reference to Jesus was when he denounced the cities of Korazin and Capernaum because they did not repent after seeing his miracles (Matthew 11:20). Jesus was especially angry at his disciples on this occasion because of their **stubborn refusal** to believe. It was not just an intellectual problem or a lack of information behind their unbelief; it was a choice not to believe.

Continuing in Hebrews . . .

And to whom did he swear that they would not enter his rest, but to those who were disobedient? So we see that they were unable to enter because of unbelief. HEBREWS 3:18–19

Disobedience and unbelief are coupled in this pair of verses as synonyms, as two expressions of the same act. Unbelief is disobedience and disobedience is unbelief. The warnings continue into the next chapter:

Therefore, while the promise of entering his rest still stands, let us fear lest any of you should seem to have failed to reach it. HEBREWS 4:1

The author then compares the life of faith with the Sabbath rest promised to God's people—a rest from our own works in imitation of God and how he rested from his works after the creation of the world. He concludes this section with an exhortation to make every effort to enter that rest, so that no one will fall short by following their example of disobedience. The emphasis of this entire passage is "hearing his voice."

- If you hear his voice, you will enter the Sabbath rest.
- If you hear his voice, you will not fall through unbelief.
- If you hear his voice, you will not be disobedient.
- If you hear his voice, you will have faith to endure.

After saying all this, he tells them how they can be sure to hear his voice.

For the word of God is living and active. HEBREWS 4:12

God's voice is his Word, and if we hear it by faith, faith will increase.

Faith grows by meditating on the Word of God.

The psalmist uses the metaphor of a tree to paint an attractive picture of the man who delights in meditating in God's Word.

But his delight is in the law of the Lord, and on his law he meditates day and night. He is like a tree planted by streams of water that yields its fruit in its season, and its leaf does not wither. In all that he does, he prospers. **PSALM 1:2–3**

The following are a few thoughts concerning this passage.

- Albert Barnes, in his commentary on the Psalms, said about this man: "He disciplines his mind to meditate habitually and intentionally. He does this at set times each day and during the brief moments of leisure and downtime of every day."[75] Meditation is not just a part of our daily devotional time. It is something we engage in all throughout our day.

- This tree is planted; it did not just grow at random. And because it was planted, there must have been a "planter," someone who put the tree exactly where it is for a specific purpose. God has planted us where we are for his divine purpose.

- The tree is not just planted, it is planted firmly. A firmly planted tree is one with an extensive root system. There is a hidden world underground that supports the tree against the elements of the world. Come what will, this tree will still be standing. This same idea is captured in Psalm 112: "Blessed are those who fear the Lord, who find great delight in his commands. Surely the righteous will never be shaken; they will be remembered forever. They will have no fear of bad news; their hearts are steadfast, trusting in the Lord. Their hearts are secure, they will have no fear; in the end they will look in triumph on their foes" (Psalm 112:1, 6–8 NIV).

- The tree is planted firmly by streams of water. Notice that the word "streams" is plural. There are more than one so that if one should fail, there are others to depend on.[76] This is a reference to the complex irrigation system used in the Middle East—a system that made parts of Egypt the most fertile and productive ground in the world. Rivers were redirected so that dozens of streams would flow in canals on the cultivated land. This produced a constant and

75 Albert Barnes, *Barnes' Notes on the Old and New Testament* (Baker Book House, 1957), comment on Psalm 1:2.

76 Charles Spurgeon, *The Treasury of David, 3 Volumes* (Hendrickson, 1876), comment on Psalm 1:3.

abundant flow of life-giving water to ensure fruitfulness regardless of weather conditions. The person who meditates constantly on God's Word does not fear when the heat comes; he will not be anxious in a year of drought nor cease to yield fruit (Jeremiah 17:8).

- Because of this endless supply of life-giving water, the tree is always green and it always yields fruit.

The last phrase of the verse, "whatever he does, he prospers," is a summary of all the above qualities. Note that there are no qualifiers connected with this phrase. The author does not say, "Whatever he does prospers, *if* it is the will of God," or, "Whatever he does prospers, *if* his motives are right." He simply states that whatever he does will prosper.

Why are there no qualifiers in this verse? Can we do anything we want—regardless if it is the will of God or not—and expect it to prosper? Certainly not. But the reason there are no qualifiers in this verse is because a man meditating on God's Word day and night will walk naturally in God's will. God's Word *is* his will, and if we constantly meditate on his Word, we will naturally walk in his will. This is because meditation produces obedience.

This Book of the Law shall not depart from your mouth, but you shall meditate on it day and night, so that you may be careful to do according to all that is written in it. For then you will make your way prosperous, and then you will have good success. JOSHUA 1:8

The word "so" in this verse indicates cause and effect. Because you meditate in the Word of God day and night, you *will* be careful to obey it.

When God said to Abraham, "I will surely bless you, and I will surely multiply your offspring as the stars of heaven and as the sand that is on the seashore. And your offspring shall possess the gate of his enemies" (Genesis 22:17), he was giving him something to meditate on during the day (sand), and something to meditate on during the night (stars).

James communicated the same idea when he said:

But whoever looks intently into the perfect law that gives freedom, and continues in it—not forgetting what they have heard, but doing it—they will be blessed in what they do. JAMES 1:25 NIV

Looking intently at the Word of God is meditating on it. If we practice this, we will be blessed in what we do.

Faith grows by patience.

Paul described Abraham's faith this way:

> No unbelief made him waver concerning the promise of God, but he grew strong in his faith as he gave glory to God. ROMANS 4:20

Abraham **grew** strong in faith. He did not necessarily start out strong in faith. If you read his story in Genesis, you know that is true. On a number of occasions, he acted in unbelief and sought to make things happen through his own efforts. But gradually his faith grew, and eventually he inherited God's promises.

Faith grows when we give it time to grow. Not everything happens overnight in God's kingdom. Not all results come immediately. Not all miracles are instantaneous. Instead, most of God's work is gradual. And because it is gradual, we must be patient.

When my oldest son was in pre-kindergarten Sunday school, his teacher brought seeds for the class to plant as an illustration of faith. Enthusiastically, he planted his seeds in the container provided by the teacher. The next Sunday he could not wait for the family to get to church so he could see his plant. But when we arrived, we saw the seed had not grown. I encouraged him that the seed was like faith, and that it would grow if we gave it time and proper care. The next Sunday, he was dismayed when he saw everyone had a little plant growing in their container—but he had nothing.

Waiting for his seed to grow had been difficult, but *now* it was excruciating. What was wrong with his seed? Did he do something wrong? Did God not love him as much as the other children? All of these thoughts went through his young mind. It got so bad, I did not want to go to church anymore! Finally, after four weeks, the seed sprouted and a little plant grew in his container. My son was happy and life was good again. Faith does grow, if it is given time and the proper care.

Conclusion

If we are believers, we already have faith. However, that faith will not do us much good unless we add the right ingredients. We have already seen three important faith additives. In the next chapter, we will examine two more.

Application

Discuss

1. Why are there so many warnings about unbelief in the Bible? What area of unbelief are you dealing with right now? Why are you finding it so difficult to believe, and what can you do to change?

    _____

    _____

    _____

2. There is a difference between hearing God's Word actively and hearing God's Word passively. The first produces faith and the second produces nothing. Are you ever guilty of hearing God's Word passively? Why do you think that is? What can you do to ensure that every time you hear God's Word, you hear it with faith?

    _____

    _____

    _____

3. Constant meditation on God's Word produces faith, obedience, and success. But it is not always easy to do. What are some of the obstacles you face that hinder you from meditating on God's Word? What is one action step you can take immediately to start increasing the amount of time you spend meditating on God's Word?

    _____

    _____

    _____

4. We inherit the promises through faith and patience. What specific promise from God are you waiting on at this time? What are the challenges you are facing as you wait? How can you encourage yourself to continue to hold onto God's promise while you wait?

_____

_____

_____

Act

Make a commitment to double the amount of time you spend in God's Word for one week. At the end of the week, evaluate the benefits you received by the exercise. Then create a method to incrementally increase your time in God's Word until you get it to the ideal place.

Meditate

So faith comes from hearing, and hearing through the word of Christ.
ROMANS 10:17

How Does Faith Grow?

Part Two

Introduction

In the last chapter, we began our examination of how faith grows. We concluded that faith grows through:

- Hearing the Word of God
- Meditating on the Word of God
- Patience

In this chapter, we will continue to look at how faith grows.

Faith grows by speaking the Word of God.

There is a strong connection in Scripture between our faith and the words of our mouth. When the disciples asked Jesus to increase their faith, he told them, "If you have faith, you can **say** . . ." (Luke 17:5–6). The author of Hebrews urged the saints to endure difficult times by holding fast to the "**confession** of their faith" (Hebrews 4:14 NASB). Paul said the very spirit of faith was connected to the words of our mouth.

> Since we have the same spirit of faith according to what has been written, "I believed, and so I spoke," we also believe, and so we also speak. 2 CORINTHIANS 4:13

Paul also said that the very process through which we are saved displays the connection between faith and speaking.

If you **declare** with your mouth, "Jesus is Lord," and **believe** in your heart that God raised him from the dead, you will be saved. For it is with your heart that you **believe** and are justified, and it is with your mouth that you **profess** your faith and are saved. ROMANS 10:9–10 NIV

Everywhere we look in Scripture, we see how important words are and how they affect our faith. Here are two reasons.

- God created with words.

When the Bible opens in Genesis 1, we see God at work speaking the worlds into existence. The first time God is mentioned, he is speaking; this is the first revelation we have of him. The phrase "God said" is repeated eleven times in the opening chapter.[77] Each time the phrase is used, something new is created. Everything God created, he created with words. Other verses confirm this fact:

By the word of the Lord the heavens were made, and by the **breath of his mouth** all their host [. . .] For he **spoke**, and it came to be; he **commanded**, and it stood firm. PSALM 33:6, 9

By faith we understand that the universe was formed at **God's command**, so that what is seen was not made out of what was visible (Hebrews 11:3 NIV). The Hebrew scholar Robert Alter said it this way:

In the biblical view, words underlie reality. God called the world into being with words. From the start, the capacity for using language set man apart from the other creatures. Spoken language, then, is the foundation of everything human and divine that transpires in the Bible.[78]

Another way the connection between God's creative acts and words is illustrated is in the cursing of the fig tree—one of the most unusual incidents in the ministry of Jesus. Many of the commentators throughout history have understood the incident to be a censure of the spiritual state of the nation of Israel. The barren fig tree, they said, symbolically represented

---

[77] Genesis 1:3, 6, 9, 11, 14, 20, 22, 24, 26, 28–29.

[78] Robert Alter, *The Art of Biblical Narrative* (Basic Books, 2nd Ed, 2011).

barren Israel[79] as reflected in their attitude toward the temple and the ministry of Jesus. These interpretations are certainly correct, but there is even more in this passage.

First of all, we must understand this incident as a teaching demonstration on the nature of faith. Jesus' own commentary when asked about the incident was, "Have faith in God." By saying this, he wanted his disciples to understand that it was an object lesson on the topic of what faith is and how it works. Jesus used two interconnected images to teach this lesson to his disciples: a barren fig tree and a barren nation. That is why the cleansing of the temple is sandwiched between the incident of the fig tree.

The story starts with a visit to the temple.

> And he entered Jerusalem and went into the temple. And when he had looked around at everything, as it was already late, he went out to Bethany with the twelve. **MARK 11:11**

We are not told what Jesus was looking at in the temple or why he chose to visit it at this time—but possibly it was to plan his strategy for the next day.

> On the following day, when they came from Bethany, he was hungry. And seeing in the distance a fig tree in leaf, he went to see if he could find anything on it. When he came to it, he found nothing but leaves, for it was not the season for figs. And he said to it, "May no one ever eat fruit from you again." And his disciples heard it. **MARK 11:12–14**

This behavior may seem strange to us. If it was not the season for figs, why should Jesus expect figs? And if it was not the season for figs, why curse the poor tree for not bearing figs? A little botanical knowledge of Palestine will help us here. The noted scholar Ernest W. G. Masterman says:

---

[79]   In the following passages—Jeremiah 24:1–9, Hosea 9:10, and Luke 13:6–9—the connection between the imagery of the fig tree and the nation of Israel is clearly demonstrated.

When the young leaves are newly appearing in April, every fig-tree which is going to bear fruit at all will have some immature figs upon it, even though "the time of figs," (i.e., of ordinary edible figs) "is not yet." These immature figs are not only eaten today, but it is sure evidence that the tree bearing them is not barren.[80]

Jesus knew it was not fig season, but he was not looking for figs. He was looking for the unripe figs about the size of small cherries that should have been on the tree. The fact that they were not was proof that the tree was barren and would not produce fruit at any season. And so Jesus spoke the inevitable result, "No one will ever eat fruit from you again." The disciples were listening, but they asked no questions. Perhaps Jesus did not appear ready to explain himself at that time. He then proceeded to Jerusalem.

And they came to Jerusalem. And he entered the temple and began to drive out those who sold and those who bought in the temple, and he overturned the tables of the money-changers and the seats of those who sold pigeons. And he would not allow anyone to carry anything through the temple. And he was teaching them and saying to them, "Is it not written, 'My house shall be called a house of prayer for all the nations?' But you have made it a den of robbers." And the chief priests and the scribes heard it and were seeking a way to destroy him, for they feared him, because all the crowd was astonished at his teaching. MARK 11:15–18

Israel had begun as a nation over 1,800 years prior to this event. The nation's beginnings were rooted in Abraham, a man of great faith. Whenever Abraham is mentioned in the New Testament, it is nearly always in the context of his faith. He had many outstanding qualities, but his faith stands out above all of them.

But now Abraham's descendants have a barren faith, a faith that, like the fig tree, will produce no fruit. There should be fruit on the spiritual tree of Israel, but, just like the barren tree, there is none. The nation had already desecrated God's presence in the temple by making it a robbers' den, and they were about to desecrate God's presence in his Son by killing him on a cross. They had destroyed the temple and were looking for ways to destroy him.

The story continues:

---

[80] Ernest W. G. Masterman, *International Standard Bible Encyclopedia* (Eerdmans, 1979).

And when evening came they went out of the city. As they passed
by in the morning, they saw the fig tree withered away to its roots.
And Peter remembered and said to him, "Rabbi, look! The fig tree
that you cursed has withered." And Jesus answered them, "Have
faith in God." MARK 11:19–22

Jesus is famous for his non sequiturs. A non sequitur is a statement that
does not logically follow the statement that preceded it. For example, if I
met you for the first time, I would introduce myself to you. If you responded
to my introduction by saying, "It will rain on Tuesday," that would be a
non sequitur. It may be a true statement, but it is out of sequence; it does
not logically follow from my greeting. The statement, "Have faith in God,"
appeared to be a non sequitur. It was not what the disciples expected to
hear from Jesus because it did not logically follow the statement, "The fig
tree you cursed has withered." You can almost hear Peter thinking, "Huh? I
know we are supposed to have faith in God, but what does that have to do
with the withered fig tree?"

But Peter did not realize that Jesus was not using a non sequitur; his
statement *did* proceed logically from Peter's question. Peter was unaware
that Jesus had contrived the whole scenario to create a memorable learning
experience, one that Peter nor the other disciples would forget.

Jesus was saying to them, "Everything about the fig tree is a lesson on
how faith works. I spoke, and it happened. That is how faith works, and that
is the example I want you to follow. That is how I want you to have faith in
God. Do not miss this lesson and end up like barren Israel."

Jesus continues:

Truly, I say to you, whoever says to this mountain, "Be taken up and
thrown into the sea," and does not doubt in his heart, but believes
that what he says will come to pass, it will be done for him. MARK 11:23

Why did Jesus preface his comments with the phrase, "I tell you the
truth"? Wasn't everything Jesus said the truth? Whenever anyone prefaces
a comment to me with a similar statement, I want to ask them, "Haven't you
been telling me the truth the whole time? Is there something I should question
about what you have been telling me? Why do you feel the sudden need to
emphasize that you are telling me the truth?" We know that Jesus always
tells the truth. Why then did he need to make that introductory statement?

In my opinion, I think Jesus knew his next statements would be so staggering and so radically unexpected that he would need to reinforce them with the strongest language possible. If that is so, then what was so staggering about his next statements?

First, Jesus said, "If *anyone* says." Jesus had just cursed the fig tree, and it had withered. That is a pretty astonishing feat. It would be easy to assume that only he could do something like that because, after all, he was the Son of God. But Jesus immediately corrected that kind of thinking when he used the word *anyone*. This is not just something that only the Son of God gets to do. *Anyone* can speak to the mountain. *Anyone* can have faith like that—from the greatest apostle to the youngest believer.

Second, Jesus said, "to *this* mountain." His use of the definite article meant he was referring to (and possibly pointing to) a specific mountain. Why is this important? Because it means we cannot spiritualize his statement to mean only mountains in a metaphorical sense. Certainly there is a metaphorical application for mountains that is applicable to this passage (for example, mountains may be seen as problems, obstacles, demonic roadblocks, etc.), but it refers primarily to a physical reality. There *is* real power in our words, and Jesus used strong language to reinforce that truth.

Third, Jesus was very specific about what we have to believe. We have to believe that *what we say will come to pass*.

There are many things we have to believe about God. We have to believe that he is (Hebrews 11:6). We have to believe he sent his Son to die for us (John 3:16). We have to believe that he rose from the dead (Romans 10:9). But as important as those things are, they are not what Jesus said we have to believe in order to move mountains. We have to believe that *what we say will come to pass*. What an astonishing, mind-boggling truth. No wonder Jesus prefaced his statements with, "I tell you the truth."

The first time I heard this passage expounded on was in a sermon from an African minister who was visiting the United States. He recounted the time he first heard this truth as a Bible school student. After hearing the message, he decided he would put it in action. Outside his dorm room there was a small hill—no mountain, certainly, but a good place to start. He closed his eyes, pointed to the hill, and said confidently, "Hill, I command you to be taken up and cast into the sea; I do not doubt in my heart, but I believe that what I say is going to happen." He opened his eyes fully expecting the hill to be gone, but to his surprise and dismay, it was not. Discouraged and confused, he finished the school term and left for summer break. He returned in the fall and was assigned his former room. Unpacking his clothes, he glanced out his window and saw that over the summer bulldozers had cleared the hill for new dormitories. He had commanded the hill to move, and it had—not how he imagined it would—but it was gone nonetheless.[81]

- Words that are spoken in faith bring victory.

For we all stumble in many ways. And if anyone does not stumble in what he says, he is a perfect man, able also to bridle his whole body. If we put bits into the mouths of horses so that they obey us, we guide their whole bodies as well. Look at the ships also: though they are so large and are driven by strong winds, they are guided by a very small rudder wherever the will of the pilot directs. **JAMES 3:2–4**

James uses two pairs of metaphors in this passage: a horse and bridle and a ship and rudder. Both pairs refer to the power of our words. Both pairs also carry the idea of destination: you ride on a horse to a particular location; you travel on a ship to another port. The idea we are supposed to understand from these metaphors is that our destination (or destiny) is closely connected with the words we speak.

In the first metaphor, James compares our words to the bridle of a horse. The bridle controls the direction of the horse. The metaphor is clear: words control our destiny the way the bridle controls the direction of the horse.

In the second metaphor, James repeats the meaning of the first and adds a few new ideas to it. He makes three statements about the ship:

- The ship is large.
- The ship is buffeted by strong winds.
- The rudder will hold the ship on course.

The application of this metaphor is also clear. The ship has a destination, and we have a destiny. The ship is large, and our destiny is significant. The ship is buffeted by strong winds, and opposing forces will try to knock us off our course. But through it all, the rudder will hold the ship on course.

---

[81] I am not suggesting that this student's words moved the hill. The bulldozers did that. But God used this unique situation to teach him a valuable spiritual lesson, and to underscore just how powerful words can be.

Our words, spoken in faith, are the rudder of our life and they will keep us on course.[82]

Faith grows by acting on the Word of God.

> So also faith by itself, if it does not have works, is dead. [. . .] Was not Abraham our father justified by works when he offered up his son Isaac on the altar? You see that faith was active along with his works, and faith was completed by his works. JAMES 2:17, 21–22

The Epistle of James deeply troubled Martin Luther because it appeared to teach justification by works. Early in his career, he even called it "an epistle of straw."[83] But he eventually understood that it was teaching an active faith, one that expressed itself in action.[84] He said:

> Faith is a living, restless thing. It cannot be inoperative. We are not saved by works; but if there be no works, there must be something amiss with faith.[85]

James said that when Abraham acted on the Word of God, it completed or perfected his faith. *The New Commentary on the Whole Bible* says it this way:

> His actions completed his faith—i.e., they manifested the full development and maturation of his faith. The seed has everything it needs to be a full-grown tree right from the start, but you can hardly say it is complete until you see the towering tree. Good deeds show that our faith is full-grown at last.

A few other Bible translations underscore this point:

- The faith was working with his works, and out of the works the **faith was perfected**. (YLT)

---

[82] Speaking God's Word is crucial to our faith development. There are a series of topical confessions for you to follow in Appendix B.

[83] Quoted in the Preface of Martin Luther's 1522 German translation of the New Testament.

[84] In Luther's writings, he quoted over half of the 108 verses in James. He obviously believed it was the word of God.

[85] Roland H. Bainton, *Here I Stand: A Life of Martin Luther* (New York: New American Library, 1950 & 1978), 259.

- You see that faith was active along with his works, and ***faith was brought to completion*** by the works. (NRSV)
- Abraham's ***faith was made perfect*** by what he did. (NCV)
- His ***faith was shown to be genuine*** by what he did. (God's Word)

From these translations, we can clearly see that actions are integral to the growth of our faith.

I have a friend who struggled with a degenerative disc problem for years. She was always in pain, and nothing she did seemed to help. She had prayed and believed God for healing for a long time, but to no avail. Finally, in a time of desperation, she heard the Lord direct her to run a marathon. Nothing seemed more impossible. She could hardly walk, how would she ever run over twenty-six miles? But in obedience to God, she put her faith in action. She trained for six months and, in January 2004, entered the Disney Marathon in Florida. She experienced pain throughout the race, but before crossing the finish line felt a "sudden twinge" and was completely healed. To this day, she has had no more problems.

She acted on the Word of the Lord and received a miracle. The cripple that Paul ministered to in Lystra had a similar experience.

> Now at Lystra there was a man sitting who could not use his feet. He was crippled from birth and had never walked. He listened to Paul speaking. And Paul, looking intently at him and seeing that he had faith to be made well, said in a loud voice, "Stand upright on your feet." And he sprang up and began walking. ACTS 14:8–10

It would have been easy for the crippled man to explain to Paul that he would be glad to stand up on his feet—if God would only heal him first. But if he had said that instead of acting on his faith, he would not have been healed. His obedient and active response to the Word of truth caused his healing. His actions combined with his faith, and together they completed his healing.

An old Scotsman operated a rowboat for transporting passengers across one of the many lochs in his native land. Carved on one oar was the word, "Faith," and on the other oar the word, "Works." When a curious passenger asked him why, he responded with a demonstration. Using just the "Faith" oar, he rowed vigorously, but they just went in circles. Switching to the "Works" oar, he rowed again with the same results—but in the opposite direction. After the demonstration, he said, "In the Christian life, works without faith are as useless as faith without works: both of them will spin you in circles and get you nowhere. But together, in cooperation, they will take you anywhere you want to go."

Conclusion

In the last two chapters, we have examined how faith grows. In the next chapter, we will look at specific examples from God's Word of faith in action.

Application

Discuss

1. Many Christians seem to have a natural resistance to confessing God's Word with boldness and consistency. They start doing it, and then various obstacles arise until slowly they abandon the practice completely. Have you had a similar experience? If so, what are some of the obstacles that have deterred you? Why were those obstacles effective in deterring you, and what can you do to ensure they will not defeat you again?

2. Our destination in life is closely connected with the words we speak. What are some of the "spiritual destinations" you desire in your life, and what confessions should you make in order to get there? What creative action step can you take to incorporate more confession in your life?

3. Our actions reveal what we believe. Describe a recent situation where your actions revealed your faith in God. Why did you respond properly to that situation? Describe another recent situation where your actions revealed your lack of faith in God. Why did you respond improperly to that situation? What did you learn from both situations that will help you the next time you face similar circumstances?

_____

_____

_____

Act

Create your own Bible confession sheet with verses that directly address a current need in your life. Spend fifteen minutes a day for a week meditating on and confessing these verses.

Meditate

It is written: "I believed; therefore I have spoken." With that same spirit of faith we also believe and therefore speak. **2 CORINTHIANS 4:13**

Faith in Action

Introduction

Throughout this book, we have examined why you need faith, what it is, and how it grows. Now, let's look at some examples of faith in action.

Paul's Shipwreck

Sometime during the Apostle Paul's third missionary journey,[86] he decided to raise a contribution for the saints in Jerusalem. A serious rift had formed among the Jewish believers against Paul because he was offering the gospel to the Gentiles without circumcision. He was passionate about healing this divide, and so he determined to visit Jerusalem with both an offering from the Gentile churches and a team of representatives from among his Gentile converts. (Possibly, he thought it would be hard for the Jewish believers to remain mad at him after he had presented them with a big check.) He explained his purpose in the letter that he wrote to the Romans at this time.

> Now, however, I am on my way to Jerusalem in the service of the Lord's people there. For Macedonia and Achaia were pleased to make a contribution for the poor among the Lord's people in Jerusalem.

---

[86] Luke records three distinct missionary journeys of Paul. The first was with Barnabas (Acts 13–14). The second was with Silas (Acts 15:36–18:22). And the third was with several companions (Acts 18:23–21:17).

They were pleased to do it, and indeed they owe it to them. For if the Gentiles have shared in the Jews' spiritual blessings, they owe it to the Jews to share with them their material blessings. ROMANS 15:25–27

When Paul arrived in Jerusalem, angry Jews from Asia Minor incited the whole city against him and tried to kill him. The Roman military intervened, and after a series of trials, took him to prison in Caesarea. Two years later, after Paul had appealed to Caesar,[87] Felix, the Roman governor, placed him on a ship heading to Rome. But before the ship got very far, they encountered significant sailing difficulties.

Much time had been lost, and sailing had already become dangerous because by now it was after the Fast. So Paul warned them, "Men, I can see that our voyage is going to be disastrous and bring great loss to ship and cargo, and to our own lives also." ACTS 27:9–10

This was not necessarily a word of knowledge or prophecy on Paul's part. It was mostly common sense. Luke tells us that the Fast was already over, a reference to the Day of Atonement. The Day of Atonement was the last day of the Jewish feast of Tabernacles, and in AD 59 (the probable year of Paul's journey) the Day of Atonement came on October 5. In the first century, the dangerous season for sailing the Mediterranean began on September 14 and lasted until November 11. After that, all navigation on the open sea ceased for the winter.[88] It was now approaching the middle of October, and Paul wisely urged them to winter where they were. They could then resume the journey in the spring, but the pilot and owner had different plans.

But the centurion, instead of listening to what Paul said, followed the advice of the pilot and of the owner of the ship. Since the harbor was unsuitable to winter in, the majority decided that we should sail on, hoping to reach Phoenix and winter there. ACTS 27:11–12

As they set out, a gentle south wind was blowing, and it appeared they would gain their purpose. But before very long, a wind of hurricane force swept down upon them. The ship was caught by the storm, and they gave way to it and were driven along. The ship took such a violent battering from the

---

[87]   One of the privileges of Roman citizenship was the right to appeal directly to Caesar if you were dissatisfied with the way you were being treated in a courtroom. Paul was born a Roman citizen and had this right.

[88]   F. F. Bruce, *Paul: Apostle of the Heart Set Free* (Eerdmans, 2000), 370.

storm that the crew started throwing cargo out to stay afloat. After nearly two desperate weeks had passed, the sailors abandoned all hope of survival.

When neither sun nor stars appeared for many days and the storm continued raging, we finally gave up all hope of being saved. ACTS 27:20

This was a very real storm that Paul and the others were in; it was not just a metaphor. But storms are often used throughout Scripture as metaphors for adversity and difficulties and the challenges of life. Here are a few examples:

Oh, that I had the wings of a dove! I would fly away and be at rest [. . .] I would hurry to my place of shelter, far from the tempest and *storm*. PSALM 55:6, 8

When the *storm* has swept by, the wicked are gone, but the righteous stand firm forever. PROVERBS 10:25

You have been a refuge for the poor, a refuge for the needy in his distress, a shelter from the *storm* and a shade from the heat. ISAIAH 25:4

Paul was in this storm for two reasons. The first reason was because the centurion and company had disobeyed the wisdom of God. Paul, God's messenger, had warned them not to continue sailing, but they refused to listen. As a result, they were all in the storm. In the same way, there are times in our lives when the storm we are experiencing is the result of disobedience. Sometimes it is the disobedience of another (as in Paul's case), and sometimes it is our own disobedience. When we find ourselves in these situations, we need to discover where we missed God's will, repent, and start doing what he originally told us to do.

But there was a second reason Paul was in the storm: he was fulfilling his destiny. Paul was on his way to Rome to testify about the Lord Jesus Christ to Caesar, the most powerful man on earth. God had said to Ananias concerning Paul that he was "My chosen instrument to proclaim my name to the Gentiles and their kings" (Acts 9:15). As the apostle to the Gentiles, he felt compelled to preach to Nero,[89] the leader of the Gentile world. And the devil would do anything he could to stop this meeting—even stir up a huge storm.

[89] Nero was the Caesar from AD 54 to 68.

Just like Paul's experience with this storm, there are also times in our lives when the storm we are experiencing is a result of fulfilling God's purpose. The enemy of our souls will stir up whatever he can to stop us from advancing toward fulfilling God's plan.

Many years ago, I found myself in a situation like this. I was experiencing a lot of pressure, and I did not know why. I did not know then what I know now about storms, and I could not figure out what the problem was. Exasperated, I set aside a time to seek God and to find out what was going on and what I needed to do about it. In desperation I cried, "God, what is my problem?" The room became very still, and I had the sense that God was about to speak. And then, very softly in my heart, I heard these words, "Your problem is that you are right in the center of my will." That was a revelation to me. I assumed I had done something wrong. I assumed that if I was in God's will, everything would be peaceful. But after researching the Scriptures, I discovered that my assumptions were wrong. I discovered that sometimes the middle of God's will can feel like a terrible storm. Here are a few confirming verses:

In fact, everyone who wants to live a godly life in Christ Jesus will be persecuted. 2 TIMOTHY 3:12

So that no one would be unsettled by these trials. For you know quite well that we are destined for them. 1 THESSALONIANS 3:3

Join with me in suffering, like a good soldier of Christ Jesus. 2 TIMOTHY 2:3

What should we do when we find ourselves in a storm like that? We should follow Paul's example. The first thing he did was to find someone with a bigger problem than his.

After they had gone a long time without food, Paul stood up before them and said: "Men, you should have taken my advice not to sail from Crete; then you would have spared yourselves this damage and loss. But now I urge you to keep up your courage, because not one of you will be lost; only the ship will be destroyed. Last night an angel of the God to whom I belong and whom I serve stood beside me and said, 'Do not be afraid, Paul. You must stand trial before Caesar; and God has graciously given you the lives of all who sail with you.'" ACTS 27:21–24

Whenever angels show up in response to someone's prayer, you can always tell what that person was praying about by what the angel said. In this example, the angel assured Paul that he would preach to Nero and that everyone on board would be saved. If that was the angel's answer, then Paul must have been praying for Nero and the men on board who did not know Christ. In the midst of a frightening and life-threatening storm, Paul refused to yield to fear or think about his own life. Instead, he found others needier than himself and prayed for them.

I have friends who pastored for many years in the southwest part of England. When I first visited them in 1995, their oldest son had recently been killed in a tragic accident while on the mission field. They were obviously under a deep burden of sorrow and despair. When I saw them again ten months later, it was also obvious that something had changed. Their countenance was bright and their outlook was positive. When we got a chance to talk, they told me what had happened.

They had realized that if they did not do something about the way they were feeling, it was going to destroy them. So they purchased a subscription to the local paper and started scanning the obituary column every day looking for parents who had lost a child. When they found someone, they would put together a care package and show up on their doorstep. When the grieving parents came to the door, they would introduce themselves and say, "We also lost a child not long ago, and we know what you are going through. If you want someone to talk with or pray with or just cry with, we are here." Not surprisingly, they had the opportunity to pray for several people and lead them to faith in Christ. In the worst storm of their lives, they found others with bigger problems than theirs. As a result, they were able to triumph over their own storm.

The next thing Paul did was he found God's purpose in the storm. He said to the entire crew:

We **must** run aground on some island. ACTS 27:26

Notice his word choice: "must." There was an island that Paul had to go to. Why? Because there was something he had to do there.

Paul, in all likelihood, would never have visited Malta if not for this storm. It was not a prominent place in the Roman empire, and it was not somewhere you normally went. But because of this storm, Paul ended up there. As a result of his visit, the gospel was preached and a church established on the island. There has been a continuous Christian witness on that island ever since.

Sometimes storms in our lives take us to places we never intended to go and never would have gone on our own. But God works in his sovereign way to accomplish his purpose in our lives, even through events that, at the time, we may think are working against us.

The final thing Paul did in the storm was to say what God said about it.

So keep up your courage, men, for I have faith in God that it will happen just as he told me. ACTS 27:25

There was a man of faith on that ship, and he had a word from God. Although Paul was the prisoner, he stood boldly on the deck of the ship and spoke God's word with confidence. In any storm of life, we should follow Paul's example. Find out what God has to say about our storm, and then boldly proclaim his Word without wavering. It will turn out for us just as he said!

Joshua and Caleb

Then Caleb silenced the people before Moses and said, "We should go up and take possession of the land, for we can certainly do it." But the men who had gone up with him said, "We can't attack those people; they are stronger than we are." And they spread among the Israelites a bad report about the land they had explored. They said, "The land we explored devours those living in it. All the people we saw there are of great size. We saw the Nephilim there (the descendants of Anak come from the Nephilim). We seemed like grasshoppers in our own eyes, and we looked the same to them." That night all the members of the community raised their voices and wept aloud. All the Israelites grumbled against Moses and Aaron, and the whole assembly said to them, "If only we had died in Egypt! Or in this wilderness! Why is the LORD bringing us to this land only to let us fall by the sword? Our wives and children will be taken as plunder. Wouldn't it be better for us to go back to Egypt?" And they said to each other, "We should choose a leader and go back to Egypt." NUMBERS 13:30–14:4

This historical event takes place sometime around 1450 BC. Moses had recently delivered God's people from Egyptian slavery and was attempting to take them into the Promised Land. God had given the people a promise, and they had a covenant with him—the land was theirs. But there was a problem: there were giants in the land.

There are always giants in the land. There are always obstacles standing in the way of the promises of God. Someone once said, "Obstacles are those frightful things you see when you take your eyes off your goals." That quote would be more accurate if it was rewritten to say, "Obstacles are those terrible things you see when you take your eyes off God's Word." If living by faith was easy, everyone would do it. The Apostle Paul understood this, and he knew that the example of the Israelites was a warning to us all.

> For I do not want you to be ignorant of the fact, brothers and sisters, that our ancestors were all under the cloud and that they all passed through the sea. They were all baptized into Moses in the cloud and in the sea. They all ate the same spiritual food and drank the same spiritual drink; for they drank from the spiritual rock that accompanied them, and that rock was Christ. Nevertheless, God was not pleased with most of them; their bodies were scattered in the wilderness. 1 CORINTHIANS 10:1–5

The primary warning to us in this passage is: "God was not pleased with **most** of them." Why was he not pleased? Because they did not believe his promise, and without faith it is impossible to please him. What was the result of their unbelief? "Their bodies were scattered over the desert." Unbelief has serious consequences. Paul knew that, and he wanted to warn us. He said:

> Do you not know that in a race all the runners run, but only one gets the prize? Run in such a way as to get the prize. 1 CORINTHIANS 9:24

I still remember the first time I read this verse. I was a new believer with little prior Bible knowledge. I also tended to be excessively literal in my interpretation of Scripture. So I was shocked when I read the words, "only one gets the prize." How could that be? Only one person? I thought, "Is that one per city, one per church, or just one?" I wasn't sure exactly what the prize was or how many people could qualify for it, but I determined at that moment that if only one was going to get it, that one would be me.

Years later, I realized that although my hermeneutical methodology[90] was all wrong, I had actually come close to understanding Paul's intended meaning. He was not saying that only one wins the prize. He was saying

---

[90] Hermeneutics is the science of accurate biblical interpretation.

that we ought to run *as if* only one wins the prize. And it would make a difference, wouldn't it, in the way we pursued the things of God if there was only one winner? Obstacles would not have the same power over our lives.

A high school football coach told a story that illustrates this idea. His team was competing for the State Championship against their rivals. They were leading 6-0 with time left for only one play. He instructed his quarterback to take the snap and down the ball. Time would run out, and they would be the champions. But his quarterback had ambitions, and he felt like his many talents had not been fully displayed in such a low scoring game. So the quarterback changed the play and called for a pass play instead. After receiving the snap, he located his receiver in the open and threw a perfect spiral to him. But at the last minute the defensive player stepped in front of the pass, intercepted it, and took off for the end zone. It looked like he would score a touchdown when at the last possible minute he was tackled from behind—by the quarterback.

Later, the two coaches discussed the last play. The losing coach was incredulous that a slow-footed quarterback could catch his fleet-footed defensive back, especially when his player had a head start. The winning coach explained it to him in simple terms: "Your player was running for a touchdown and a State Championship, but my player was running for HIS LIFE!"

How you run does make a difference.

How do we run in such a way as to get the prize? We follow the example of Joshua and Caleb. Out of that whole generation of Israelites, they were the only two people who received God's promise. The people of Israel did not win the prize and enter the land because they believed in the giants more than they believed in the promise, and only people of faith inherit the land. God's testimony concerning the faith of Caleb was:

> But because my servant Caleb has a different spirit and follows me wholeheartedly, I will bring him into the land he went to, and his descendants will inherit it. NUMBERS 14:24

Joshua and Caleb gave us an example to follow.

- They believed God's promises more than they believed the testimony of their physical senses.
- They declared God's promises while facing great obstacles.

We all have our own personal giants that continually try to deter us from our promised land. But if we follow the faith of Joshua and Caleb, we will win the prize.

Jairus and the Woman

A large crowd gathered around Jesus expecting him to do miracles. People had come from miles around, bringing their sick with them. They were all watching and waiting and hoping. But through the middle of the crowd came a man who could not wait. His daughter was dying and he was determined to have Jesus heal her.

> Then one of the synagogue leaders, named Jairus, came, and when he saw Jesus, he fell at his feet. He pleaded earnestly with him, "My little daughter is dying. Please come and put your hands on her so that she will be healed and live." MARK 5:22–23 NIV

"She **will be** healed," he said. Jairus was certain. His faith was unwavering.

If Jesus was politically correct, he would have instructed Jairus to wait his turn. There were many who had been there longer than he. Jairus would have to wait—it was only fair. But that is not what happened.

> And he went with him. And a great crowd followed him and thronged about him. MARK 5:24

Jesus responds to faith. There were many that day that had needs, some probably as great as that of Jairus, but none of them received help. Jairus received a miracle, but everyone else went home disappointed. Well, not quite everyone. There was one other person who believed that day. She also received a miracle.

Life had been difficult for this woman. She had been subject to bleeding for twelve years. Many doctors had promised a cure, but they had just taken her money and treated her badly. She was worse now than when she started.

But then she heard about Jesus. They said he could heal the sick, cure the lame, and raise the dead. And as she listened to the stories, something began to happen within her. Faith was born and began to grow. Finally, she determined she would go to Jesus and receive her healing.

When she approached Jesus that day, she kept saying to herself what she had probably said so many times before—"If I just touch his garments, I will be healed. If I just touch his garments, I **will** be healed." As Jesus passed by, she reached out and touched his garment.

And immediately the flow of blood dried up, and she felt in her body that she was healed of her disease. MARK 5:29

Hundreds had pressed against Jesus that day, and hundreds had touched his garments. But there was something different about this woman. She really believed.

And Jesus, perceiving in himself that power had gone out from him, immediately turned about in the crowd and said, "Who touched my garments?" And his disciples said to him, "You see the crowd pressing around you, and yet you say, 'Who touched me?'" And he looked around to see who had done it. But the woman, knowing what had happened to her, came in fear and trembling and fell down before him and told him the whole truth. And he said to her, "Daughter, your faith has made you well; go in peace, and be healed of your disease." MARK 5:30–34

She put her faith in action and received a miracle from Jesus that day.

While Jesus was delayed with the woman, men came from the home of Jairus with the news Jairus had dreaded, "Your daughter is dead; why bother the teacher any more?" Ignoring the bad report, Jesus said to Jairus, "Don't be afraid; just believe, and she will be healed." Jairus obviously did what Jesus told him to do because before the day was over, Jairus was eating a meal with his twelve-year-old daughter.

Jairus put his faith in action and received a miracle from Jesus that day.

Conclusion

Faith requires action. Men and women in the Bible put their faith in action as a testimony for us to follow their example.

Application

Discuss

1. Have you ever experienced a storm in your life as the result of disobedience? What did you do to get out of it? Have you ever experienced a storm in your life as the result of following God's destiny for your life? What did you learn from it that will help you the next time a storm comes?

    _____

    _____

    _____

2. In the midst of a great storm, Paul boldly declared God's Word concerning the situation. Do you find it difficult to speak God's Word when you are in the middle of a storm? Why? What can you do to correct this and change?

    _____

    _____

    _____

3. What would change about your life if Paul's statement in 1 Corinthians 9:24 was literal and only one got the prize? What **should** change in your life now that you know he is saying that we ought to run as **if** only one wins the prize? What action steps will you take immediately to institute those changes?

    _____

    _____

    _____

4. What are the main giants in your life right now that are keeping you from inheriting your promised land? What will you do to defeat them?

_____

_____

_____

Act

Read Acts 27. Find as many principles of faith in the text as you can. Select one and create a plan to implement it in your life.

Meditate

So take heart, men, for I have faith in God that it will be exactly as I have been told. ACTS 27:25

10

Faith and God's Word

Part One

Introduction

Men and women of faith have one thing in common: they are passionately in love with God's Word.

The Bible is the most widely distributed book in history. It has been the primary agent for cultural transformation in the world for nearly two thousand years. It was the foundation of Western culture, the bedrock of its educational system, and the inspiration of its literature, music, and art. No other book has had such a vast and formative effect on the history of the world as the Holy Bible.[91]

Yet no other book in history has been more maligned, denounced, and vilified. It has elicited the most defamatory attacks from intellectuals, skeptics, and critics for centuries. It seems that no one has been able to remain neutral about the Bible.

However, the Bible is more than just a shaper of cultures and a source of controversy; it is also our very life. Health, joy, peace, and true liberty abound within its pages. It gives wisdom beyond our years and health to our body. It provides a light to our feet and a lamp to our path. It is more precious than gold and more valuable than diamonds. It is the bread of heaven

---

[91]   There is more general information Bible history in Appendix A.

that nourishes and sustains us. It will make us prosperous and successful in every venture as we study and meditate upon it every day.

The Bible is the only written revelation God has given to man. It is the final authority in all matters of faith and practice. It reveals who God is and what he has planned for his creation. It is his personal love letter to his people. One of the last things Moses said to his people just before he died was,

> Take to heart all the words by which I am warning you today, that you may command them to your children, that they may be careful to do all the words of this law. For it is no empty word for you, but your very life, and by this word you shall live long in the land that you are going over the Jordan to possess. DEUTERONOMY 32:46–47

Because God's Word is our life, we must have the proper scriptural attitude toward it. In this chapter and the next, we will look at four attitudes we should have towards God's Word.

Our Attitude toward God's Word

The first attitude we should have towards God's Word is desperation.

Why should we be desperate for God's Word? There are many reasons, but I want to focus on one in particular. God's Word is the primary change agent in our life. When I say "primary change agent," I mean that the Bible is the main tool God uses to change us into his image. And we desperately need to change. There are so many areas in our life where we fall short, so many things that weigh us down, and so many sins that so easily entangle us.

How are we going to change? Should we exert ourselves more? Should we try harder? I have been down that road before, and I can assure you it is a dead-end street. My religious upbringing was very strong on trying harder. And because I am a naturally determined individual and have a reasonably well-developed will, I was able to make some progress against sin by just trying harder. But the main problem I always found with that approach was it made me "the hero of the story." And anything that makes me the hero of the story and not God is pride. And pride always leads to a fall. My very attempts to change only strengthened my inability to change.

So how do we change? Jesus gave us some insight when he prayed,

> Sanctify them in the truth; your word is truth. JOHN 17:17

Sanctification is the process by which God conforms us into his image. It begins the moment we are born again, and it continues until we die. The essence of what Jesus said in his prayer was, "Change them into your image, and do it through the agent of truth—your Word." God's Word is the primary agent of change in our life. This truth is confirmed throughout the Scriptures.

We see it in the life of Joshua. When Joshua took over the leadership of Israel, he was faced with a daunting task. Moses was dead, and God now expected him to lead three million recalcitrant Israelites into a land of giants. How did he feel about his task? He was terrified (any normally intelligent person would have been). We know he was terrified because God said to him three times, "Be strong and courageous" (Joshua 1:6–7, 9).[92]

I can almost hear Joshua thinking, "God, I know you have commanded me not to be afraid, but for some reason, I am still afraid. Do you have anything else to offer? Do you have any tangible means to help me get rid of this fear?" God certainly did. He said,

This Book of the Law shall not depart from your mouth, but you shall meditate on it day and night, so that you may be careful to do according to all that is written in it. For then you will make your way prosperous, and then you will have good success. JOSHUA 1:8

God told Joshua that if he would meditate on his Word day and night, the Word would cause him to be careful to do everything written in it. The action "meditate day and night" and the result "careful to do" is connected in this verse by the phrase "so that." The phrase "so that" serves as the causal link between the action and the result. In other words, meditation would produce obedience—a changed heart.

The next link in the chain is the word "then." The action "be careful to obey" will produce the result of prosperity and success.

Meditation ➜ Obedience/Life Change ➜ Prosperity/Success

Meditation does not produce prosperity; it produces life-changing obedience. And obedience produces prosperity. That is an important distinction. If you remove the all-important middle step of obedience/life change, meditation can deteriorate into a metaphysical and ritualistic attempt

[92] God intensified each exhortation. The first time God said, "Be strong and courageous." The second time he said, "Be strong and very courageous." The third time he said, "I command you to be strong and courageous."

to manipulate God into getting what you want. It is the same mentality a religious man has with his prayer beads: he thinks that if he says enough prayers the exact way, God will be required to give him what he wants. But meditation on God's Word is not a magic formula. It is the primary change agent God uses to change us into his image.

So the answer to all Joshua's concerns was meditation upon the Word of God. It was the primary change agent for Joshua, and it is the primary change agent for us. What worked for Joshua will work for us.

We also see this principle in the life of Moses. He said,

> Now what I am commanding you today is not too difficult for you or beyond your reach. DEUTERONOMY 30:11 NIV

When I read these words a few years ago, they startled me.[93] A little background to Deuteronomy will help you understand my surprise. The word *deuteronomy* comes from two Greek words meaning *second* and *law*. The book consists of a series of sermons Moses delivered to the people before they went into the Promised Land and before he went into Paradise. In these sermons he restated the essence of the law he had delivered in Exodus and Leviticus. So when Moses says, "what I am commanding you today," he was referring to the entire Old Testament law: all 613 commands.

Can you understand why these words startled me? Not too many people throughout history have been successful in obeying all the commandments. How then could Moses have the audacity to suggest that they are not too difficult or out of reach? To discover the answer to that question, I had to read a bit farther. He continues,

> It is not in heaven, that you should say, "Who will ascend to heaven for us and bring it to us, that we may hear it and do it?" Neither is it beyond the sea, that you should say, "Who will go over the sea for us and bring it to us, that we may hear it and do it?" But the word is very near you. It is in your mouth and in your heart, so that you can do it. DEUTERONOMY 30:12–14

That was the answer to my question. If I keep the Word of God in my heart (meditation) and in my mouth (confession), I will obey it. The Word will cause me to obey because it is the primary agent of change in my life. Paul said to the church in Thessalonica,

---

[93] If we are reading God's word carefully, we will probably be startled fairly often.

And for this reason we also constantly thank God that when you received from us the word of God's message, you accepted it not as the word of men, but for what it really is, the word of God, *which also performs its work in you who believe.* 1 THESSALONIANS 2:13 NASB

Notice the last phrase, "which also performs its work in you who believe." What work? That depends on what work you need done. There is a basic principle in life that every seed produces after its own kind. This is certainly true in the natural word, and it's also true in the spiritual world. If we plant Bible verses on love in our heart, those words will do their work: they will produce love in our heart. If we plant Bible verses on boldness, those words will do their work: they will produce boldness. Whatever work we need done in our life, if we plant God's Word concerning it in our heart, we should expect a harvest.

Jesus told his disciples a parable that elaborates on this point.

And he said, "The kingdom of God is as if a man should scatter seed on the ground. He sleeps and rises night and day, and the seed sprouts and grows; he knows not how. The earth produces by itself, first the blade, then the ear, then the full grain in the ear. But when the grain is ripe, at once he puts in the sickle, because the harvest has come." MARK 4:26–29

I have always loved this passage of Scripture. It illustrates a simple but profound biblical principle: God's Word, sown in faith, will produce a harvest every time.

Notice that the farmer has certain responsibilities, and that the soil and the seed have certain responsibilities. We are the farmer in the parable, and so it is important that we understand exactly what our responsibilities are. If we do not, we may try to do something that only the soil and seed can do.

The farmer is responsible to:

- Sow seed.
- Wait patiently.
- Keep a daily routine.[94]

The seed and the soil are responsible to:

---

[94] This is implied in the phrase: "Goes to bed at night and gets up by day." More on this later.

- Grow and produce results.

Growth is not the farmer's responsibility. Results are not the farmer's responsibility. Growth and results are the responsibility of the seed and of the soil. The farmer will always get in trouble when he takes responsibility for growth and results; they are not his responsibility.

The *seed* sprouts up and grows—how, he himself does not know. The *soil produces crops by itself.*[95]

The farmer does not need a master's degree in agriculture from the University of Jerusalem. He does not need to understand how the process works. He just needs to know (and believe) that when the seed and the soil get together, they produce a harvest. God's Word, sown in faith, will produce a harvest every time.

> *The parable of Mark 4:26–29 is a continuation of the parable of Mark 4:1–20. Both parables have three components in common: the sower (the one who gives the Word), the seed (the Word), and the soil (the one who receives the Word). The first parable emphasizes the one who receives the Word and the condition of his heart: hard, rocky, thorny, or good. Jesus explained each type of soil and compared them to different heart attitudes among those who heard the Word. The second parable emphasizes the* attitude *of the sower toward the whole process of sowing and reaping. Neither parable emphasizes the seed because it is assumed that the Word will always produce results. The only variable is the sower and the receiver.*

Since the seed and the soil are not our responsibility, and since they will work regardless of whether we understand how, let us concentrate on the farmer's responsibilities.

First, an explanation of the metaphors that Jesus used and how I am applying them in this chapter. The seed is the Word of God, and the soil is the human heart. There are many applications to the principles Jesus taught in this section, but the primary one I am using is the process of how we experience life-changing transformation. So the seed is not just the Word of God; it is the Word of God that **we** sow. And the soil is not just the human heart; it is **our** human heart. When I say God's Word, sown in faith, will

---

[95] This parable assumes that the heart (soil) is the good heart referred to in the proceeding parable.

reap a harvest every time, I mean it will reap a harvest of change in **our** life when **we** sow it in faith.

Responsibility #1: Sow Seeds.

What motivates the farmer to sow his seeds so faithfully? Why does he work so hard in this activity?

The answer is simple: the farmer has confidence that the seed and the soil will produce a crop. Without this essential faith in the process, he would not invest his time. This is the foundation upon which every harvest is based: confidence in the seed, confidence in the soil, and confidence in the process. So we could read this passage like this:

> The kingdom of God is like a man who sows the Word of God into his heart, and goes to bed at night and gets up by day, and God's Word sprouts up and grows—how, he himself does not know. The heart produces crops by itself.

We sow the Word of God in our heart when we speak it out of our mouth. Thirty-four years ago, I began the discipline of speaking God's Word the first thing in the morning. I began this process because I had confidence in the seed. I knew that if I sowed God's Word in my heart, it would produce a harvest.

Responsibility #2: Wait Patiently.

The NASB says, "he goes to bed at night and gets up by day." No other translation uses these exact words, but all of them carry the idea of time passing.

The normal operation of the kingdom of God is that growth takes time. There are occasional miracles, but generally there is a necessary time delay between planting and reaping. And that is what causes us so much trouble. We want instant results. We want immediate change. We want to speak to mountains and see them move before our very eyes. But unfortunately, life does not often work that way. Even when miracles do happen, there is usually a significant period of waiting beforehand.

Because life does not work that way, we need to wait patiently. And we can wait because we have confidence in the seed. God's Word will do its work in our life. Time is not our enemy. Time is working for us. Time is on our side.

In the early eighties, I heard a report of an island in the South Pacific where it had not rained in a particular region for eighteen years. But then the monsoon came. For three straight weeks it rained so hard no one went out. When the rain finally stopped, the islanders were surprised to discover green vegetation where it had once been barren. Seeds had remained in the ground those many years, dormant but not dead. All that was needed was rain.

Faith is like that. God's Word sown in our heart may lie dormant for many years. But when God sends the rain, a harvest results.

We will continue this section in chapter eleven.

Application

Discuss

1. Have you ever used the "try harder" method of spiritual transformation? What were the results?

2. The Bible is the primary agent God uses to change our life. What are some other substitutes that people use? Why are the other methods so appealing? What are some of the substitutes you have used? Why?

3. How would you rate your ability to wait on the fulfillment of God's promises? Do you tend to be more patient or impatient? Why? What can you do to increase your patience?

Act

Select an area of your life that needs change. Find five to ten Bible verses that address that area. Meditate and confess those verses several times a day.

Meditate

This Book of the Law shall not depart from your mouth, but you shall meditate on it day and night, so that you may be careful to do according to all that is written in it. For then you will make your way prosperous, and then you will have good success. JOSHUA 1:8

11

Faith and God's Word

Part Two

Introduction

In the last chapter we began to look at the four attitudes we must have towards God's Word. This chapter continues our examination of the first attitude: desperation.

Responsibility #3: Keep a Daily Routine.

"He goes to bed at night, he gets up by day." This sounds so boring, so monotonous. But that is how real growth happens. It rarely comes through big events. It is usually in the mundane routine that progress is made.

The Chinese Bamboo Tree exhibits an interesting growth pattern that illustrates this point. The first year it is planted, nothing happens. The second year there is no apparent growth. The third and fourth year is the same. But in the fifth year, the tree sprouts and grows ninety feet in six weeks. It can grow three feet in a day and several inches in an hour. There are times when you can sit and watch it grow. Five years of faithful labor is finally rewarded by nearly miraculous growth. Daily routines add up over time to produce astounding results.

In the book *Good to Great*, Jim Collins compares the great companies he studied to a massive, 5,000-pound flywheel. In his metaphor, your job is to turn the flywheel. It takes a tremendous amount of energy to get it started, but finally it begins to move. After a few hours of exhausting labor, you have pushed it one turn. Another hour and you have completed another turn. But slowly momentum begins to build. Finally you hit a moment of breakthrough. The flywheel hurls forward, spinning by its own power.

Collins then asks the question, "What was the one big push that made the flywheel go fast?" The answer is, of course, there wasn't one push that made the difference. It was the accumulation of effort applied in a consistent direction.[96]

That is the power of a daily routine. God's Word, consistently sown in faith, will produce a harvest. And it will change our life.

I am sure we could all make a list of areas of change we need in our lives right now. (If you find it difficult to think of any areas, you could circulate a list among your family and friends and watch it grow rapidly.) The answer to those stubborn areas that we struggle with is God's Word—the primary agent of change. Remember what Peter wrote,

> He has granted to us his precious and very great promises, so that through them you may become *partakers of the divine nature*, having escaped from the corruption that is in the world because of sinful desire. **2 PETER 1:4**

Partaking of the divine nature is sanctification, and sanctification happens through his promises—the primary agent of change. That is why we are desperate for God's Word. This desperation will produce in us a desire to accumulate as much of God's Word as we can. The psalmist said,

> Your word I have *treasured* in my heart. **PSALM 119:11 NASB**

To *treasure* means "to hoard in great quantities for future use." When a severe storm or hurricane threatens a community, there is always a mad rush to hoard essential commodities. People will stand in line for hours and endure any inconvenience to ensure that they will not run short of what they need to live. This is the attitude expressed by the psalmist: he would endure any inconvenience to store up the Word of God in his heart.

We had a gasoline shortage in our city. A friend of mine, coming from another city and unaware of the shortage, arrived in town with his tank nearly empty. He tried several stations, but could find no gasoline. He eventually found one station that had gas, but there were over one hundred

---

[96] Jim Collins, *Good to Great: Why Some Companies Make the Leap...and Others Don't* (HarperBusiness, 1st Ed., 2011), 164–165.

cars waiting to fill their tanks. Fights began to break out in the parking lot among people afraid they would be stranded. He eventually left the station in fear of his life.

If people were as concerned with hoarding God's Word as they were with hoarding a little gasoline during a shortage, it would be a different world.

When Moses told God's people that, "man does not live by bread alone, but man lives by every word that comes from the mouth of the Lord" (Deuteronomy 8:3), the people understood exactly what he meant. Bread was the basic food of the Jews, the staple of their diet. It was present at every meal. So the Word of God was to be the staple of their spiritual diet; without it they would not survive. That is desperation. And that is the right attitude to have towards God's Word.

The second attitude we should have towards God's Word is devotion.

> And they *devoted* themselves to the apostles' teaching. ACTS 2:42

Immediately after Pentecost, the new believers began devoting themselves to the Word of God. The first recorded fruit of the new birth was devotion to God's Word. This is the normal response for new believers. It will vary in intensity from person to person, but generally new believers will find a new desire to read and learn about God in the Bible.

The word translated *devoting* in this verse comes from the Greek word *proskartereo*. It is a strong word that means "to be steadfastly attentive to, to give unremitting care to, to persist obstinately in, and to continue unceasingly with great intensity and single-mindedness."[97] A person with this attitude will be steadfast, unmovable, constant in pursuit, unshakable, resolute, and unwavering. Sometimes a word needs a picture to help us grasp its power and full meaning. The following are three pictures to help us understand *proskartereo*.

The first picture of *proskartereo* is Clubber Lang, Rocky's antagonist in the movie *Rocky III*. Fans of the *Rocky* movies generally agree that *Rocky III* was the best of all—primarily because it featured the best bad guy: Clubber Lang. Lang is the quintessential antagonist. He is someone we love to hate.

---

[97]   W. E. Vine, *Expository Dictionary of New Testament Words* (Zondervan, 1982).

Clubber Lang was single-minded in his devotion to the supreme object of his life: to be the heavyweight champion of the world. In one memorable scene, he described the intense focus of his life to a group of reporters.

LANG: I live alone, I train alone, and when I win the title, I'll win the title alone.

REPORTER: Clubber, do you hate Rocky Balboa?

LANG: No, but I pity the fool. And I will destroy anyone who stands in my way.

REPORTER: What is your prediction for the fight?

LANG: Pain, I predict pain.

Clubber Lang's focused passion provides us with a powerful metaphor of the biblical concept of devotion to God's Word.

The second picture of *proskartereo* is Dan Gable. Gable was a wrestler, one of the best America ever produced. Throughout his high school and college career he was never beaten—until his last match his senior year of college. His record was 182-1. But that loss just made Dan Gable mad. He was a terror for the next two years in international competition while preparing for the Olympics. He said in a magazine interview during this time that occasionally he would wake up in the night wondering what the Russians were doing. He would not go back to sleep without doing pushups and sit-ups until he was exhausted. He said,

> When I would get tired and want to stop, I would wonder what my next opponent was doing. I would wonder if he was still working out. I would try to visualize him. When I could see him still working, I would start pushing myself. When I could see him headed to the showers, I would push myself harder.[98]

When the Olympics finally arrived, he won the gold medal, defeating every opponent. Amazingly, no one scored even one point against him. That is *proskartereo*.

The third picture of *proskartereo* began on October 31, 1517, when an obscure Augustinian monk tacked ninety-five statements on the door of the Wittenberg Castle Church in Germany. He only wanted to initiate a scholarly debate, but instead he started a firestorm. This small event

---

[98] Mike Chapman, *Wrestling Tough*, (Human Kinetics, 2005), 155.

became the tipping point for one of the most significant events in history: the Protestant Reformation. The man was Martin Luther.

Luther's ideas swept through Germany in the next two weeks and through Europe within two months. By 1520, they had caused such a stir that Pope Leo X issued a formal edict (called a papal bull) demanding that Luther recant his views within sixty days. Luther responded by burning the papal bull in a public ceremony.

In April of the next year, Luther was summoned to the city of Worms for what he thought would be a discussion of his teachings. When he arrived, he discovered that there would be no discussion. This was a trial and Luther had two options: recant or die.

He stood before Charles V, the king of Spain, Germany, the Netherlands, and parts of Italy, Hungary, and Eastern Europe. Charles was also the Holy Roman Emperor and the most powerful man in the world. He had one agenda: silence this upstart monk once and for all. Charles would brook no compromise; Luther's utter defeat was his sole purpose.

Luther was momentarily daunted by Charles and his retinue. He asked for a day to consider his course. The next day, he stood before the council and said,

> Unless I am refuted and convicted by testimonies of the Scriptures or by clear arguments since I believe neither the Pope nor the Councils alone; it being evident that they have often erred and contradicted themselves, I am conquered by the Holy Scriptures quoted by me, and my conscience is bound in the word of God: I can not and will not recant anything, since it is unsafe and dangerous to do anything against the conscience. Here I stand. I can do no other. God help me![99]

That is *proskartereo*—"steadfast, unmovable, constant in pursuit, unshakable, resolute, and unwavering." And that is the attitude of devotion we should have toward the Word of God.

---

[99] Philip Schaff, *History of the Christian Church, Vol 7* (Hendrickson, 3rd Edition, 2006), Chap. 55.

The third attitude we should have towards God's Word is desire.

> Like newborn infants, long for the pure spiritual milk, that by it
> you may grow up into salvation. 1 PETER 2:2

Peter wanted his readers to be as eager for the nourishment of the Word
as babies are for milk—to yearn for it with great intensity. He exhorted them
first to cast out impure desires and motives (1 Peter 2:1), and then to feed
on the wholesome spiritual food of God's Word that produces growth. We
should approach the Word with clean hearts and minds in eager anticipation,
with a desire to grow spiritually.[100] Like the Bereans:

> Now these Jews were more noble than those in Thessalonica; they
> received the word with all eagerness, examining the Scriptures daily
> to see if these things were so. ACTS 17:11

The word *eagerness* in this passage means "animated by great interest
and intense desire." The word *examining* means "to inquire into in detail; to
investigate or scrutinize." These new believers scrutinized the Word of God
with great interest and intense desire.

For Christmas in 1989, I bought my two sons (then age eight and six)
their first Nintendo game system. It came with two games: Duck Hunt, and
the ever-popular Super Mario Bros. They especially loved the Mario Bros.
game. They conspired every day to be the first one to defeat the dragon,
save the princess, and conquer the game. (I beat them both and saved the
princess first. After that, I retired from gaming and have not played since.)
We had a lot of fun together playing that game.

But besides the thrilling possibility of winning the game, the thing that
was the most fun about playing was discovering hidden benefits in each
level. What a thrill it was when we broke a group of bricks and revealed a
hidden 1-Up mushroom (a 1-Up mushroom gave you an extra life—a valuable
commodity when battling fire-breathing dragons). Or the time we discovered
the Warp Zone that allowed you to bypass certain levels and advance farther
in the game. It was the possibility that there was always something new to
discover that kept us returning to the game time and again.

---

[100] John F. Walvoord and Roy B. Zuck, *The Bible Knowledge Commentary: Old Testament and
New Testament* (David C. Cook, 2002).

This must have been how the Bereans felt about searching God's Word, and this is how we should feel about it. There are 1-Up mushrooms and Warp Zones hidden everywhere. And each new discovery gives us increased power to battle dragons.

The fourth attitude we should have towards God's Word is delight.

> Your words were found, and I ate them, and your words became to me a joy and the delight of my heart, for I am called by your name, O Lord, God of hosts. JEREMIAH 15:16

The word translated *joy* in this passage comes from an original Hebrew word that means *a state of joyful exuberance.* The word *delight* refers to the jubilant mirth associated with attending a festival.

When my two boys were small, I took them to Six Flags in Georgia for a day of "jubilant mirth." I told them they could eat whatever they wanted throughout the day—in reasonable quantities and at regular intervals. My older son quickly chose a treat that looked good to him. But my younger son took his time to select the perfect delicacy (he was a sugar connoisseur at a young age). I watched him observing people eating various goodies. I could see him calculating the sugar rush in his mind.

Finally, he made his choice. He pointed to someone feasting on blue cotton candy and said, "That's what I want." I replied, "Son, you have chosen wisely."

Since he had never eaten cotton candy before, I had to disciple him in the fine art of eating it. "Pull a large section off and place it in your mouth," I advised. "Then do not move. Allow it to dissolve slowly in your mouth."

He followed my directions with precision. He placed a significant quantity of the cotton candy in his mouth and held it perfectly still. As it dissolved, I saw his face light up. I thought, "That is exactly what Jeremiah was describing." The look on his face was pure "jubilant mirth."

The experience of eating the cotton candy is a perfect picture of our attitude toward the Word of God. Maybe Jeremiah should have said it this way, "Your words became for me like blue cotton candy!"

I did have a friend tell me after he heard me speak on this topic that he hated cotton candy. I was incredulous that such people existed on the earth. But he assured me it was true. I could only advise him to substitute what had the same effect upon him as cotton candy had upon my son. Maybe,

"Your words became for me like warm chocolate cookies," or "Your words became for me like a perfectly cooked filet mignon!"

It is encouraging to me that Jeremiah said, "Your words **became** for me a joy and delight of my heart." The word **became** refers to a process. Jeremiah is saying that the Word did not start off as a complete joy and delight. It grew and matured over time. This kind of delight in God's Word does not come overnight. Steady application and continual habit develop it. It is a process.

Another story will illustrate the delight we have in God's Word. My friend told me about her three-year-old niece. The girl's parents were very health-conscious and regulated her diet strictly. She was prohibited from eating sweets or anything with sugar. So she had no experience with cookies, cake, or ice cream, and she certainly had never sampled blue cotton candy. (I understand her parents' concern. When my two sons were young, we tried the same experiment. It only lasted about six months. I am convinced they have spent every day since then trying to make up for lost time.)

The parents, however, made one small miscalculation. They enrolled her for a brief time in a daycare. One fateful day in the daycare, another child had a birthday celebration. The celebration was abundantly supplied with many tantalizing delicacies including the pièce de résistance: chocolate covered cupcakes. After one bite the child was convinced of her life mission: to get as much of this stuff as she possibly could.

This event went unnoticed by the parents. But a few weeks later several of their relatives gathered together for a surprise party for another family member. At the appropriate time, the host brought out a massive chocolate cake for the celebration. When the daughter saw the cake, she remembered her recent experience, and, to the eternal chagrin of her parents, she began screaming uncontrollably, "Cake, cake, cake. I want CAKE!"

Maybe we can learn something from this three-year-old girl. The next time we sit to read or study God's Word, we might try screaming out, "Bible, Bible, Bible. I want BIBLE!"

Conclusion

God's Word is the fuel for our faith. As we daily feed upon it, our desire for it will grow. And as it does, faith will grow accordingly.

Application

Discuss

1. Daily routines add up over time to produce astounding results. What daily routines have you established that you are faithful to keep? What difference have they made in your life? What new routines do you need to establish to accomplish what you want? What has prevented you from establishing those routines, and what action steps can you take to begin?

2. In your own words, describe the attitude of *proskartereo*. How does your current devotion to God's Word compare? What is the biggest personal obstacle keeping you from increased devotion, and what can you do about overcoming it?

3. Is God's Word like blue cotton candy to you? If yes, why? If no, has there ever been a time in your life when it was? What has changed, and what can you do to restore your delight in God's Word?

Act

Read Psalm 119. See how many verses you can find that confirm the attitudes of desperation, delight, desire, and devotion.

Meditate

He has granted to us his precious and very great promises, so that through them you may become partakers of the divine nature, having escaped from the corruption that is in the world because of sinful desire. 2 PETER 1:4

12

Faith in the Covenant

Remember that you were at that time separated from Christ, alienated from the commonwealth of Israel and strangers to the covenants of promise, having no hope and without God in the world. EPHESIANS 2:12

A man separated from Christ is a stranger to Christ's covenants—this man does not know what they are, and he is not eligible for their provisions. But once a man is joined to Christ, God's covenants become his possession. As Charles Spurgeon once said,

> God's dealings with men have always had a covenant character. It has so pleased Him to arrange it that He will not deal with us except through a covenant, nor can we deal with Him except in the same manner.[101]

However, to appropriate these covenant promises, we must first know what they are.

Several years ago, a friend of mine purchased a high-end VCR.[102] I recognized the model as a very pricey item with many features, including

---

[101] Charles Haddon Spurgeon, "The Blood of the Covenant," Blue Letter Bible, updated 2019, https://www.blueletterbible.org/Comm/spurgeon_charles/sermons/1186.cfm, 1.

[102] Some may not remember the VCR, or, video cassette recorder. It was how you watched rented movies before the digital revolution.

the ability to do some simple editing. When I asked him why he bought it, he said, "My girls like to watch Disney movies."

Surprised, I said, "You can certainly watch movies on this machine, but do you know what else you can do?" He handed me the thick manual that accompanied the product and said, "I started to read this, but it was too complicated."

I tried to explain some of the many features of the machine, but he was obviously uninterested. He had a feature-rich VCR, but was content to get only the very basic use out of it.

I often think how descriptive this is of many Christians. They have received a feature-rich covenant, but are often content to get only the basic use of it. Like my friend, they find the "manual" too complicated. Even though they are officially under the covenant, they are in practical reality "strangers to the covenants of promise."

There are several covenants God has made with man, but we will concentrate on the covenant he made with Abraham and how it relates to us today. The person who is in Christ has become an heir of the promises God made to Abraham.

> Know then that it is those of faith who are the sons of Abraham.
> So then, those who are of faith are blessed along with Abraham,
> the man of faith. And if you are Christ's, then you are Abraham's
> offspring, heirs according to promise. GALATIANS 3:7, 9, 29

When Paul says that we are "heirs according to the promise," he means that whatever Abraham received, we can receive. Or, to say it another way, "Whatever Abraham got, I get." If that is true then I should try to discover exactly what Abraham got—because whatever he got, I get.

I am always interested when I hear about a great blessing someone received. But I must confess I pay a little more attention when I know that whatever they got, I will also get. I am happy for Abraham and everything he got—and I am glad to hear his story. But I am even more interested in his story because it describes what is mine also.

So then, what did God promise to Abraham? The first account of God's personal dealings with Abraham are recorded in the twelfth chapter of Genesis.

> Now the Lord said to Abram, "Go from your country and your
> kindred and your father's house to the land that I will show you.
> And I will make of you a great nation, and I will bless you and make

your name great, so that you will be a blessing. I will bless those who bless you, and him who dishonors you I will curse, and in you all the families of the earth shall be blessed." **GENESIS 12:1-3**

God promised seven things to Abraham in this passage. He said,

- I will make you into a great nation.
- I will bless you.
- I will make your name great.
- You will be a blessing.
- I will bless those who bless you.
- I will curse those who dishonor you.
- All families on the earth will be blessed through you.

These are great promises for Abraham. But what makes them so exciting for us today is that they are also promises for us—because we are children of Abraham, and "Whatever Abraham got, I get!"

God said, "I will make your name great." What is the advantage of a great name? It gives you influence. God is saying to Abraham, "I will give you great influence." This is promised to us also as heirs of Abraham's blessing.

I had a professional athlete speak at my church once. He was very well known in our community and the meeting attracted a considerable amount of attention. A large crowd was on hand to hear him speak. He had little public speaking experience, was poorly prepared, and did not communicate well. But he had a name. And that name gave him influence. People listened to his every word; and when he gave the altar call, many responded. All because of a name.

Remember: "Whatever Abraham got, I get." Although some of the promises were obviously specific to Abraham (for example, "In you all the families of the earth will be blessed"), the essence of God's promises to Abraham are ours.

The second account of God's personal dealings with Abraham is recorded in the fifteenth chapter of Genesis. This passage augments and clarifies the promises God has already made.

After these things the word of the Lord came to Abram in a vision: "Fear not, Abram, I am your shield; your reward shall be very great." But Abram said, "O Lord God, what will you give me, for I continue childless, and the heir of my house is Eliezer of Damascus?" And Abram said, "Behold, you have given me no offspring, and a member of my household will be my heir." And behold, the word of the Lord came to him: "This man shall not be your heir; your very own son shall be your heir." And he brought him outside and said, "Look toward heaven, and number the stars, if you are able to number them." Then he said to him, "So shall your offspring be." And he believed the Lord, and he counted it to him as righteousness. **GENESIS 15:1–6**

God promised Abraham that his descendants would be as plentiful as the stars of the heavens, and Abraham received the promise by faith (Romans 4:13). But Abraham was still in need of further confirmation. And so God condescended to his weakness and gave him the greatest assurance he could—he made a blood covenant with him.

But he said, "O Lord God, how am I to know that I shall possess it?" **GENESIS 15:8**

Abraham's question in this verse, "How am I to know that I shall possess it?" may seem strange in the light of the previous statement in verse six: "And he believed the Lord." But Abraham's faith was tenuous, in need of certainty. God did not reprove him for weak faith. Instead, he provided him with incontrovertible proof of his intentions. And he did so in a way that Abraham was sure to understand: he cut a covenant with him. Andrew Murray said,

In his infinite condescension to our human weakness and need, God has sought to make use of all the aspects of human covenants to give us perfect confidence in him.[103]

To provide the confirmation Abraham needed, God instructed him to prepare the elements for the covenant ceremony.

And he said to him, "I am the Lord who brought you out from Ur of the Chaldeans to give you this land to possess." But he said, "O Lord God, how am I to know that I shall possess it?" He said to him, "Bring me a heifer three years old, a female goat three years old, a ram three years old, a turtledove, and a young pigeon." And he brought him all these, cut them in half, and laid each half over against the other. But he did not cut the birds in half. And when

---

[103] Andrew Murray, *The Two Covenants* (Merchant Books, 2013), 2.

birds of prey came down on the carcasses, Abram drove them away. As the sun was going down, a deep sleep fell on Abram. And behold, dreadful and great darkness fell upon him. **GENESIS 15:7–12**

In the covenant ceremony, animals were cut in two and each half placed opposite each other to form a path for the parties to walk through. This bound the parties to keep the terms of the covenant under penalty of death. If one party violated the covenant, the other pledged to do to him as they had done to the severed animals. The covenant ceremony was a visceral experience, one you would never forget. Walking a path covered with blood and entrails and the stench of freshly killed animals would remain indelibly etched in your memory.

But this covenant ceremony was a little different than the ones Abraham was accustomed to. In the traditional ceremony, both parties would walk through the bloody path—signifying that each was bound to the terms of the covenant. But in this ceremony only God walked the path, signifying that the promise was all of grace. "That is why it depends on faith, in order that the promise may rest on grace and be guaranteed to all his offspring—not only to the adherent of the law but also to the one who shares the faith of Abraham, who is the father of us all" (Romans 4:16).

When the sun had gone down and it was dark, behold, a smoking fire pot and a flaming torch passed between these pieces. On that day the Lord made a covenant with Abram. **GENESIS 15:17–18**

The smoking oven and the flaming torch were symbols of God's presence. He revealed himself in smoke and fire on Mount Sinai at the giving of the Ten Commandments (Exodus 19:18), and he revealed himself in the pillar of fire and the pillar of smoke as he led them through the wilderness (Exodus 13:21).

God assured Abraham of his promise in the strongest way possible.

God's divinely chosen cure for our unbelief is the Covenant into which he has entered with us.[104]

The third account of God's personal dealings with Abraham is recorded in the seventeenth chapter of Genesis.

---

[104] Andrew Murray, *The Two Covenants* (Merchant Books, 2013), 3.

When Abram was ninety-nine years old the Lord appeared to
Abram and said to him, "I am God Almighty; walk before me, and
be blameless, that I may make my covenant between me and you,
and may multiply you greatly." Then Abram fell on his face. And
God said to him, "Behold, my covenant is with you, and you shall
be the father of a multitude of nations. No longer shall your name
be called Abram, but your name shall be Abraham, for I have made
you the father of a multitude of nations. I will make you exceedingly
fruitful, and I will make you into nations, and kings shall come
from you. And I will establish my covenant between me and you
and your offspring after you throughout their generations for an
everlasting covenant, to be God to you and to your offspring after
you." GENESIS 17:1–7

Every time God appeared to Abraham, he restated the covenant and
expanded it. There are four essential promises in this section.

- I will multiply you greatly.
- You will be the father of a multitude of nations.
- I will make you exceedingly fruitful.
- Kings shall come from you.[105]

The question we should ask now is, "Did God keep his promise?"

God's promise was to Abraham and all his descendants. Beginning with
Isaac and then Jacob, God's blessing to Abraham is clearly in force.

And Isaac sowed in that land and reaped in the same year a
hundredfold. The Lord blessed him, and the man became rich,
and gained more and more until he became very wealthy. He had
possessions of flocks and herds and many servants, so that the
Philistines envied him. GENESIS 26:12–14

The astonishing covenantal blessings bestowed on Isaac are even more
amazing because it was a year of famine (Genesis 26:1). Certainly God kept
his promise to Abraham's first descendant. Did it continue with Isaac's
son Jacob?

---

[105] Kings are leaders. God promised Abraham his influence would extend all the way to the
leaders of society.

And God said to him, "I am God Almighty: be fruitful and multiply. A nation and a company of nations shall come from you, and kings shall come from your own body. The land that I gave to Abraham and Isaac I will give to you, and I will give the land to your offspring after you." GENESIS 35:11–12

Since God kept his promise to Abraham's son and grandson, and since he cannot lie, we can have perfect confidence that the covenant he made with Abraham is working for us today.

But what does it mean for us? God's covenant promise to Abraham that he would be heir of the world is the same covenant promise we can claim to see the nations of the world brought into the kingdom of God.

For the promise to Abraham and his offspring that he would be heir of the world did not come through the law but through the righteousness of faith. ROMANS 4:13

This statement sums up God's many promises to Abraham (and to his descendants): you will be heir of the world. As Abraham's descendants, we go into all the world to preach the gospel not as foreign invaders, but as rightful heirs claiming what belongs to us in Christ.

The author of the letter to the Hebrews confirmed the surety of God's covenant to us in this rich passage:

For when God made a promise to Abraham, since he had no one greater by whom to swear, he swore by himself. HEBREWS 6:13

An oath is a solemn declaration to validate a promise. When you make an oath you appeal to someone greater than yourself to attest to the truth of your statement and certify the validity of your promise. You bind yourself to legal or moral sanctions for failing to carry out your sworn pledge, usually involving the penalty of divine retribution. When an American citizen places his hand upon the Bible and swears in a court of law, saying, "I solemnly swear to tell the truth, the whole truth, and nothing but the truth, so help me God," he is saying in effect, "May all the curses of this book come upon me if I willfully tell a lie."

When God swore by himself, he bound himself under a curse if he would not fulfill his promise. That is how sacred his oath is.

Saying, "Surely I will bless you and multiply you." HEBREWS 6:14

The literal translation of this passage is, "Surely blessing I will bless you, and multiplying I will multiply you." The double repetition of both blessing and multiplying is a Hebraic formula for an oath. It is a mode of expression that signifies emphasis and certainty.

For people swear by something greater than themselves, and in all their disputes an oath is final for confirmation. HEBREWS 6:16

When I was a kid and my friends doubted something I was claiming, they could always call my bluff by asking the ultimate question, "Do you swear to God?" If I was lying or exaggerating (which was most of the time) I would always back down at that point. But if I was telling the truth I would say in solemn and lugubrious tones, "I swear to God." When I said that, all challenges to my veracity ended. We did not understand all the reasons why, but we knew that there was something potentially dangerous about swearing to God, and if someone did it, they could not be doubted.

So when God desired to show more convincingly to the heirs of the promise the unchangeable character of his purpose, he guaranteed it with an oath. HEBREWS 6:17

This is such a powerful promise, it is good to read it in several versions.

God desired to show more convincingly to the heirs of the promise *the unchangeable character of his purpose.* RSV

God wanted to prove that his promise was true to those who would get what he promised. And he wanted them to understand clearly that his purposes never change. NCV

God also bound himself with an oath, so that those who received the promise could be perfectly sure that he would never change his mind. NLT

The author continues.

So that by two unchangeable things, in which it is impossible for God to lie, we who have fled for refuge might have strong encouragement to hold fast to the hope set before us. We have this as a sure and steadfast anchor of the soul. HEBREWS 6:18–19

The two unchangeable things are God's Word and God's oath. One is enough to secure complete and implicit trust, but God went the extra mile to show the unchangeableness of his promise. The word *unchangeable* is from the Greek word *ametathetos* which means "unable to be changed." It was used in the covenant documents of the first century to refer to a will that could not be changed for any reason. That certainly should produce strong encouragement.

Conclusion

A clear understanding of God's covenant is a great source of encouragement to our faith. As we study it and meditate upon it, it will build our faith and increase our confidence in God's promises. As Andrew Murray said,

> To many a man, who has never thought much of the Covenant, a true and living faith in it would mean the transformation of his whole life.[106]

Application

Discuss

1. Which of the seven promises God made to Abraham in Genesis 12 is the most appealing to you? Why? What can you do to appropriate it in your life in a greater way?

---

[106] See Note 104.

2. Andrew Murray said, "God's divinely chosen cure for our unbelief is the Covenant into which God has entered with us." What emotional effect does God's covenant have on you, and how does it help to cure your unbelief?

_____

_____

_____

Act

Read the account of the life of Abraham in Genesis 12:1–25:8. Record all the signs of God's covenant you can find in those verses.

Meditate

And if you are Christ's, then you are Abraham's offspring, heirs according to promise. GALATIANS 3:29

13

Faith and Prosperity

Part One

Introduction

I was confused about money and prosperity when I started following Jesus. I had been raised in a religious tradition that tended to promote poverty as a spiritual virtue, and my middle-class upbringing fit easily into that mindset. Those factors combined to convince me that someone with money would have a hard time being a real Christian. I also saw many passages of Scripture that, at the time, seemed to confirm my view.

Later, as I became a student of Church history, I discovered that I was not the only one confused about money. In the introduction to an issue of the *Christian History* magazine concerning the Church's view of money, the editors stated,

> After the two millennia of its existence, the Church still struggles to find its way through the money maze.[107]

Over time, as my mind became renewed to God's Word, I stumbled on (and stumbled over) other scriptures that seemed to present an entirely different perspective on money than the one I started with. For example:

---

[107] *Christian History*, "Money in Christian History," Part II, Issue 19, July 1988.

You shall remember the Lord your God, for it is he who gives you power to get wealth, that he may confirm his covenant that he swore to your fathers, as it is this day. DEUTERONOMY 8:18

The blessing of the Lord makes rich, and he adds no sorrow with it. PROVERBS 10:22

There are no easy or simplistic answers to the questions of prosperity and to the proper relationship between believers and money. But it is vital for our faith life that we develop and live by a biblical view of money.

In this chapter and the next we will attempt to examine some of the important biblical teachings concerning money and prosperity.

A Brief History

Throughout the long history of the Church, many have held the view that money is a detriment to holiness. I call this view "sanctified poverty."

This viewpoint was rarely seen in Judaism, the historical antecedent of Christianity. Because the Jews recognized Abraham as their founder—and Abraham was a wealthy man—most Jews have been comfortable with wealth. They have never seen it as a deterrent to genuine spirituality.

In contrast, the idea that wealth is a hindrance to true spirituality did take root early in the history of the Church. There were several reasons why.

First, Jesus, unlike Abraham, was not a wealthy man. Many early Church leaders chose to emulate Christ's lifestyle. Because Jesus was poor, they reasoned, the highest form of spirituality was voluntary poverty. Listen to the thoughts of a few of the early Church Fathers.

Those who are rich in this world cannot be useful to the Lord unless their riches are cut down.[108]

Wealth is of itself sufficient to puff up and corrupt the souls of its possessors and to turn them from the path by which salvation is to be attained.[109]

---

[108] Alexander Roberts, *Ante-Nicene Fathers Volume 2: Fathers of the Second Century: Hermes, Tatian, Athenagoras, Theophilus, and Clement of Alexandria*, trans. James Donaldson and Arthur Coxe (Henry M. Piironen, 2013), 15.

[109] Alexander Roberts, *Ante-Nicene Fathers Volume 2: Fathers of the Second Century: Hermes, Tatian, Athenagoras, Theophilus, and Clement of Alexandria*, trans. James Donaldson and Arthur Coxe (Henry M. Piironen, 2013), 591.

Riches are not only to be scorned, but are full of peril. A person becomes perfect and complete when he sells all his goods and distributes them to the poor.[110]

Another influence that contributed to the negative attitude the early Christian community had toward money came through its engagement with Greek philosophy. Starting with Justin Martyr and the Apologetic Fathers[111] in the middle of the second century, Church leaders became enamored with making Christianity more relevant to the educated classes. Since the education of that day was rooted in Greek thought, the Fathers reasoned they would have to find areas of agreement and common ground with that worldview. This approach did make Christianity more palatable for some, but it also had serious negative consequences.

The lure of Greek philosophical speculation was nearly irresistible to Christian apologists. They incorporated aspects of Greek wisdom, and therefore Greek dualism, into their defenses of the orthodox faith. The result was intellectual schizophrenia—philosophical syncretism. The Christian philosophers attempted to combine irreconcilable systems: Greek philosophy and biblical revelation.[112]

Greek dualism[113] saw a radical difference between the nonmaterial and the material world. The soul, they said, was nonmaterial and therefore good, but the body was material and therefore evil. In this view, the body and all material things were depreciated. A significant number of the early Church Fathers, influenced by these Greek thinkers, incorporated this view into the scriptural concept of the flesh and the spirit. As this idea slowly permeated Christian thought, it made anything associated with the material world evil (or at least prone to evil) and therefore something to be shunned.

---

[110] Alexander Roberts, *Ante-Nicene Fathers, vol 5: Hippolytus, Cyprian, Caius, Novation, Appendix* (Eerdmans, 1988), 453.

[111] The Apologetic Fathers defended the faith against pagan attacks and attempted to win legal recognition and intellectual acceptance for Christianity. They were from a higher social class with more extensive education and generally took a philosophical approach in their writings.

[112] Gary North, *Unholy Spirits: Occultism and New Age Humanism* (Dominion Press, 1988), 30.

[113] Dualism is the view that the world consists of and can be explained by two fundamental entities (usually opposites), such as spirit and matter.

This is also why the Church advocated celibacy as the highest form of Christian devotion.[114] Again, a few representative quotes from the Church Fathers:

> You would find many among us, both men and women, growing old unmarried in hope of living in closer communion with God.[115]

> How many are there who from the moment of their baptism set the seal of virginity on their flesh. How many after equal mutual consent cancel the debt of matrimony and become voluntary eunuchs for the sake of their yearning after the celestial kingdom.[116]

Marriage was not viewed as sinful (there was too much biblical evidence to the contrary), but celibacy was deemed the higher state and the one that would guarantee a closer walk with God. This flirtation with Greek thought also led to their advocating an extreme asceticism.

The most extreme case of asceticism was Simeon Stylites (AD 390–459). Simeon entered a monastery at an early age. He would eat only once a week—except during Lent when he would fast the whole forty days. He laced his body tightly with a cord that pressed through to the bones; removing it required excruciating pain. After his extreme actions got him kicked out of the monastery, he then spent some time as a hermit on a mountain with an iron chain on his feet. When this failed to satisfy him, he invented a new sort of holiness. He built a 2' x 3' platform on a pillar and determined to live there the rest of his life. At first the pillar was only a few feet high, but as he reached toward heaven and perfection, he continued to extend it until at his death, thirty-six years later, it was sixty feet high. He stayed on the pillar for his entire life, exposed to the sun, rain, and cold striving after a superhuman holiness.[117]

---

[114] This is also why they rejected the literal interpretation of the Song of Solomon and instead viewed it as allegorical. They could not believe that God would allow what amounts to a sex manual to be included in the canon of Holy Scripture.

[115] Alexander Roberts, *Ante-Nicene Fathers Volume 2: Fathers of the Second Century: Hermes, Tatian, Athenagoras, Theophilus, and Clement of Alexandria*, trans. James Donaldson and Arthur Coxe (Henry M. Piironen, 2013), 146.

[116] Alexander Roberts, *The Ante-Nicene Fathers, Vol. 4: Tertullian, Part 4/Minucius Felix/Commodian/Origen, Parts 1 & 2* (Eerdmans, 1988), 42.

[117] Adapted from Philip Schaff, *History of the Christian Church, Vol 7* (Hendrickson, 3rd Edition, 2006).

Asceticism is the practice of self-denial and renunciation of worldly pleasure in order to attain a higher degree of spirituality. It often requires abstinence from food, drink, or sexual activity, as in fasting or celibacy. It may also require physical pain or discomfort, such as endurance of extreme heat or cold or self-punishment. It may require withdrawal from the material world to a life of meditation.[118]

It is easy to see how this attitude toward the material world would affect the Church's view concerning money and prosperity. Money was a part of the evil, material world; it should be avoided. Poverty became a requirement—at least for those who wanted to live the highest life possible.

When the emperor Constantine published the Edict of Milan in AD 313, granting full freedom to all existing forms of worship with special reference to Christianity, a new era in the Church's relationship to material prosperity began. Constantine erected magnificent church buildings in prominent cities and made large donations to the Church. Prosperity and financial blessing were now in vogue.

But there was a price to pay. The emperor ruled Christian bishops as his civil servants and demanded unconditional obedience to official pronouncements, even when they interfered with Church matters. Even more significant, however, was that the Christian name had now become a passport to political, military, and social promotion. As a result, thousands joined the Church, many of whom were more politically ambitious than religiously motivated. Many assumed roles in the Church without experiencing conversion; large segments of Church membership consisted of nothing more than baptized pagans.

The Christianizing of the State was also a secularizing of the Church; the temporal gain of Christianity canceled by great spiritual loss. The Church could now act upon the State, but so could the State act upon the Church. The bishops became prominent State officials. Their dioceses expanded, and their power and revenue increased. All classes, even the emperor himself, showed them tokens of reverence such as elevated titles and kneeling.

Francis of Assisi took the concept of voluntary poverty to new levels. He determined that no one would ever be poorer than he was. Whenever he would meet a beggar dressed worse than he was, he would immediately exchange his clothes with him.

[118] Microsoft Encarta Reference Library, 2002.

Francis often referred to money as "dung." He thought it ought to be shunned as the devil himself. He hated materialism in any form. When some of his followers asked for Bibles to teach the Scriptures, he recoiled. He believed that once you own a book, you need a candle to read it by, a pen for making notes, a desk to write on, a chair for the desk, a room for the desk, a house for the room, a servant to clean house, and on and on without end.

A rich person once left a sack of money on the altar of the Church of St. Mary of the Portiuncula. One of Francis' followers removed the sack and placed it on the window sill. When Francis discovered that he had touched the sack with his hands, he rebuked him severely. He commanded him to carry the sack in his mouth so that his hands would not touch it, and remove it to a pile of animal excrement outside.

It is unlikely that anyone ever desired poverty as much as Francis.

In this worldly climate, poverty looked like the genuinely spiritual alternative. It was a rebuke to the worldliness and greed of the official Church. Countless thousands fled to the monasteries throughout the Middle Ages to save their souls and keep themselves unstained from the world. They took vows of poverty and swore to own no property. Once again, true spirituality and poverty seemed inextricably linked.

The rediscovery of the doctrine of justification by faith during the Protestant Reformation radically altered this view. The Reformers rejected the glorification of poverty. Monastic movements that began as works of charity had become means of seeking salvation.[119]

Luther undercut this medieval religious ideology of poverty with his doctrine of justification by grace alone apart from human works. Since righteousness before God is gained by grace alone [. . .] there is no salvific value in being poor.[120]

The Reformers not only cut the theological ties to poverty and spirituality, but they laid the groundwork for biblical prosperity. In Alister McGrath's extensive study of Protestantism, *Christianity's Dangerous Idea*, he reviewed the ideas of sociologist Max Weber and the connection between the doctrines of grace and economic prosperity.

---

[119] John R. Muether, "Money and the Bible: A Survey of the History of Biblical Interpretation on Money and Wealth," *Christian History*, Issue 14, April, 1987.

[120] Carter Lindberg, *The European Reformations* (John Wiley & Sons, 2010), 114.

Under Catholicism, the accumulation of capital was seen as intrinsically sinful; under Calvinism, it was seen as praiseworthy [. . .] Calvinism, according to Weber, thus generated the psychological preconditions essential to the development of modern capitalism [. . .] Calvinism made commercial success respectable by declaring that the virtues that lay behind it—such as thrift, austerity, and discipline—were themselves acceptable in God's sight.[121]

Despite this new approach to prosperity, almost five hundred years after the Reformation a general confusion and disagreement still permeates much contemporary discussion about money. Many groups and movements have added their views to the mix including Anabaptists, Puritans, the Social Gospel Movement, Liberation Theology, Christian Theonomy, and the Word of Faith.

So what does the Bible teach on this important topic? The overwhelming testimony of Scripture and history is: if an individual or a society consistently and continually obeys God and his Word, that person or people will increase in wealth.

The blessed life begins with a biblical view of money and prosperity. Our thoughts determine our actions. If we want to experience the fullness of God's promises, we must get our thinking right. With that in mind, let's examine what the Bible says about prosperity.

Scriptural Foundation for Prosperity

There are several reasons why we should have faith for prosperity.

The first reason to have faith for prosperity is God's covenantal promises.

Scripture affirms that prosperity has always been a provision of God's covenant—both in the Old Testament and in the New Testament. When God made his covenant with Abraham, he promised to bless Abraham exceedingly. The Scripture testifies that God fulfilled his promise.

Now Abram was very rich in livestock, in silver, and in gold. And the Lord had blessed Abraham in all things. GENESIS 13:2; 24:1

---

[121] Alister McGrath, *Christianity's Dangerous Idea* (HarperOne, Reprint Edition, 2008), 330–331.

The Lord has greatly blessed my master [Abraham], and he has become great. He has given him flocks and herds, silver and gold, male servants and female servants, camels and donkeys. GENESIS 24:35

God extended his covenant promise to Abraham's progeny. First to Isaac . . .

And Isaac sowed in that land and reaped in the same year a hundredfold. The Lord blessed him, and the man became rich, and gained more and more until he became very wealthy. He had possessions of flocks and herds and many servants, so that the Philistines envied him. GENESIS 26:12–14

. . . and then to all his descendants.

You shall remember the Lord your God, for it is he who gives you power to get wealth, that he may confirm his covenant that he swore to your fathers, as it is this day. DEUTERONOMY 8:18

The blessing that God promised Abraham carried over to us in the New Covenant.

So that in Christ Jesus the blessing of Abraham might come to the Gentiles, so that we might receive the promised Spirit through faith. GALATIANS 3:14

Abraham's blessing is to those who are in Christ. Christ redeemed us from the curse of poverty and provided for our prosperity through the sacrifice of himself.

For you know the grace of our Lord Jesus Christ, that though he was rich, yet for your sake he became poor, so that you by his poverty might become rich. 2 CORINTHIANS 8:9

This is the Great Exchange—the Cosmic Role Reversal. Hollywood has produced over 170 films with the theme of role reversal, but the greatest role reversal in history was when God became a man. This principle relates to several different ideas found in the New Testament. Here are a few examples:

- Christ was righteousness; we were sin. He became sin so that we who were sin could become his righteousness (2 Corinthians 5:21).
- Christ was life; we were dead. He took upon himself physical death so that we who were dead could live in him (Romans 4:25; 5:10).

He did not become sin so that we could follow his example and become sin. He did not become death so that we could follow his example and become death. It was a Cosmic Role Reversal, a Great Exchange. We see the same principle concerning material wealth.

Christ was rich; we were poor. He became poor so that we could become rich through his poverty. He did not become poor so that we should follow his example and become poor ourselves, but that we could be delivered from poverty and experience his blessings.

The literary context of this passage (2 Corinthians 8:9) is found in chapters eight and nine. Both chapters concern the monetary contribution Paul was raising for the church in Jerusalem. Both chapters are about money. You can certainly apply some of the verses to spiritual prosperity, but Paul's primary intent was clearly financial and material. People who insist that Paul's statement in 8:9 refers to spiritual blessings have missed the entire point of the verse.

The second reason to have faith for prosperity is the blessing promised to those who give.

Scripture affirms that God has promised a financial blessing upon those who give—both in the Old Testament and in the New Testament. First we will look at the Old Testament.

Honor the Lord with your wealth and with the firstfruits of all your produce; then your barns will be filled with plenty, and your vats will be bursting with wine. PROVERBS 3:9–10

One gives freely, yet grows all the richer; another withholds what he should give, and only suffers want. Whoever brings blessing will be enriched, and one who waters will himself be watered. PROVERBS 11:24–25

This theme continues in the New Testament.

Give, and it will be given to you. Good measure, pressed down, shaken together, running over, will be put into your lap. For with the measure you use it will be measured back to you. LUKE 6:38

I have received full payment, and more. I am well supplied, having received from Epaphroditus the gifts you sent, a fragrant offering, a sacrifice acceptable and pleasing to God. And my God will supply every need of yours according to his riches in glory in Christ Jesus. **PHILIPPIANS 4:18–19**

The Philippian church had consistently provided for Paul's needs. They provided for him when he left Philippi around AD 49 (Philippians 4:15–17). They provided for him during the contribution for Jerusalem around AD 56 (2 Corinthians 8:1–4). And they provided for him with an offering delivered by Epaphroditus during his first Roman imprisonment around AD 61 (Philippians 2:25). Because of their faithful giving, Paul could promise them that God would meet their every need.

The third reason to have faith for prosperity is the promises God has given to believers with godly and righteous character.

Scripture affirms that God has promised a financial blessing upon those who manifest godliness in their character—both in the Old Testament and in the New Testament. First in the Old Testament . . .

Praise the Lord! Blessed is the man who fears the Lord, who greatly delights in his commandments. His offspring will be mighty in the land; the generation of the upright will be blessed. Wealth and riches are in his house, and his righteousness endures forever. **PSALM 112:1–3**

For the Lord God is a sun and shield; the Lord bestows favor and honor. No good thing does he withhold from those who walk uprightly. **PSALM 84:11**

. . . then in the New Testament.

But seek first the kingdom of God and his righteousness, and all these things will be added to you. **MATTHEW 6:33**

These biblical promises regarding prosperity belong to us as God's people. We can claim them and expect God to do what he said he would do. But there are other promises and principles in the Bible that temper and augment these promises. In the next chapter, we will examine five admonitions that will help us to have a deeper comprehension of God's plan for prosperity.

Application

Discuss

1. How has your background and upbringing affected your views about money and prosperity? Can you detect any traces of the sanctified poverty viewpoint in your life? Where does it show up, and what can you do to change it?

    _____

    _____

    _____

2. Many people have a difficult time accepting the biblical teaching of financial prosperity. List all the reasons you think that might be. What can we do to overcome those objections?

    _____

    _____

    _____

Act

Read 2 Corinthians 8:1–9:15. List all the principles related to prosperity you can find in these two chapters.

Meditate

The blessing of the Lord makes rich, and he adds no sorrow with it.
PROVERBS 10:22

14

Faith and Prosperity

Part Two

Introduction

In the last chapter, we examined the historical foundations of some of our attitudes about money and prosperity. We also looked at scriptural reasons why prosperity is God's will. Now we will explore five admonitions the Bible gives us concerning money.

Admonitions Concerning Money

Money is power. That is what makes it so appealing. That is also what makes it so dangerous. Power is always dangerous—in whatever form it takes. There are many examples. Electricity is a natural power that brings great blessing to life. But it can be exceedingly dangerous—even fatal—if not handled with great care. Charisma is power. It can be a great blessing to influence people for good. It can also be used to damage and destroy people.

In the same way, money can be a great blessing for good or a great curse for evil. Because of this, the Scriptures provide an abundance of cautionary advice, warnings, and even commands concerning money. Here are a few.

Do not assume that God is required to bless everyone equally.

First-century Jews believed that material wealth was a sign of God's covenantal blessing. If you were rich, it was because God had smiled upon you. When the rich, young ruler turned from following Jesus because he considered the cost too high, Jesus shocked his disciples when he said:

> And Jesus said to his disciples, "Truly, I say to you, only with difficulty will a rich person enter the kingdom of heaven. Again I tell you, it is easier for a camel to go through the eye of a needle than for a rich person to enter the kingdom of God." MATTHEW 19:23-24

This statement so astonished the disciples they said, "Then who can be saved?" Their thought was, if it is hard for a rich man to get saved—with all the material evidence of God's favor—what chance does anyone have? Peter, looking out for his own interests and representing the entire group, spoke up and said, "We have left everything to follow you. What then will there be for us?" Jesus assured them they would receive a hundred times as much in this life and eternal life as well. However, lest they start calculating their profits too quickly, he then told them a parable to temper the promise he had just made.

In this parable, a landowner went out early in the morning to hire men to work in his vineyard. He found a group of men and agreed to pay them a denarius for the day. He went out again at the third, sixth, and ninth hour to hire more men. About an hour before quitting time, he found another group and hired them.

When evening came, it was time to pay the men. He lined the workers up beginning with the last ones and going on to the first. Much to everyone's astonishment, those workers who had worked an hour each received a full-day's wage. When the ones who were hired first saw that, they expected to receive even more. But when they also received a day's wage, they grumbled against the landowner saying, "You have made them equal to us who have borne the burden of the day and the scorching heat." The clear implication was: "You are not being fair. We worked longer, and we deserve more than they."

But the landowner answered, "Am I not allowed to do what I choose with what belongs to me? Or do you begrudge my generosity?"

The moral of the story is simple: God is sovereign in the allocation of material prosperity. It all belongs to him, and he can give as much as he wants to whomever he wants. His generosity is not based on inexorable laws that he is required to keep, but on the free choice of his will.

I have a friend who is big, fast, and strong. It is possible in our culture to trade those commodities for a large amount of cash. He did. He played professional football for ten years. Conversely, God made me skinny, weak, and slow. He did give me other abilities, but not the kind the NFL was interested in. My friend probably made more money in those ten years than I have made in my entire working life. Does that mean he had more faith then I did? Maybe, but not necessarily. God gave him abilities that were more marketable in our current economy.

This does not imply that there are not clear biblical principles regarding wealth and prosperity, and that these principles are available to every believer. There are, but God is still sovereign in the allocation of his possessions. And if we do not understand that, we will fall into the same moral trap that these men in the parable did: envy.

I knew a man several years ago who expected to receive a sizeable inheritance from a very wealthy relative. While I was happy for him, I struggled a bit with this arrangement. I knew him well and I did not think he had nearly as much faith as me. I did not think he even understood faith very well. But he was about to get hugely blessed by God while I continued to struggle financially. It did not seem to me that God was playing by the rules.

That experience (and many others like it) helped to underscore the plain biblical teaching that God is sovereign in the allocation of his possessions. I must be faithful to believe his Word, obey his commands, and trust in his provision. But in the end, he has his own plans to allocate what is his.

I have often wondered why this is so. I do not know all the reasons, but I am sure that one reason is that God uses money to test our heart.

Be aware that God uses money to test the heart.

Jesus once told a parable about a dishonest and crafty steward who squandered his master's possessions. He concluded the story with the following statements concerning money:

> One who is faithful in a very little is also faithful in much, and one who is dishonest in a very little is also dishonest in much. If then you have not been faithful in the unrighteous wealth, who will entrust to you the true riches? And if you have not been faithful in that which is another's, who will give you that which is your own? LUKE 16:10–12

These statements make it clear that God's purpose in money extends beyond our prosperity. He watches how we handle money and uses that to test where our heart is. We see this same principle in God's dealing with the Israelites. Moses said to them before they went into the Promised Land:

> Take care lest you forget the Lord your God by not keeping his commandments and his rules and his statutes, which I command you today, lest, when you have eaten and are full and have built good houses and live in them, and when your herds and flocks multiply and your silver and gold is multiplied and all that you have is multiplied, then your heart be lifted up, and you forget the Lord your God. DEUTERONOMY 8:11–14

God was going to give them fine houses, large flocks, and abundant gold and silver—all definite signs of prosperity. But before God would give them these blessings, he led them through a testing period.

> [He] led you through the great and terrifying wilderness, with its fiery serpents and scorpions and thirsty ground where there was no water, who brought you water out of the flinty rock, who fed you in the wilderness with manna that your fathers did not know, that he might humble you and test you, to do you good in the end. DEUTERONOMY 8:15–16

The important part of the above verse is the phrase, "to do you good in the end." The goal of the test was not to keep them broke and needy but to purify their heart so that they could truly enjoy his blessings. God knew that greed would destroy them if it went unchecked, and he wanted to make sure that did not happen.

Be on your guard against every form of greed.

> Someone in the crowd said to him, "Teacher, tell my brother to divide the inheritance with me." LUKE 12:13

In first-century Judaism, the rabbis served as judges in all types of civil and legal issues, so it was not unusual that this man would petition Jesus in this way. The man had seemingly been cheated out of what was legally and morally due him and he sought reparations. But Jesus refused to engage the problem and said in response, "Who made me a judge over you?"

So far there is nothing unusual in this story. However, Jesus then makes a statement that must have startled the man and the crowd.

Then he said to them, "Watch out! Be on your guard against all kinds of greed; life does not consist in an abundance of possessions."
LUKE 12:15 NIV

Apparently, this man's desire for an equal share of the inheritance—something that was rightfully his—was a cover for greed. Jesus followed his statement with a story of a rich man whose lands produced a good crop. This man was so prosperous he contemplated a secure future of ease and pleasure. He said to himself,

And I will say to my soul, "Soul, you have ample goods laid up for many years; relax, eat, drink, be merry." **LUKE 12:19**

But that was not God's assessment of his future.

But God said to him, "Fool! This night your soul is required of you, and the things you have prepared, whose will they be?" So is the one who lays up treasure for himself and is not rich toward God.
LUKE 12:20–21

Surely this parable must have been an eye-opening rebuke to the man who had never considered the possibility that his vigorous attempts to provide for himself were an insidious covering for greed. That is how subtle greed is, and that is why Jesus issued a double warning: "Watch out" and "Be on your guard." One warning was not enough. Greed is too dangerous.

Listen to some of the warnings in Scripture.

For from within, out of the heart of man, come evil thoughts, sexual immorality, theft, murder, adultery, *coveting* . . . **MARK 7:21–22**

For you may be sure of this, that everyone who is sexually immoral or impure, or who is *covetous* **that is, an idolater,** has no inheritance in the kingdom of Christ and God. **EPHESIANS 5:5**

But those who desire to be rich fall into temptation, into a snare, into many senseless and harmful desires that plunge people into ruin and destruction. For the love of money is a root of all kinds of evils. It is through this craving that some have wandered away from the faith and pierced themselves with many pangs. **1 TIMOTHY 6:9–10**

Although we usually consider greed to be a rich man's sin, it has no economic boundaries. Augustine wrote in his commentary on Psalm 72 that greed was a sin that tempted the poor as much as the rich: "It is not a matter of income but of desire," he said. "Look at the rich man standing beside you; perhaps he has a lot of money on him but no avarice in him; while you, who have no money, have an abundance of avarice."

Pursue biblical contentment.

> Not that I am speaking of being in need, for I have learned in whatever situation I am to be content. I know how to be brought low, and I know how to abound. In any and every circumstance, I have learned the secret of facing plenty and hunger, abundance and need. I can do all things through him who strengthens me.
> **PHILIPPIANS 4:11–13**

There are forces in this world that pressure us to be discontent. Over 1,500 commercial messages target Americans every day; companies spend more than $200 billion on advertising in the United States each year. The primary purpose of most of this advertising is to create discontentment. They want us to feel that something is missing in our life because we do not have their product. Former advertising executive Ray Locke said,

> Next to Christianity, advertising is the greatest force in the world. And I say that without sacrilege or disrespect. Advertising makes people discontented. It makes them want things they don't have. Without discontent, there is no progress, no achievement.[122]

A website mocking commercial advertisement offered these suggestions for potential advertisers.[123]

1. Appeal to a sense of inadequacy or inferiority in your audience.
2. Offer a fundamentally better life in exchange for their money.
3. Whenever possible, associate sex and wealth with your product.

In contrast to this worldly discontent, the Bible teaches contentment.

I use the phrase *biblical contentment* deliberately because there is a difference between contentment as it is usually defined and contentment as it is defined in the Bible. The dictionary defines contentment as complete satisfaction with what you have. That definition, while partly true, is

---

[122] Ana White, "Selling Discontent," Ray Locke quote, on New Dream website, http://www.newdream.org/newsletter/discontent.php (site discontinued).

[123] http://www.themanjones.com (site discontinued).

scripturally incomplete and could easily lead to complacency. A proper biblical definition of contentment needs to add the quality of ambition.

Ambition is a strong desire for achievement, and it is a godly characteristic. When Jesus said, "Whoever wants to become great among you must be your servant," he appealed to the disciples' natural ambitions ("wants to become great") to direct them toward a godly aim ("must be your servant").

Paul was an ambitious man—before and after his conversion. Before his conversion, he was "more extremely zealous for his ancestral traditions" (Galatians 1:14 NASB) than most of his contemporaries. As a Christian, he "worked harder than any of them" (1 Corinthians 15:10).

In the same letter that Paul described his contentment (chapter four), he described his ambition.

I want to know Christ and [. . .] attain to the resurrection from the dead. Not that I have already obtained all this [. . .] but I press on to take hold of that for which Christ Jesus took hold of me [. . .] one thing I do: Forgetting what is behind and straining toward what is ahead, I press on toward the goal to win the prize for which God has called me heavenward in Christ Jesus (Philippians 3:10–14 NIV).

Notice the words Paul used: attain, press on, take hold of, straining, and win. They all represent a strong desire for achievement. He was ambitious and contented at the same time. This is a good picture of biblical contentment.

So biblical contentment requires the combination of two things: (1) a deep satisfaction with what we have, and (2) a godly desire for more—to the glory of God. On one hand, we should be content with the money and standard of living we have. On the other hand, we should be ambitious for more so that we can help more people.

Give generously.

The Old Testament requirement for giving was based upon the tithe. The New Testament requirement for giving is based on generosity. But how do we define generosity? Because it may mean different things to different people, God gives us the starting point for generosity: the tithe. Here is an example.

During one of my trips to England, I visited the great cathedral at York. There was no admission charge to enter, but they did have a "suggested donation" of three pounds. I could have walked in for only two pounds, or one pound, or for free. There was no admission fee. But what the suggested donation sign said in essence was, "This is what it takes for us to keep the church maintained. You can be generous and give us more, but your generosity has not started until you get to the three-pound mark."

There are some similarities between the suggested donation at York Cathedral and the tithe. First, you do not need to pay the donation to get in the cathedral, and you certainly do not have to pay the tithe to get into Christ's Church. Second, the suggested donation is just the starting place; there are no limits as to how much you can give. The tithe is also just the starting place; you can certainly give much more.

No metaphor is perfect and, in this case, I would not want you to think that the tithe is just a suggested donation. It is not. It is essential. But until you give the tithe, you have not yet been generous. Generosity begins after the tithe, and generosity is the standard for New Testament giving. Here is a great example from the life of John Wesley.

In 1731, Wesley began to limit his expenses so that he would have more money to give to the poor. He recorded in his journal that his income that year was £30, and his living expenses were £28, so he had £2 to give away. The next year, his income doubled, but he still lived on £28 and gave £32 away. In the third year his income jumped to £90, but again he lived on £28, giving £62 away. The fourth year he made £120, lived again on £28 and gave £92 to the poor.

Wesley believed that with increasing income, the Christian should increase his standard of giving more than his standard of living. He began this practice when he was at Oxford, and he continued it throughout his life. Even when his income rose into the thousands of pounds (a vast sum by modern standards), he lived simply and quickly gave his surplus money away.

One year his income was slightly over £1,400; he gave all away except £30. He was afraid of laying up treasures on earth, so the money went out in charity as quickly as it came in as income. He reported that he never had as much as £100 at one time. Wesley limited his expenditures by not buying the kinds of things generally considered essential for a man in his station of life. In 1776, the English tax commissioners inspected his return and wrote back, "[We] cannot doubt but you have plate for which you have hitherto neglected to make entry." They assumed that a man of his prominence certainly had silver dinnerware in his house, and they wanted him to pay the proper tax on it. Wesley wrote back, "I have two silver spoons at London and two at Bristol. This is all the plate I have at present, and I shall not buy any more while so many round me want bread."[124]

Wesley's giving standards were his own personal conviction and do not apply to all believers. But his life certainly was a testimony of generosity.

Why People Do Not Prosper

If prosperity is God's will, then why is it that many do not prosper? There are several reasons given in the Bible for why this is. Here are a few.

They rob God of the tithe and offerings.

> Will man rob God? Yet you are robbing me. But you say, "How have we robbed you?" In your tithes and contributions. You are cursed with a curse, for you are robbing me, the whole nation of you. MALACHI 3:8–9

They cannot handle the temptations of wealth.

> But godliness with contentment is great gain, for we brought nothing into the world, and we cannot take anything out of the world. But if we have food and clothing, with these we will be content. But those who desire to be rich fall into temptation, into a snare, into many senseless and harmful desires that plunge people into ruin and destruction. For the love of money is a root of all kinds of evils. It is through this craving that some have wandered away from the faith and pierced themselves with many pangs. But as for you, O man of God, flee these things. 1 TIMOTHY 6:6–11

They are under a curse of poverty.

> But if you will not obey the voice of the Lord your God or be careful to do all his commandments and his statutes that I command you today, then all these curses shall come upon you and overtake you. Cursed shall you be in the city, and cursed shall you be in the field. Cursed shall be your basket and your kneading bowl. Cursed

---

[124] Funding the Great Commission Illustrations," Generous Church, updated 2019, https://www.generouschurch.com/illustrations-on-funding-the-great-commission.

shall be the fruit of your womb and the fruit of your ground, the increase of your herds and the young of your flock. Cursed shall you be when you come in, and cursed shall you be when you go out. DEUTERONOMY 28:15–19

Conclusion

The overwhelming testimony of Scripture and history is, "When an individual or a society consistently and continually obeys God and his Word, that person or people will increase in wealth." When we renew our minds to that fact, we will experience God's prosperity and abundance.

Application

Discuss

1. Why is it so tempting to believe that God should bless everyone equally? Have you ever been tempted to question God's fairness in his allocation of blessings? What were the circumstances, and how did you overcome the temptation?

    _____

    _____

    _____

2. Because greed expresses itself in many ways, Jesus warned us to be on guard against every form of greed. What form of greed is particularly challenging for you to resist? Why? How have you learned to battle it, and what else can you do in the future?

    _____

    _____

    _____

3. Biblical contentment combines a deep satisfaction with what we have, along with a godly desire for more. Do you have biblical contentment in your life concerning prosperity? If yes, why? If no, why not, and what can you do about it?

_____

_____

_____

Act

Using a concordance or an online reference aid, find as many verses as you can on generosity. Select the five that stand out to you the most and think about how they apply to your life. Record your thoughts for future reference.

Meditate

Take care, and be on your guard against all covetousness, for one's life does not consist in the abundance of his possessions. LUKE 12:15

15

Faith for Healing

Part One

Introduction

Faith for healing is one of the great challenges we face. Because of man's sin in the Eden, the curse of sickness and disease is rife in this fallen world. The devil knows that sickness incapacitates us physically, hindering our ministry and limiting our influence. He also knows that it hinders us psychologically from boldly proclaiming the Word of God. For this reason, we must daily renew our minds to understand and believe the promises of God concerning healing and divine health.

Because we may find that our greatest faith challenge is in our health, we must be aware of the many reasons why we should have faith for divine healing.

The first reason to have faith for healing is God's covenantal promises.

Scripture affirms that healing has always been a provision of God's Covenant—both in the Old Testament and in the New Testament. First we will look at the Old Covenant.

> If you will diligently listen to the voice of the Lord your God, and do that which is right in his eyes, and give ear to his commandments and keep all his statutes, I will put none of the diseases on you that I put on the Egyptians, for I am the Lord, your healer. EXODUS 15:26

This is the first mention of the healing provision in Scripture. It is important to note that it came three days after God opened the Red Sea and delivered his people from the Egyptians. It came at the very beginning of their journey; a journey that Paul said was a picture of our journey in Christ.

Forty years later, God reiterated his promise just before his people were about to go into the Promised Land.

> And because you listen to these rules and keep and do them, the Lord your God will keep with you the covenant and the steadfast love that he swore to your fathers. He will love you, bless you, and multiply you. He will also bless the fruit of your womb and the fruit of your ground, your grain and your wine and your oil, the increase of your herds and the young of your flock, in the land that he swore to your fathers to give you. You shall be blessed above all peoples. There shall not be male or female barren among you or among your livestock. And the Lord will take away from you all sickness, and none of the evil diseases of Egypt, which you knew, will he inflict on you, but he will lay them on all who hate you. DEUTERONOMY 7:12–15

His covenant is all-inclusive. Besides divine health, it also covers increase, prosperity, and childbearing.

Another testimony to God's covenantal provision of healing is what happens if his covenant is rejected. Deuteronomy 28:15–61 records the results of disobedience. The following is a brief excerpt:

> If you are not careful to do all the words of this law that are written in this book, that you may fear this glorious and awesome name, the Lord your God, then the Lord will bring on you and your offspring extraordinary afflictions, afflictions severe and lasting, and sicknesses grievous and lasting. And he will bring upon you again all the diseases of Egypt, of which you were afraid, and they shall cling to you. Every sickness also and every affliction that is not recorded in the book of this law, the Lord will bring upon you, until you are destroyed. DEUTERONOMY 28:58–61

As we examine this passage, it is plain that sickness is the result of the curse of the law. It is also plain from the New Testament that we are redeemed from the curse of the law.

Christ redeemed us from the curse of the law by becoming a curse for us—for it is written, "Cursed is everyone who is hanged on a tree." GALATIANS 3:13

God's covenantal promises for healing continue in the book of Psalms.

Bless the Lord, O my soul, and forget not all his benefits, who forgives all your iniquity, who heals all your diseases. PSALM 103:2–3

When the Psalmist juxtaposes forgiveness and healing, he implies a theme we will elaborate on later: the atoning blood that forgives is the same atoning blood that heals.

In Psalm 107:20–21, healing is a manifestation of one of the fruits of God's covenant love.

He sent out his word and healed them, and delivered them from their destruction. Let them thank the Lord for his steadfast love, for his wondrous works to the children of man. PSALM 107:20–21

The phrase *unfailing love* is translated from the Hebrew word *chesed* (pronounced kheh' sed). It is a rich and full word that is used 240 times in the Old Testament. It can mean steadfast love, mercy, or favor. It is a covenant word that applies primarily to God's particular love for his chosen and covenant people. The entire history of God's covenantal relationship with Israel can be summarized in terms of *chesed*. It is the one permanent element in the flux of covenantal history. Even the creation is the result of God's *chesed* (Psalm 136:5–9). His *chesed* lasts for a "thousand generations" (Deuteronomy 7:9), indeed "forever" (Psalm 136:1–26).[125]

This theme of God's covenant promises for healing continues in the New Testament, finding its fullest manifestation in the ministry of Jesus.

And Jesus went throughout all the cities and villages, teaching in their synagogues and proclaiming the gospel of the kingdom and healing every disease and every affliction. MATTHEW 9:35

That evening at sundown they brought to him all who were sick or oppressed by demons. And the whole city was gathered together at the door. And he healed many who were sick with various diseases. MARK 1:32–34

---

[125] W. E. Vine, *Expository Dictionary of New Testament Words* (Zondervan, 1982).

Before Jesus' departure, he assured his disciples that they would display the same power they saw in him.

And these signs will accompany those who believe: in my name [. . .] they will lay their hands on the sick, and they will recover. **MARK 16:17–18**

This promise was abundantly demonstrated in the ministry of the disciples.

And a man lame from birth was being carried, whom they laid daily at the gate of the temple that is called the Beautiful Gate to ask alms of those entering the temple [. . .] And Peter directed his gaze at him [. . .] and said, "Look at us. [. . .] I have no silver and gold, but what I do have I give to you. In the name of Jesus Christ of Nazareth, rise up and walk." And he took him by the right hand and raised him up, and immediately his feet and ankles were made strong. And leaping up, he stood and began to walk. **ACTS 3:2–8**

And God was doing extraordinary miracles by the hands of Paul, so that even handkerchiefs or aprons that had touched his skin were carried away to the sick, and their diseases left them. **ACTS 19:11–12**

If this is how God acted in both the Old and New Testaments, then we have confidence that he will act the same way in our day, for Scripture confirms that he never changes—both in the Old and New Testament.

For I the Lord do not change. **MALACHI 3:6**

Jesus Christ is the same yesterday and today and forever. **HEBREWS 13:8**

This verse, "Jesus Christ is the same yesterday and today and forever," was the motto of one of the most famous healing evangelists in the history of the United States: Aimee Semple McPherson. At her Oakland, California evangelistic Crusade in 1921, the skeptic L. J. De Souza attended the meetings to find people who did not get healed. He wrote a letter to the editor of the San Jose Mercury Herald calling for a "thorough investigation of the so-called healings." The American Medical Association of San Francisco sent representatives to the Crusade to examine the results of her healing ministry. The report stated that the work of Aimee Semple

McPherson met with their approval in every way, that the healing was "genuine, beneficial, and wonderful."[126]

If God healed people in the Old Testament, and Jesus healed people in the New Testament, and the disciples healed people after Jesus left, and if he never changes, then we should expect that he will heal people today. Because, "Every good gift and every perfect gift is from above, coming down from the Father of lights with whom there is no variation or shadow due to change" (James 1:17).

The second reason to have faith for healing is the sacrifice of Jesus.

The Scripture affirms that Christ died for sins *and* for sicknesses. First in the Old Testament . . .

Surely He took up our infirmities and carried our sorrows, yet we considered Him stricken by God, smitten by Him, and afflicted. But He was pierced for our transgressions, He was crushed for our iniquities; the punishment that brought us peace was upon Him, and by His wounds we are healed. ISAIAH 53:4–5 BSB

The English Standard Version (ESV) translates the word *infirmities* from the Hebrew word *choliy*. This word is used twenty-two more times in the Old Testament. Nineteen of the times, it is translated *disease*, *illness*, *affliction*, or *sickness* (the other three times it is translated *injury* or *evil*). The ESV translates the word *sorrows* from the Hebrew word *makob*. This word is used fourteen more times in the Old Testament. Eleven of the times it is translated *pain* or *suffering* (the other three times it is translated *afflictions*, *woes*, or *grief*). This is strong evidence that the infirmities and griefs that the suffering servant carried and bore are supposed to be understood as physical sickness and pain.

. . . and then in the New Testament.

---

[126] Daniel Mark Epstein, *Sister Aimee: The Life of Aimee Semple McPherson* (Mariner Books, 1994), 233.

That evening they brought to him many who were oppressed by demons, and he cast out the spirits with a word and healed all who were sick. This was to fulfill what was spoken by the prophet Isaiah: "He took our illnesses and bore our diseases." **MATTHEW 8:16–17**

Matthew makes it plain that Isaiah's infirmities and sorrow should be understood as sicknesses and diseases. Peter also confirms what Isaiah wrote.

He himself bore our sins in his body on the tree, that we might die to sin and live to righteousness. By his wounds you have been healed. **1 PETER 2:24**

A. B. Simpson, the founder of the Christian and Missionary Alliance denomination, claimed,

Divine healing is part of the redemption work of Jesus Christ. Its foundation stone is the cross of Calvary.[127]

Man is both a material and a spiritual being. And both natures have been equally affected by the fall. His body is exposed to disease; his soul is corrupted by sin. We would therefore expect that any complete scheme of redemption would include both natures, and provide for the restoration of his physical as well as the renovation of his spiritual life.[128]

A. B. Simpson's testimony of divine healing.

For more than twenty years I was a sufferer from many physical infirmities and disabilities. I became the pastor of a large city church at twenty-one, and plunging headlong into my work I broke down in one year with heart trouble. Slowly recovering in part, I labored on for years with the aid of constant remedies and preventives.

God knows how many hundred times in my earlier ministry when preaching in my pulpit it seemed that I must fall in the midst of the service. It usually took me till Wednesday to get over the effects of the Sabbath sermon, and about Thursday I was ready to begin to get ready for the next Sabbath.

---

[127] A. B. Simpson, *The Four-Fold Gospel* (CampHill, PA: Christian Publications, Inc., Revised Edition, 1984), 47.

[128] A. B. Simpson, *The Gospel of Healing* (CreateSpace Publishing, New Edition, 2013), Chap. 1.

A prominent physician told me that I had not strength enough left to last more than a few months. He required my taking immediate measures for the preservation of my life and usefulness.

While recovering, I heard many people testify that they had been healed by simply trusting the Word of Christ, just as they would for their salvation. It drove me to my Bible. I determined that I must settle this matter one way or the other. With my Bible open, and with no one to help or guide me, I became convinced that this was part of Christ's glorious Gospel for a sinful and suffering world, and the purchase of His blessed Cross, for all who would believe and receive His Word.

I could not believe this and then refuse to take it for myself. And so one afternoon I went out into the woods and there I raised my right hand to Heaven and I made to God these three great and eternal pledges:

- *I solemnly accept this truth as part of Thy Word, and I shall never question it.*
- *I take the Lord Jesus as my physical life, for all the needs of my body until all my life-work is done.*
- *I solemnly agree to use this blessing for the glory of God, and the good of others.*

I arose. It had only been a few moments, but I knew that something was done. Every fiber of my soul was tingling with a sense of God's presence. I do not know whether my body felt better or not—I know I did not care or want to feel it—it was so glorious to believe it simply, and to know that henceforth He had it in hand.

Then came the test of faith. A subtle voice whispered: "Now you have decided to take God as your healer, it would help if you should just go down to Dr. Cullis' cottage and get him to pray with you." I listened to it for a moment without really thinking. The next, a blow seemed to strike my brain, which made me reel for a moment as a man stunned. I staggered and cried: "Lord, what have I done?" In a moment the thought came very quickly, "That would have been alright before this, but you have just settled this matter forever, and told God you will never doubt that it is done."

I saw it like a flash of lightning, and in that moment I understood what faith meant. I saw that when a thing was settled with God, it was never to be unsettled. When it was done, it was never to be undone or done over again in any sense that could involve a doubt of the finality of the committal already made.

In the early days of the work of faith to which God afterwards called me, I was helped by a holy fear of doubting God. This word often shone like a living fire in my Bible: "If any man draw back, My soul shall have no pleasure in him." What the enemy desired was to get some element of doubt about the certainty and completeness of the transaction just closed, and God mercifully held me back from it.

That night we had a service in our hotel, and I was permitted to speak. I told how I had lately seen the Lord Jesus and His blessed Gospel in a deeper fullness, as the Healer of the body, and had taken him for myself, and knew that He would be faithful and sufficient.

Nearby was a mountain 3,000 feet high—I was asked to join a little party that were to ascend it. I shrank back at once. Then came the searching thought, "If you fear or refuse to go, it is because you do not believe that God has healed you. If you have taken Him for your strength, need you fear to do anything to which He calls you?" I felt it was God's thought. I felt my fear would be, in this case, pure unbelief, and I told God that in His strength I would go.

And so I ascended that mountain. At first it seemed as if it would almost take my last breath. I felt all the old weakness and physical dread; I found I had in myself no more strength than ever. But over against my weakness and suffering I became conscious that there was another Presence. There was a Divine strength reached out to me if I would have it, take it, claim it, hold it, and persevere in it. On one side there seemed to press upon me a weight of Death, on the other an Infinite Life. And I became overwhelmed with the one, or uplifted with the other, just as I shrank or pressed forward, just as I feared or trusted. Thank God, from that time I have had a new heart in this breast, literally as well as spiritually, and Christ has been its glorious life![129]

Application

Discuss

1. Many people find that healing is their greatest faith challenge. Is that true for you? Why or why not? If yes, what can you do to overcome that challenge?

_____

_____

_____

[129] A. B. Simpson, *The Four-Fold Gospel* (CampHill, PA: Christian Publications, Inc., Revised Edition, 1984).

2. What principles regarding faith for healing stand out in the testimony of A. B. Simpson? Which of these principles is most pertinent to your life right now? Why? How can you implement them in your life?

_____

_____

_____

Act

Look at Appendix D: Healing. Select several individuals from the list and read the verses associated with them. Record the principles of faith for healing you find in their stories.

Meditate

Surely he has borne our griefs and carried our sorrows; yet we esteemed him stricken, smitten by God, and afflicted. But he was pierced for our transgressions; he was crushed for our iniquities; upon him was the chastisement that brought us peace, and with his wounds we are healed.
ISAIAH 53:4–5

16

Faith for Healing

Part Two

Introduction

In the last chapter, we looked at two reasons we should have faith for healing: God's covenantal promises and the sacrifice of Jesus.

The third reason to have faith for healing is Christ's destruction of all the works of the enemy.

Sickness is a work of Satan.

> Now he was teaching in one of the synagogues on the Sabbath. And behold, there was a woman who had had a disabling spirit for eighteen years. She was bent over and could not fully straighten herself. When Jesus saw her, he called her over and said to her, "Woman, you are freed from your disability." And he laid his hands on her, and immediately she was made straight, and she glorified God. But the ruler of the synagogue, indignant because Jesus had healed on the Sabbath, said to the people, "There are six days in which work ought to be done. Come on those days and be healed, and not on the Sabbath day." Then the Lord answered him, "You hypocrites! Does not each of you on the Sabbath untie his ox or his donkey from the manger and lead it away to water it? And ought not this woman, a daughter of Abraham **whom Satan bound for eighteen years**, be loosed from this bond on the Sabbath day?"
> LUKE 13:10–16

Jesus made a point to remind the Pharisees that this woman was a daughter of Abraham—a child of the covenant—and as such, she should not be bound even one more day.

Peter reiterated the same idea in his sermon to Cornelius' household.

You yourselves know [. . .] how God anointed Jesus of Nazareth with the Holy Spirit and with power. He went about doing good and healing all who were oppressed by the devil, for God was with him. ACTS 10:37–38

Christ healed all those who were sick through the oppression of the devil. He destroyed all the works of Satan through his life, his death, and his resurrection.

Since therefore the children share in flesh and blood, he himself likewise partook of the same things, that through death he might destroy the one who has the power of death, that is, the devil, and deliver all those who through fear of death were subject to lifelong slavery. HEBREWS 2:14–15

He disarmed the rulers and authorities and put them to open shame, by triumphing over them in him. COLOSSIANS 2:15

The Healing Methods of Jesus

Jesus utilized many methods to heal the sick. There are twenty-one specific healings[130] recorded in the Gospels. The following is a compendium of the method Jesus used in each case.

- Three times, Jesus laid his hands on people (the leper, the man with dropsy, and the slave's right ear).
- Six times, Jesus spoke the Word to people (the centurion's servant, the paralytic on the roof, the Syrophoenician woman, the dead man of Nain, the man at the pool, and Lazarus).
- Four times, Jesus touched and spoke to people (Peter's mother-in-law, the two blind men, Jairus' daughter, and blind Bartimaeus).

---

[130] The term "specific healings" refers to healings where something is known about the people who were healed. There are at least thirteen other references in the Gospels to general healing: Matthew 4:23, 24; 8:16, 17; 9:35; 12:15; 14:35, 36; 15:30, 31; Mark 1:32–34; 6:54–56; 3:9, 10; Luke 4:40; 6:17–19; 7:21, 22; 9:11.

- Four times, Jesus commanded them to do something in faith (the man with the withered hand, the ten lepers, the child of the royal official, the man born blind).
- One time, Jesus was touched by someone in faith (the woman with the issue of blood).
- Two times, Jesus used other unique methods (the deaf and dumb man, the blind man and the walking trees).
- One time, Jesus used an undisclosed method (the demon-possessed blind and dumb man).

In seven of the above situations, people came to Jesus for healing. Eight times, others were brought to Jesus for healing. Six times, Jesus went to them for healing. Out of the twenty-one recorded incidents, the text indicates that seven were healed by their own faith (the centurion's servant, the paralytic on the roof, the woman with the issue of blood, the two blind men, the Syrophoenician woman, blind Bartimaeus, and the leper).

Why People Do Not Get Healed

Not everyone got healed in the Bible, and current experience tells us that not everyone gets healed today. This is a very challenging problem to many people and one that can cause much confusion. There are no easy answers to this dilemma, but the Bible does record at least five reasons why people do not get healed.

The first reason is unbelief.

When Jesus returned to his hometown after a season of ministry, the inhabitants took offense at him and challenged his message and ministry.

> And on the Sabbath he began to teach in the synagogue, and many who heard him were astonished, saying, "Where did this man get these things? What is the wisdom given to him? How are such mighty works done by his hands? Is not this the carpenter, the son of Mary and brother of James and Joses and Judas and Simon? And are not his sisters here with us?" And they took offense at him. . . . And he could do no mighty work there, except that he laid his hands on a few sick people and healed them. And he marveled because of their unbelief. MARK 6:2–3, 5–6

If people did not believe in Jesus' healing ministry while he was on the earth performing astonishing miracles before their eyes, we should not be surprised that people would have a difficult time believing in Jesus' healing ministry now that he is gone and mere men and women are the ones doing the praying.

The problem of unbelief is a prominent cause in why many people do not get healed, but one that must be handled with great care, grace, and sensitivity. Many people have had the painful experience of not being healed and then having to endure the censure and judgment of others.

The second reason is unconfessed sin.

> Is anyone among you sick? Let him call for the elders of the church, and let them pray over him, anointing him with oil in the name of the Lord. And the prayer of faith will save the one who is sick, and the Lord will raise him up. And if he has committed sins, he will be forgiven. Therefore, confess your sins to one another and pray for one another, that you may be healed. The prayer of a righteous person has great power as it is working. JAMES 5:14–16

It is instructive that James says the prayer of faith *will* heal the sick, not might heal the sick, or will heal the sick *if* it is God's will. It is assumed that it is God's will to heal the sick. The only qualifier in this passage is the sixteenth verse: "Therefore confess your sins to another and pray for one another that you may be healed." The implication seems to be that unconfessed sin may hinder the process in some way and prohibit the person from being healed.

David had a similar experience. When he failed to remove the deceit in his spirit by confessing his sin, his physical body suffered.

> Blessed is the man against whom the Lord counts no iniquity, and in whose spirit there is no deceit. For when I kept silent, my bones wasted away through my groaning all day long. For day and night your hand was heavy upon me; my strength was dried up as by the heat of summer. I acknowledged my sin to you, and I did not cover my iniquity; I said, "I will confess my transgressions to the Lord," and you forgave the iniquity of my sin. PSALM 32:2–5

This is another area that requires extreme sensitivity. The Bible teaches that unconfessed sin is a potential problem and so we must teach it, but it can cause severe damage to people if not explained carefully. The enemy will take advantage of this one and whisper in our hearts that we are not healed because there is unconfessed sin in our life. This is where we need the shield of faith and the breastplate of righteousness if we are to stand firm and receive our healing.

The third reason is a lack of revealed knowledge.

My people are destroyed for lack of knowledge. HOSEA 4:6

It is a truism that you cannot benefit from something you do not know you have. If someone puts a thousand dollars in your bank account and neglects to tell you, you will not benefit from the money—at least not until your next statement arrives. Then knowledge will enable you to benefit from the blessing.

If you are not aware of the provision God has made in Christ for your healing, it is not likely that you will benefit from it. I do not mean "aware" in the sense of mere cognizance. In spiritual matters, mere knowledge is not enough; it requires illumination. The biblical doctrine of illumination teaches that the Bible is qualitatively different from all other books and that it requires God-given assistance to understand it. Man's unregenerate mind cannot apprehend spiritual truths without divine assistance. "The natural person does not accept the things of the Spirit of God, for they are folly to him, and he is not able to understand them because they are spiritually discerned" (1 Corinthians 2:14).

Illumination is the ministry of the Holy Spirit enlightening those who are in a right relationship with him to comprehend the Word of God.

Then he opened their minds to understand the Scriptures. LUKE 24:45

Illumination of God's Word for divine healing will come as we meditate on his Word.

Kenneth Hagin's testimony of divine healing.

I received healing of a deformed heart and an incurable blood disease while on my deathbed because I believed these words in Mark 11:24 which were spoken from the lips of Jesus: " . . . What things soever ye desire, when ye pray, believe that ye receive them, and ye shall have them."

I received the revelation of that scripture in August 1934. I was bedfast and paralyzed because of an incurable heart condition and was so helpless I couldn't even bathe myself.

One particular night as I lay dying, I quoted Mark 11:24 all night long. I never slept a wink; I just quoted that verse of Scripture over and over again, probably more than a thousand times. I still didn't know exactly what it meant, but at that time, it was the only glimmer of hope I had.

I said, "Lord, You said when You were here on the earth, 'What things soever ye desire . . .' and I desire a well body. Father, You said that when I prayed, I was to believe. Well, I've prayed and I've believed." I added, "Dear Lord Jesus, if You stood right here by my bedside and I could see You with my physical eyes, and You told me, 'Son, your problem is you don't believe,' I would have to say to You, 'Dear Lord Jesus, You're lying about it because I do believe.'" I said that to the Lord in all sincerity, not in tones of arrogance. I really thought I was believing.

As I was talking to the Lord, telling Him I did believe His Word and that the problem was not with my believing, I heard these words down on the inside of me: "You do believe all right—as far as you know."

I knew what the Lord was saying to me. You see, you can't believe beyond actual knowledge of God's Word. Therefore, in order for me to believe more of God's Word and receive the desired result, I had to know more of God's Word.

Then I heard the Holy Spirit quote the rest of that verse: " . . . BELIEVE THAT YE RECEIVE THEM, AND YE SHALL HAVE THEM."

Suddenly, I got the revelation of that scripture and I saw where I had been missing it! I was only quoting part of Mark 11:24: "What things soever ye desire, when ye pray, believe . . . " But I wasn't quoting the last part of that verse, which says " . . . believe that ye RECEIVE them, and ye shall have them."

I said to the Lord, "Now I know what I've got to do. I've got to begin to believe I receive healing for my paralyzed body right now, while I'm still lying here helpless. While I'm lying here bedfast, I've got to believe I receive healing for my deformed heart and incurable blood disease."

By believing I received my healing when I prayed for healing, I was made completely well from the top of my head to the soles of my feet. When I saw what Mark 11:24 was saying and began to put it into practice, the paralysis disappeared, the blood disease left me, and my heart became normal and healthy. More than fifty-five years have come and gone, and I'm still healed. Praise God forevermore![131]

---

[131]   Adapted from *The Word of Faith*, The Testimony of Kenneth Hagin, August 1990, YEE Ministries, http://www.oocities.org/ymwmw/kennethhagin.html.

The fourth reason is not judging the body rightly.

> Let a person examine himself, then, and so eat of the bread and
> drink of the cup. For anyone who eats and drinks without discerning
> the body eats and drinks judgment on himself. That is why many
> of you are weak and ill, and some have died. 1 CORINTHIANS 11:28–30

This is a challenging passage of Scripture and one that commentators
offer contrary opinions concerning. But one thing is clear: some Christians
in Corinth were sick and some had died because they did not recognize
the body of the Lord. The purpose of this section is not to examine all the
details of what it means to not recognize the body of the Lord. The purpose
of this section is to show that, despite the clear provisions of Scripture for
healing, not everyone gets healed.

The fifth reason is God's judgment.

> When you are assembled in the name of the Lord Jesus and my
> spirit is present, with the power of our Lord Jesus, you are to deliver
> this man to Satan for the destruction of the flesh, so that his spirit
> may be saved in the day of the Lord. 1 CORINTHIANS 5:4–5

This passage is even more challenging than the previous one. However,
it probably refers to an expression of excommunication. By removing this
man from the protection of the Church and God's covenant, he would be
exposed to the devil and therefore subject to the physical torment. The
eminent scholar Theodore Beza said in reference to this passage,

> In the Scriptures there are but two kingdoms recognized—the
> kingdom of God and the kingdom of the world, which is under the
> control of Satan. To exclude a man from one is to subject him to
> the dominion of the other.[132]

Albert Barnes, in his *Notes on the New Testament*, said about this passage,

> There can be no doubt that excommunication is here intended,
> and that, by excommunication, the offender was in some sense
> placed under the control of Satan. It is further evident that by

---

[132] Albert Barnes, *Notes on the New Testament* (Kregel Classics, 8th Edition).

being thus placed under him the offender would be subject to corporal inflictions by the agency of Satan, which are here called the "destruction of the flesh."[133]

Conclusion

The Bible is clear in its teaching that divine healing is available for everyone who believes. It is not faith in our faith, but faith in God's power and his love for us.

I do not like the term, Faith Healing. While faith is a very precious grace, yet it is only the medium of the communication of God's infinite love and power, and we must never put it in the place of God Himself. There I am glad the subject is expressed in the words Divine healing, or "Healing through Faith in Jesus;" not healing by faith, but THROUGH faith; through faith in Jesus, by the power of God.[134]

Application

Discuss

1. Why is it important to know that sickness is a work of Satan? What difference would it make in our ability to believe for healing if we thought that our sickness might be from God?

_____

_____

_____

---

[133] See Note 132.

[134] Alexander Dowie, *Talks with Ministers on Divine Healing,* (Chicago: International Divine Healing Association, 1892), 1.

2. What principles regarding faith for healing stand out in the testimony
    of Kenneth Hagin? Which of these principles is most pertinent to your
    life right now? Why? How can you implement them in your life?

    _____

    _____

    _____

3. Why is it important to know some of the reasons why people do not get
    healed? What are some potential dangers to having that knowledge?

    _____

    _____

    _____

4. Why is unbelief about healing so pervasive in the modern church, and
    in what ways has that unbelief affected you? What can you do to rid
    yourself of the effects of unbelief?

    _____

    _____

    _____

Act

Select several more individuals from the list in Appendix D and read the
verses associated with them. Record the principles of faith for healing that
you find in their stories.

Meditate

You yourselves know [. . .] how God anointed Jesus of Nazareth with the
Holy Spirit and with power. He went about doing good and healing all who
were oppressed by the devil, for God was with him. ACTS 10:37–38

17

The Faith Fight

Part One

Introduction

There have been many long wars throughout history. The Hundred Years' War lasted 116 years.[135] The Crusades lasted almost 200 years.[136] The war between the Isles of Scilly and the Netherlands lasted 335 years (although no shot was ever fired). However, the longest war in history has been the one fought for the souls of men. It began in the Garden of Eden, and it will end at the last trumpet. The war was declared when God spoke these words:

> I will put enmity[137] between you and the woman, and between your offspring and her offspring; he shall bruise your head,[138] and you shall bruise his heel. GENESIS 3:15

---

[135] The Hundred Years' War was a series of wars fought between England and France between 1337 and 1453.

[136] The first Crusade was proclaimed by Pope Urban II in 1095. The eighth Crusade ended in 1291 when the crusader city of Acre fell, ending the Christian presence in the Holy Land.

[137] The dictionary defines enmity as, "the extreme ill will and deep-seated hatred that exists between enemies."

[138] The New Commentary on the Whole Bible says that a serpent's poison is lodged in its head, and a bruise on that part of its anatomy is fatal.

Matthew Henry commented on this verse saying, "A perpetual quarrel is here commenced between the kingdom of God and the devil; war is proclaimed between the seed of the woman and the seed of the serpent."[139]

Many Christian commentators since the second century have called this the Protevangelium (Lat.), the "first preaching of the gospel." It has also been described as "the Bible in embryo, the sum of all history and prophecy in a germ." It is a prediction of continual hostility between good and evil, between man and the satanic forces that oppose his moral well-being, and between the people of God and the unregenerate world system in which they live.[140]

This is the faith fight, and we will dedicate the next two chapters to examining it.

The Fight of Faith

When Paul admonished Timothy to "fight the good fight of the faith" (1 Timothy 6:12), he used the word *agonizomai* to describe this battle. The word derives from the root *agon*, the place where people gathered to witness the great athletic contests of Greece. The word gradually came to mean the individual contests themselves and eventually, by the time of Paul's letter, the broader meaning of intense conflict or battle. The extended meaning of *agonizomai* is to struggle, contend with an adversary, engage in conflict, strain every nerve to attain an object, and put forth every effort and toil. It provides us with a good description of the faith fight.

The Christian life *is* a fight, but not in the traditional sense of that word. Our fight has already been won by the death, resurrection, and victory of Christ. We belong to the only army in history sure of the outcome of the war—even before all the battles have been fought. Paul declared the victory when he said,

> He disarmed the rulers and authorities and put them to open shame, by triumphing over them in him. COLOSSIANS 2:15

Albert Barnes commented on this verse, saying,

[139] Matthew Henry, *Commentary on the Whole Bible, 6 Volumes* (Hendrickson, 2014).

[140] W. A. Criswell, *The Believer's Study Bible: New King James Version*, (Thomas Nelson, Inc., 1991), Note on Genesis 2:15.

The terms used in this verse are all military, and the idea is, that Christ has completely subdued our enemies by his death. A complete victory was achieved, so that everything is now in subjection to him.[141]

Paul used the metaphor of a Roman general and his treatment of defeated foes. The first thing a victorious general would do was to strip off the armor and other valuables of his enemy. The New Century Version of this verse says, "God *stripped* the spiritual rulers and powers of their authority." The original Greek word translated *stripped* means "to take the spoils of a defeated enemy."

> The Savior, by his death, wrested the dominion from them, and seized upon what they had captured as a conqueror seizes upon his prey. Satan and his legions had invaded the earth and drawn its inhabitants into captivity, and subjected them to their evil reign. Christ, by his death, subdues the invaders and recaptures those whom they had subdued.[142]

After the Roman general had despoiled his enemies, he would then lead them in a triumphal march to humiliate them and to inspire the adoring crowds.

> A conqueror, returning from a victory, would display in a triumphal procession the kings and princes whom he had taken, and the spoils of victory. Paul says that this was now done "openly"—that is, it was in the face of the whole universe—a glorious triumph over all the powers of hell. It does not refer to any public display on the earth, but to the grand victory as achieved in view of the universe, by which Christ, as a conqueror, dragged Satan and his legions at his triumphal car.[143]

Prior to the cross, Jesus referred to the devil as the ruler of this world (John 12:31; 14:30; 16:11). The Greek word John used for world was *kosmos*. This word referred to the physical universe. After the cross, Paul also referred to the devil as the prince of this world. However, he used a different word. The word he used was *aion* which denotes "an age, or period

---

[141] Albert Barnes, *Barnes' Notes on the Old and New Testament* (Baker Book House, 1957).

[142] See Note 141.

[143] See Note 141.

marked by certain spiritual or moral characteristics." *Aion* is always to be distinguished from *kosmos*.[144]

The use of two different words implies that something has changed. The devil formerly had authority in the world. But Jesus stripped him of that authority. Now he just has authority over the "sons of disobedience" who yield to the spirit of the age. Jesus said,

> Now is the judgment of this world; now will the ruler of this world be cast out. JOHN 12:31

If Christ has vanquished all his enemies and destroyed him who once had the power of death, why is there still a fight? If the enemy is defeated, why do we need to continue to battle?

We still have a fight because of the following realities:

1. Christ's victory is complete, but he requires that we enforce it.
2. We are often ignorant of who our enemy is and how he operates.
3. The enemy is defeated, but he can still speak and deceive us.
4. Man's sin and fall have tilted the world toward apathy and resistance to God.

We will examine each of these in the remainder of this chapter.

Enforcing Christ's Victory

Man's fall in Eden separated him from God, enslaved him to sin, and made him captive to the devil. God came to earth as a man, paid man's debt, and destroyed the works of the devil.

> The reason the Son of God appeared was to destroy the works of the devil. 1 JOHN 3:8

At Calvary, Jesus destroyed the authority of the enemy. But the enemy will not yield willingly; he must be forcibly evacuated—and that is the job of the Church. Redeemed man is now mandated to enforce the victory of Calvary.

If you owned an empty building in the downtown area of a big city, you would post signs throughout the property prohibiting unlawful occupation. If people ignored your signs and started moving in, you would have to take legal action and engage the police to enforce the law and evacuate the

---

[144] W. E. Vine, *Expository Dictionary of New Testament Words* (Zondervan, 1982).

squatters. If you did not enforce the law, they would continue to reside illegally on your property.

This is the situation the Church is in today. Christ has won the victory for us and defeated our enemy. Signs have been posted, but the enemy will not leave willingly. It is now our job to enforce his victory. There are unlawful occupants on our property, and we must drive them out.

During the Lord's time on earth, he trained his disciples to enforce his authority upon the enemy. Upon his ascension, he instructed his disciples to continue the work until all creation had heard the gospel of his kingdom and all things had been placed under his feet. And he gave us authority to accomplish the task. The mandate is still our responsibility, and the authority is still ours.

All authority in heaven and on earth has been given to me. Go therefore and make disciples of all nations . . . MATTHEW 28:18-19

We go in his authority and in his name to enforce his victory. In Paul's letter to the Ephesians, he detailed the extent of Christ's authority.

And what is the immeasurable greatness of his power toward us who believe, according to the working of his great might that he worked in Christ when he raised him from the dead and seated him at his right hand in the heavenly places, far above all rule and authority and power and dominion, and above every name that is named, not only in this age but also in the one to come. EPHESIANS 1:19-21

Christ's authority is far above anyone or anything in this universe. And we share in that authority.

And he put all things under his feet and gave him as head over all things to the church, which is his body, the fullness of him who fills all in all. EPHESIANS 1:22-23

He is head over all things and we are his body. We are positioned with him in heavenly places of authority.

. . . and raised us up with him and seated us with him in the heavenly places in Christ Jesus. EPHESIANS 2:6

But with all that authority invested in us, it will do us very little good if we do not actively impose Christ's victory. The enemy will continue to live in our buildings until we kick him out.

Knowing Our Enemy

One reason that the enemy continues to camp out in territory that is no longer his is because of wrong views we have of him. A proper scriptural understanding of our enemy is vital to victory. There are several things we need to know about our enemy.

We have an enemy.

Jim Wilson, a highly decorated commissioned United States Naval officer, wrote about the spiritual application of military principles. He said,

> Before we can be secure from attacks by an enemy we must know there is an enemy. The nation that has no enemy is very secure. The nation that has an enemy but does not think so is very insecure.[145]

We have a real enemy and it is incumbent upon us to be aware of him and his activity.

> For we do not wrestle against flesh and blood, but against the rulers, against the authorities, against the cosmic powers over this present darkness, against the spiritual forces of evil in the heavenly places. EPHESIANS 6:12

The enemy is not as powerful as he wants us to believe.

Christians often make two mistakes about the devil. The first mistake is: they magnify him.

The artists of the Middle Ages and the Renaissance tended to paint angels as pudgy babies and demons as ferocious monsters. Anyone betting on a fight between those two groups would have to wager on the demons. The 1973 box-office hit, *The Exorcist*, painted a similar picture for modern viewers. Many subsequent films have added to that image. But that is a false and dangerous view of the enemy. It produces fear and withdrawal.

The enemy also tries to get us to believe a false view of the war we are fighting. His view looks like the first *Star Wars* movie: believers are a small band of rebels fighting with truth on their side but very few weapons, against a monolithic evil empire with seemly invincible weapons (i.e., the Death

---

[145] Jim Wilson, *Principles of War: A Handbook on Strategic Evangelism* (Canon Press, 2009), 43.

Star). The actual view of the war is: the enemy is a band of ill-equipped and strife-ridden guerillas fighting against the most powerful weapons known to man.

God and the devil are not on equal ground. Satan is a created being, not even close to rivaling God in power, glory, and might. We must beware of seeing God and the devil as equal enemies locked in mortal combat. This is not a battle between Obi-Wan Kenobi and Darth Vader, or between Gandalf and Saruman. This is a battle between an elephant and an ant, or a T-Rex and a rat.

The enemy should not be underestimated.

The second, and opposite, mistake Christians make regarding the enemy is to underestimate him. Peter warned the churches scattered throughout Asia Minor to:

> Be sober-minded; be watchful. Your adversary the devil prowls around like a roaring lion, seeking someone to devour. **1 PETER 5:8**

Because we have a real enemy, we must be sober-minded and watchful. Other translations add nuances of meaning to Peter's exhortation.

> Discipline yourselves, keep alert. (NRSV)

> Be careful—watch out for attacks. (TLB)

> Be of sober spirit, be on the alert. (NASB)

> Control yourselves and be careful! (NCV)

> Keep your mind clear, and be alert. (God's Word)

These warnings would be unnecessary if the enemy were harmless. Unfortunately, that is not the case. Augustine once said: "Christ is called 'a lion' in Revelation 5:5 because of his courage; the devil, because of his ferocity. The one lion comes to conquer, the other to hurt."[146] The word *roaring* that Peter used denotes the howl of a beast in fierce hunger.[147]

---

[146] Martin Vincent, *Vincent's Word Studies in the New Testament (4 Volumes)* (Peabody, MA: Hendrickson, 1886), Note on 1 Peter 5:8.

[147] See Note 146.

Whenever an upset occurs in a sports competition, it is usually because the favored team underestimated the other team.[148] It is dangerous to discount the devil and underestimate his cunning.

We must not be unaware of the enemy's schemes.

The enemy has many schemes that he has developed and perfected over many years.

> In order that Satan might not outwit us. For we are not unaware of his schemes. **2 CORINTHIANS 2:11 NIV**

> Put on the whole armor of God, that you may be able to stand against the schemes of the devil. **EPHESIANS 6:11**

The Greek word Paul used in these verses for *schemes* is *methodeia*. It refers to "devious and systematic plans using cunning and strategy, designed especially for doing damage and causing harm." The enemy has a systematic plan for destroying us,[149] and we must be aware of what it is.

> Intelligence of an enemy requires knowing who he is, his intentions, and his methods of operating. This prevents deception and surprise.[150]

Early one morning, a man in upstate New York got in his car to go to work. The car, however, would not start. He opened the hood to check his battery and found that someone had taken it during the night. The next morning he found a new battery on his car with a note attached. The note told the story of a man and his pregnant wife on their way to the hospital to deliver their first child. Their car had died right in front of his house and because of the hour of the night and the concern about their unborn child, they panicked and took the battery. Attached to the note was a picture of their new baby, a sincere apology, and two tickets to a Broadway show playing at that time in New York City.

---

[148] For example, the 1980 U.S. Olympic hockey team. They were severe underdogs going into the competition and their opponents did not take them seriously.

[149] There used to be a popular tract that began with these words: "God loves you and has a wonderful plan for your life." A corollary truth might be: "The devil hates you and has a terrible plan for your life."

[150] Jim Wilson, *Principles of War: A Handbook on Strategic Evangelism* (Canon Press, 2009), 44.

Encouraged that they had been able to help this young couple, the man and his wife drove the two hours to the city, and enjoyed the reward of a Broadway play. When they arrived home late that night, they found that everything in their house was gone. They had been the victims of a devious and systematic scheme. The thieves, knowing exactly when they would be gone and for how long, backed a trailer up to the house and took everything.

In the same way, military leaders study the enemy to know his modus operandi and to assess his strength and weakness. Athletes watch game footage of their opponents, carefully studying them to prepare for the coming encounter. We study the Bible to see how the enemy operates so we do not succumb to his schemes. Here are a few of his schemes listed in Scripture.

His first scheme is deception.

Deception is the deliberate attempt to get someone to believe what is not true. It is the essence of warfare.

> Now the serpent was more crafty than any other beast of the field that the Lord God had made. He said to the woman, "Did God actually say, 'You shall not eat of any tree in the garden'?" **GENESIS 3:1**

Satan is first introduced as cunning and subtle, the sly deceiver who twists God's truth. The hermeneutical principle of First Mention[151] states that the first mention of a topic sets a precedent for future understanding and interpretation of that topic. The first mention is the first link in a long chain of revelation, a seed that has within it the full truth to be developed in subsequent references. Satan is a deceiver from the beginning to the end.[152] When he lies, he speaks out of his own character, for he is a liar and the father of lies (John 8:44).

The legendary Chinese general Sun Tzu wrote the earliest military treatise, *The Art of War*, around 500 BC. In it, he described Chinese weapons, command systems, communications, discipline, grade distinctions, strategy, and logistics.[153] Much of what he taught about warfare is applicable to the life of faith and our battle with the enemy. Here is his description of war:

---

[151] Hermeneutics is the art and science of interpreting the Bible accurately.

[152] Revelation 20:3: "And threw him into the pit, and shut it and sealed it over him, so that he might not deceive the nations any longer."

[153] *Microsoft Encarta Reference Library,* 2002.

All war is deception. Even though you are competent, appear to be incompetent. Though effective, appear to be ineffective. When you are going to attack nearby, make it look as if you are going to go a long way; when you are going to attack far away, make it look as if you are going just a short distance. When you want to go right, make it appear you want to go left.[154]

This is the enemy's primary scheme.

Conclusion

In the next chapter, we will continue to examine the schemes of the enemy. Then we will look at the weapons of our warfare.

Application

Discuss

1. How different does the fight of faith become when you know that all the battles have already been won? Why is it difficult sometimes to remember that and to act like it is true? How can we change our perspective?

_____

_____

_____

2. Do you tend to overestimate or underestimate the devil's power and influence? Why? What can you do to correct that perspective?

_____

_____

_____

---

[154] Sun Tzu, *The Art of War* (Filiquarian, First Thus Edition, 2007), 2.

3. When was the last time you fell for the enemy's scheme of deception? Why were you tricked? What can you do to protect yourself in the future?

_____

_____

_____

Act

Study the two accounts of Jesus' temptation in the wilderness (Matthew 4:1–11; Luke 4:1–13). Record everything you can find about how to deal with the devil and temptation in your life.

Meditate

The reason the Son of God appeared was to destroy the works of the devil.
1 JOHN 3:8

18

The Faith Fight

Part Two

Introduction

In the last chapter, we examined what the fight of faith is and why we need to fight it. In this chapter, we will continue to examine the enemy's schemes. Then we will look at the weapons of our warfare.

His second scheme is accusation.

Accusation is the act of charging someone with a shortcoming, an error, or a crime.

> For the accuser of our brothers has been thrown down, who accuses them day and night before our God. REVELATION 12:10

The word *devil* derives from the Greek word *diabolos* that refers to a slanderer, or one who falsely and maliciously accuses others. The enemy uses this weapon in four different ways:

- He accuses the believer to himself.
- He accuses the believer to God.
- He accuses God to the believer.
- He accuses one believer to another.

His third scheme is isolation.

> Whoever isolates himself seeks his own desire; he breaks out against all sound judgment. **PROVERBS 18:1**

Anyone who has seen nature programs that show lions hunting in the wild knows that a lion will look for the beast that has strayed from the herd. Once it has located an isolated stray, it will slowly and silently stalk the prospective victim, cutting off escape routes and trying not to be seen until it is about one hundred feet away. Then with a burst of speed, the lion will run toward the prey, grab it, and throw it to the ground.

The two main ways the devil isolates believers is through unforgiveness and strife.

His fourth scheme is temptation.

Temptation is the act of inciting immoral desire or craving in someone.

> For this reason, when I could bear it no longer, I sent to learn about your faith, for fear that somehow the tempter had tempted you and our labor would be in vain. **1 THESSALONIANS 3:5**

The devil tempted Eve with the lust of the flesh ("When the woman saw that the tree was good for food"), the lust of the eyes ("that it was a delight to the eyes"), and the boastful pride of life ("the tree was to be desired to make one wise") (Genesis 3:6). He tried the same temptations on Jesus in the wilderness—the lust of the flesh ("tell this stone to become bread"), the lust of the eyes ("he showed him all the kingdoms of the world"), and the boastful pride of life ("if you are the Son of God, throw yourself down from here") (Matthew 4:3–9).

Temptation is a powerful weapon against our soul. Here is a pointed example:

An obese medieval ruler named Crassus was usurped by his brother and removed from the throne. His brother confined him to a prison with a small opening. The opening was large enough for a normal-sized man to crawl out but too small for the corpulent Crassus. His brother promised him his freedom and his kingdom restored if he would lose enough weight to slip out of his prison. He then ordered massive quantities of the finest delicacies taken to Crassus' prison every day. Crassus, unable to resist the temptation, died in prison.

There are many other schemes the enemy uses, but all of them have one thing in common: his speaking voice.

The Enemy's Voice

Although the enemy is defeated, he still has one remaining weapon: the power of his voice.

There is a great scene in J. R. R. Tolkien's epic story *The Lord of the Rings* that illustrates this idea well. The Ents have defeated the traitor Saruman at the Battle of Isengard. His vast empire is in ruins before him. Gandalf, Aragorn, and representatives from the free peoples of Middle Earth confront him with a final chance to repent of his treachery. As they prepare to approach him, Gandalf issues a stern warning to the company, "Beware his voice." Here is Tolkien's description of Saruman's voice:

> Suddenly another voice spoke, low and melodious, its very sound an enchantment. Those who listened unwarily to that voice [. . .] remembered only that it was a delight to hear the voice speaking, all that it said seemed wise and reasonable. For some the spell lasted only while the voice spoke to them, and when it spoke to another they smiled, as men do who see through a juggler's trick while others gape at it. For many the sound of the voice alone was enough to hold them enthralled; but for those whom it conquered the spell endured when they were far away, and ever they heard that soft voice whispering and urging them. But none were unmoved; none rejected its pleas and its commands without an effort of mind and will.[155]

This is a powerful picture of our own adversary: broken, defeated, and powerless, but still speaking, still beguiling, still deceiving. And for those who listen to his voice, they are defeated.

A Fallen World

Paul reminded the Ephesians that they formerly walked "according to the course of this world." This is an important phrase for us to understand in our fight of faith. The course of this world is the tendency in our fallen world for everything to go from order to disorder. It is reflected in the second law of thermodynamics which states that disorder will tend to increase over

---

[155] J.R.R. Tolkien, *The Lord of the Rings: One Volume* (Great Britain: HarperCollins Publishers, 2004), Chap. 10.

time. Simply stated, everything in this world rusts, decays, and eventually wears out.

Because of this, living by faith is like paddling upstream in a canoe. You do not have to make a deliberate decision to turn around. All you have to do is stop paddling. The course of the stream will do the rest. You do not have to make a deliberate decision to stop living by faith. The forces of this world will pull you back if you do not exert a continuous effort.

When I was young, I wore braces to straighten my teeth. After the braces were removed, I failed to wear my retainer and my teeth returned to their original position. All my adult life, I was self-conscious about my teeth, and finally, at the age of thirty-nine, I returned to the orthodontist to repeat the ordeal. Eighteen months and several thousand dollars later, my teeth were straight again. As I left the office after my last check up, the orthodontist said to me, "The forces that misshaped your teeth to begin with are still in place. If you do not wear your retainer, your teeth will revert to their former position." This time, I have not made the same mistake; my retainer is in place at night.

The forces that misshaped our lives before conversion are still in place. When we gain ground through appropriating the life-transforming power of God's Word, we must hold that ground or those forces will push us back to where we were before.

This is illustrated in the armor of a first-century Roman soldier. Although the armor was effective in battle, it was wearisome on the long marches and difficult to don every day. As the army grew progressively slack and undisciplined, the soldiers received permission to discard some of the more cumbersome articles of armor, most notably the helmet and breastplate. But in contrast, Paul urged us to put on the *full* armor of God and not discard any portion of it because of laziness, apathy, or fatigue. This is a continual battle that every believer must fight. As Thomas Jefferson once said,

The price of freedom is eternal vigilance.[156]

The Weapons of Our Warfare in Ephesians Six

So far, we have examined why we need to fight the fight of faith. Now we will examine how we do it.

---

[156] This quote is attributed to Jefferson, but the original source is unknown.

The most extensive list of our weapons is found in Ephesians 6:13–17. We will examine this passage one verse at a time.

Therefore take up the whole armor of God, that you may be able to withstand in the evil day, and having done all, to stand firm.
EPHESIANS 6:13

Paul used the armor of a Roman soldier as a metaphor for our spiritual weapons. He urged us to put on the full armor of God to stand against the schemes and attacks of the enemy. No one can put on the armor for another person. The individual must consciously put it on themselves. Failure to do so may result in casualty.

Paul makes it plain that the evil day *will* come. There is no way around it if we live in this world. At birth we were dropped into an active war zone, and the sooner we come to terms with that fact, the better off we will be. The first step in this fight of faith is to embrace the right attitude about the fight. It is to understand that the kingdom of God advances through conflict. It is to declare boldly, "I love the fight."

Now on one hand, I do not actually love the fight. I would much prefer to have an easy life in a thatched cottage in a quaint English village enjoying cream tea and daily walks in the woods. But on the other hand, I do love the fight because that is where the victory is. The fight is what makes us strong. I've heard a story told that illustrates this point.

After the Cecropia moth experiences metamorphosis, it beats its wings to break the cocoon and free itself. This process takes about two hours to complete. A young boy wandered along and saw the struggling moth. He peeled back the cocoon to help free it. But the moth was unable to fly. The two-hour process is what makes the wings strong enough for flight.

The fight is what makes us strong. We must embrace the fight if we want a chance of winning. This is a biblical "theology of violence."

From the days of John the Baptist until now the kingdom of heaven has suffered violence, and the violent take it by force. **MATTHEW 11:12**

I once had a conversation with a young married couple who were deeply involved with the New Age Movement. The husband explained their philosophy this way: "I believe the universe is our friend. We must learn to go with the flow and comply passively with the currents of the universe. Resistance is what causes stress and anxiety. We should allow the universe to take us where it wants without any hindrance." I responded, "That could be a wonderful philosophy except for one tiny problem: what if the universe is not our friend? What if there are forces out there that are hostile to us, forces that want nothing more than our complete destruction?"

They did not appreciate my advice, but it is a scriptural fact. There are forces in the universe that are hostile to us, and if we remain passive they will destroy us. It is a fight to the death, and the enemy will give us no quarter.

As the Roman civilization became more decadent, their lust for violent sport increased. To satiate the craving for action, the authorities chained two combatants together and placed them in a small ring. There was only one rule to this game: the match ended when one of the wrestlers was dead. This illustration highlights the necessary attitude for victory in the spiritual fight: fight to the death. The enemy will not grow tired and acquiesce. The only choices are to fight or die.

> Stand therefore, having fastened on the belt of truth, and having put on the breastplate of righteousness, and, as shoes for your feet, having put on the readiness given by the gospel of peace.
> EPHESIANS 6:14–15

The belt was the main support of the armor; it kept all the parts of the armor in their proper place. The breastplate consisted of two parts, one to cover the soldier's front and the other to cover his back.

The Roman soldier wore sandals bound by thongs over the instep and around the ankle, with soles thickly studded with nails. The word translated *readiness* was sometimes used in the sense of a firm foundation, which would make this passage mean something like: *having put on the firm foundation of the gospel of peace as shoes for your feet.*[157] A clear understanding of truth and righteousness will give us our traction on the slippery slopes of spiritual combat.

> In all circumstances take up the shield of faith, with which you can extinguish all the flaming darts of the evil one. EPHESIANS 6:16

The ESV translates this verse "in all circumstances," but other commentators translate it "over all," implying that the shield of faith is the covering over all the armor—an accurate historical and spiritual picture. For the Roman shield represented here is not the short round shield for hand-to-hand

---

[157] Martin Vincent, *Vincent's Word Studies in the New Testament, Volume 3* (Peabody, MA: Hendrickson, 1886).

combat, but the full body shield of the heavy infantry[158] that covered all the armor of the soldier. This is an accurate picture of the role of faith—a complete covering for every part of our life.

The shield was covered with linen and leather to extinguish the fire-tipped arrows of the enemy. The ancient fire dart was an arrow with a flammable head used to set fire to wood and tents.

The Roman historian Livy tells of a huge dart used at the siege of Saguntum which was propelled by twisted ropes. "There was used by the Saguntines a missile weapon called *falarica*, with the shaft of fir, and round in other parts, except toward the point, where the iron projected. This part, which was square, they bound around with flax and pitch. It had an iron head three feet in length, so that it could pierce through the body with the armor. But what caused the greatest fear was that this weapon, even though it stuck in the shield and did not penetrate the body, when it was discharged with the middle part on fire, and bore along a much greater flame produced by the mere motion, obliged the armor to be thrown down, and exposed the soldier to succeeding blows."[159]

I grew up watching the Wile E. Coyote and Roadrunner cartoons. In one memorable episode, the coyote (*Carnivorous eatibus anythingus*) purchased a device from the Acme Corporation that would shoot multiple arrows like a Gatling gun. His goal was to aim the device at the roadrunner (*Accelerati incredibilus*) and to stick him with enough arrows to finally defeat him. Unfortunately, the device misfired and dozens of arrows pierced the hapless and perpetually inept coyote.

I think this is an accurate picture of believers who do not know how to use the shield of faith. The enemy has pierced them with so many fiery darts that they are no significant threat to him.

And take the helmet of salvation, and the sword of the Spirit, which is the word of God. EPHESIANS 6:17

The sword of the Spirit is the only offensive weapon in the list. The *machaira* was a short, two-edged sword carried by Roman legionaries, who wielded it with deadly accuracy. It was extremely difficult to approach a soldier well-trained in the use of the machaira; the sword was short and

---

[158] The shield was four feet long by two-and-a-half feet wide and curved on the inner side.

[159] See Note 157.

could be moved rapidly. Because it was two-edged, it was possible to strike on either side without changing its position in the hand. Its razor-sharp point could pierce armor.[160]

Jesus gave us an example of how to use the sword of the Spirit when he wielded it in his battle with the devil in the wilderness. Three times, he resisted the enemy's temptations with quotations from Scripture.[161]

Other Weapons of Our Warfare

We will conclude this section by looking at the weapons of praise and the name of Jesus.

Praise

When Martin Luther would get discouraged, he would say to his friend and associate Philip Melanchthon, "Let us sing the forty-sixth Psalm." He wrote the hymn "A Mighty Fortress" based upon that psalm. Perhaps no other song captured the spirit of the Protestant Reformation like this song. It was the song that martyrs sang as they gave their life for Christ. It was the song that refugees sang as they were forced to flee their native land. No wonder it has been called the "Battle Hymn of the Reformation." Here is an excerpt from the hymn:

> And though this world, with devils filled,
> Should threaten to undo us,
> We will not fear, for God hath willed
> His truth to triumph through us.
> The Prince of Darkness grim,
> We tremble not for him;
> His rage we can endure,
> For lo, his doom is sure;
> One little word shall fell him.

The power of praise is demonstrated convincingly in two Bible events, one in the New Testament and one in the Old Testament.

---

[160] W. A. Criswell, *The Believer's Study Bible: New King James Version,* (Thomas Nelson, Inc., 1991).

[161] All three of Jesus' responses were from the book of Deuteronomy.

When Paul cast a spirit of divination out of a slave girl in Philippi, her owners realized that their source of profit was gone. They hauled Paul and Silas before the civil authorities who beat them and cast them into prison. About midnight, Paul and Silas started complaining about how difficult and unfair ministry life was . . . or, not exactly. Here is the actual account:

> About midnight Paul and Silas were praying and singing hymns to God, and the prisoners were listening to them. ACTS 16:25

Bloody, beaten, and chained, they still praised. And they did not praise because they knew an earthquake would come if they did. They did not praise because they had read a book about the personal benefits of praise. They praised because they were honored to be considered worthy to suffer for his name. They praised simply because of who God is and not for what they would get. That kind of praise works miracles.

> And suddenly there was a great earthquake, so that the foundations of the prison were shaken. And immediately all the doors were opened, and everyone's bonds were unfastened. ACTS 16:26

A violent earthquake would shake the foundations of a prison and possibly cause the doors to fly open, but it would not loosen every prisoner's chains. That was a miracle—a miracle designed to show the liberating power of praise.

This same theme was displayed during the reign of King Jehoshaphat. A vast army of Moabites and Ammonites came to make war on him. The king proclaimed a fast and the people called on the name of the Lord in a solemn assembly. Then the word of the Lord came to the prophet and he said,

> Listen, all Judah and inhabitants of Jerusalem and King Jehoshaphat: Thus says the Lord to you, "Do not be afraid and do not be dismayed at this great horde, for the battle is not yours but God's."
> 2 CHRONICLES 20:15

In response to this word, Jehoshaphat appointed men to sing and praise the Lord, saying, "Give thanks to the Lord, for his steadfast love endures forever."

> And when they began to sing and praise, the Lord set an ambush against the men of Ammon, Moab, and Mount Seir, who had come against Judah, so that they were routed. When Judah came to the

205

watchtower of the wilderness, they looked toward the horde, and behold, there were dead bodies lying on the ground; none had escaped. 2 CHRONICLES 20:22–24

When Jehoshaphat and his men went to carry off the plunder, there were so many items of value that it took three days to collect it.

The Name of Jesus

Jesus has given us the power of attorney to use his name.

In that day you will ask nothing of me. Truly, truly, I say to you, whatever you ask of the Father in my name, he will give it to you.
JOHN 16:23

The power of attorney is the legal right to designate someone else to act on your behalf on matters that you specify. The person who executes the power of attorney is called the principal. The person designated to act is called the agent. The principal designates that the agent is authorized to act on the principal's behalf—to stand in the shoes of the principal—for whatever purpose the principal permits.

The name of Jesus unlocks the blessings of heaven.

And his name—by faith in his name—has made this man strong whom you see and know, and the faith that is through Jesus has given the man this perfect health in the presence of you all. ACTS 3:16

The name of Jesus will do the same things today that Jesus did during his earthly ministry.

Truly, truly, I say to you, whoever believes in me will also do the works that I do; and greater works than these will he do, because I am going to the Father. Whatever you ask in my name, this I will do, that the Father may be glorified in the Son. If you ask me anything in my name, I will do it. JOHN 14:12–14

Conclusion

The battle is the Lord's and he has given us invincible weapons. The only way we can be defeated is if we refuse to fight or we quit too soon. But if we will remain in the battle, we can be sure that he "always leads us in triumphal procession in Christ" (2 Corinthians 2:14 NIV).

Application

Discuss

1. Which scheme of the enemy are you the most prone to: accusation, isolation, or temptation? Why? What can you do to strengthen yourself against that scheme?

_____

_____

_____

2. What piece of your spiritual armor are you most likely to discard or fail to don? Why?

_____

_____

_____

Act

Study the believer's spiritual armor in Ephesians 6:10–19. Record your thoughts. Look for ways to apply the armor in a more tangible way in your daily life.

Meditate

Therefore take up the whole armor of God, that you may be able to withstand in the evil day, and having done all, to stand firm. EPHESIANS 6:13

Appendix A

Bible History

General Facts

- The word "Bible" comes from the Greek word "biblos" which simply means "book." The Bible is "the Book."
- Over forty different authors from diverse vocations on three continents wrote the Bible over a period of more than 1,500 years. They used a variety of literary types, including history, law (civil, criminal, ethical, ritual), poetry, treatise, philosophical musing, parable, wisdom literature, narrative, diatribe, allegory, biography, personal correspondence, travelogue, prophesy, and apocalyptic literature.
- The Bible has been translated into more languages than any book in the world. According to the statistical summary provided by the United Bible Societies' World Report, as of January 2019, the whole Bible had been translated into 692 languages and dialects, and parts of it into another 2,670.[162]
- In the thirteenth century, Stephen Langton, the archbishop of Canterbury, divided the Bible into the chapter divisions we use today. In 1551, Robert Estienne (sometimes referred to as Robert

---

[162] "Key Facts about Bible Access," United Bible Societies, United Bible Societies (UBS), https://www.unitedbiblesocieties.org/key-facts-bible-access/.

Stephens or just Stephanus) added the verse references found in all modern Bibles.

- The Old Testament was written primarily in Hebrew (a few sections were written in Aramaic[163]). The New Testament was written in common marketplace Greek (not classical or modern Greek).
- There are sixty-six books in the Bible: thirty-nine in the Old Testament, and twenty-seven in the New Testament.
- The first five books of the Old Testament are called the Pentateuch.[164]
- The Old Testament is divided into three parts: history, poetry, and prophecy. There are seventeen history books,[165] five poetry books,[166] and seventeen prophecy books.[167]
- The New Testament is divided into four parts: gospel,[168] history, epistle, and apocalypse.
- The Gospels are accounts of the life and ministry of Jesus Christ, arranged not as biographies or chronological narratives,[169] but as theological sermons to meet the needs of a particular group.
- The Gospels record material that is historical, but cannot be considered historical in the same way the term is used today. Apart from Luke, the Gospels do not claim to be chronological. They contain very little information about Christ's early life and spend an excessive amount of time reporting the events of the Passion Week.

---

[163] The Aramaic portions of the Old Testament are the following: Ezra 4:8–6:18; 7:11–26; Daniel 2:4–7:28; Genesis 31:47 (two words); Jeremiah 10:11. The language in which they are written used to be called Chaldee, but is now generally known simply as Biblical Aramaic (*International Standard Bible Encyclopedia*).

[164] The word *pentateuch* comes from two Greek words: *penta*, which means *five*, and *teuch*, which means *book*. The term was first used by Origen to denote what the Jews of his time called the Torah (teaching). The Torah is the holiest and most beloved of the sacred writings of the Jews (*Microsoft Encarta Reference Library, 2002*).

[165] Genesis, Exodus, Leviticus, Numbers, Deuteronomy, Joshua, Judges, Ruth, 1 & 2 Samuel, 1 & 2 Kings, 1 & 2 Chronicles, Ezra, Nehemiah, and Esther.

[166] Job, Psalms, Proverbs, Ecclesiastes, and Song of Solomon.

[167] The five Major Prophets are: Isaiah, Jeremiah, Lamentations, Ezekiel, Daniel. The twelve Minor Prophets are: Hosea, Joel, Amos, Obadiah, Jonah, Micah, Nahum, Habakkuk, Zephaniah, Haggai, Zechariah, and Malachi.

[168] The Gospels are often included under the History heading.

[169] A Gospel *includes* biography and chronological narrative, but that is not its primary purpose.

- The first three Gospels (Matthew, Mark, and Luke) are similar to one another in structure, content, and wording. They are called the Synoptics (from a Greek word meaning "to see together"). They concentrate on Jesus' Galilean ministry and public discourses. The fourth Gospel, John, concentrates on his Judean ministry and private discourses.
- There is one book of history: Acts. Luke's history had a limited scope. He did not focus on the biographies of the apostles, Church organization, or the general growth of the Church. Instead, he showed how the Church expanded from the isolated city of Jerusalem to the great metropolis of Rome.
- There are twenty-one epistles.[170] The epistle was a common literary form in the first-century Greco-Roman world. It usually consisted of a standard greeting, thanksgiving, message, and farewell.
- There is one apocalypse: Revelation. Apocalypse, a genre popular in the first century, concerns the end of the world and the salvation of the righteous. It uses an abundance of symbols, visions, and prophecies.

The Formulation of the Canon

The word "canon" comes from a Greek word meaning a "measuring rod." It is used to describe the inspired books of the Bible. The word "canonicity" refers to the process whereby the early Church Fathers determined which books were divinely inspired and had the seal of divine authority. The New

---

[170] Thirteen books are called Pauline: Romans, 1 & 2 Corinthians, Galatians, Ephesians, Philippians, Colossians, 1 & 2 Thessalonians, 1 & 2 Timothy, Titus, Philemon; and eight are called General: Hebrews, James, 1 & 2 Peter, 1, 2 & 3 John, and Jude.

Testament Canon was the result of 350 years of prayer and research.[171] Many forces contributed to its final form. Here are a few of them:

- There was a need for an authoritative voice to proclaim the message of the apostles who were all dead by the end of the first century. Oral tradition would continue to deteriorate over the years, and they needed a written canon for accurate instruction because there were many spurious writings claiming to be inspired. For example, the Apocalypse of Adam, the Gospel of Philip,[172] the Acts of Peter, the Acts of Thomas, etc.
- There was a need to know which books were authoritative for doctrine, and which were merely edifying. For example, what should be done with Clement's letter to the Corinthians, written in AD 95? A number of the churches reasoned that since Clement was a disciple of Paul (Philippians 4:3), the letter should be authoritative. (In the end, Clement's letter was rightly considered merely edifying and not canonical.)
- There was a need for a true canon to answer the false ones developing (for example, the canon that the heretic Marcion[173] established around AD 150).
- There was a need to establish finality in revelation. Various sects and cults propagated ideas of continuing revelation and new messages coming from God.

---

[171] The final form of the canon developed gradually. Clement of Rome (AD 95) mentioned at least eight New Testament books in a letter. Polycarp (AD 108) acknowledged fifteen letters. Irenaeus (AD 185) acknowledged twenty-one books. Hippolytus (AD 170–235) recognized twenty-two books. The Muratorian Canon (AD 170) included all the New Testament books except Hebrews, James, and 3 John. Athanasius (AD 367) cited the twenty-seven books of the New Testament as being the only true books. The Council of Laodicea (AD 363), the Council of Hippo (AD 393) and the Council of Carthage (AD 397) all affirmed that only the twenty-seven books of the New Testament were to be read in the churches. "When the Synod of Hippo listed the twenty-seven books of the New Testament, it did not confer upon them any authority which they did not already possess, but simply recorded their previously established canonicity" (F. F. Bruce, *The Books and the Parchments*, 113).

[172] Referred to frequently in the runaway bestseller The DaVinci Code as the "sacred text" that explains the truth about the marriage of Jesus and Mary Magdalene.

[173] Marcion rejected the Old Testament and removed all New Testament writings apart from Paul's letters and parts of Luke's gospel.

- There was a need to decide which books to die for. For example, in AD 302, the emperor Diocletian issued an edict to uproot Christianity by burning Bibles and destroying churches. Christians caught with the sacred books could be killed.

There were at least four tests applied to the various books to determine their authenticity.

- The first was apostolicity: Was the author an apostle or did he have a connection with an apostle? Mark was not considered an apostle, but he wrote under Peter's authority. Luke also was not considered an apostle, but he wrote under Paul's authority.
- The second was acceptance: Did the Church at large accept the book? By this rule, spurious or false books were rejected. However, this rule also delayed the recognition of some legitimate books. For example, James, Jude, 2 Peter, and Revelation were some of the last books accepted into the canon because not all the churches initially recognized their inspiration.
- The third was content: Was the book consistent with orthodox teaching?
- The fourth was inspiration: Did the book reflect the quality of inspiration?

Understanding the Bible

- There are five concepts we must be familiar with to have a proper understanding of the Bible: revelation, inspiration, inerrancy, illumination, and interpretation.
- Revelation means that God manifests himself to particular persons at definite times and places, enabling those persons to enter into a redemptive relationship with him.[174] There are two kinds of revelation: general and special.

---

[174] "Nobody would know the truth about God, or be able to relate to Him in a personal way, had not God first acted to make Himself known" (J. I. Packer, *Concise Theology: A Guide to Historic Christian Beliefs*).

- General revelation is God's communication of himself to all persons at all times and in all places.[175] Special revelation is God's authoritative Word conveyed objectively and propositionally through the exclusive medium of the Bible.[176]

- John Calvin explained the difference between the two with this analogy: "Just as old men with weak vision, if you thrust before them a most beautiful volume, even if they recognize it to be some sort of writing, yet can scarcely construe two words, but with the aid of spectacles will begin to read distinctly; so Scripture, gathering up the otherwise confused knowledge of God in our minds, having dispersed our dullness, clearly shows us the true God. This is a special gift of God to instruct the church."

- Inspiration is the supernatural influence on the Bible authors, making their writings infallible and an exact expression of God's mind and will[177] (2 Peter 1:20–21; 2 Timothy 3:16–17). The authors retained their individual personalities as thinkers and writers.

- Inerrancy means that the Bible is fully true in all it teaches and affirms.[178] Inerrancy allows for popular expressions, approximations, phenomenal language, and variety in details in explaining the same event. It also allows for variety in style. John's gospel was written in the simple style of an unlearned fisherman; Luke's gospel was written with the sophisticated vocabulary of an educated person; Paul's epistles were written with the logic of a debater.

---

[175] There are three manifestations of general revelation. Nature reveals God's glory (Romans 1:20). Providence reveals God's love (Matthew 5:45). Conscience reveals God's holiness (Romans 2:14–15).

[176] There are three other manifestations of special revelation. The first is miraculous events—God manifesting himself in history. (For example, the parting of the Red Sea.) The second is divine speech—God revealing himself through human language. (For example, Joseph's dream to move his family to Egypt until the death of Herod.) The third is visible manifestations—God showing himself in visible form. (For example, the Lord appearing to Abraham by the oaks of Mamre in Genesis 18.)

[177] "Inspiration is the supernatural influence exerted on the sacred writers by the Spirit of God, by virtue of which their writings are given Divine trustworthiness" (*International Standard Bible Encyclopedia*, Vol. 3, 1453).

[178] "The Scriptures possess the quality of freedom from error. They are exempt from the liability to mistake, incapable of error. In all their teachings they are in perfect accord with the truth" (E. J. Young, *Thy Word is Truth*, 113).

- Illumination is the ministry of the Holy Spirit whereby he enlightens those who are in a right relationship with him to comprehend the written Word of God. The Bible is God-breathed and is qualitatively different from all other literature. Therefore, it is necessary that man receive God-given help in understanding the Bible (1 Corinthians 2:11, 14; Luke 24:45).
- Interpretation is the human process of cooperating with the divine process of illumination. It is the careful and systematic analysis of a text to discover the intended meaning. The goal of interpretation is to determine the meaning of the text in its original context—what the author meant when he wrote to his original readers.

Interpretation

The Bible's central message is so plainly stated that the most unlearned of those who have ears to hear and eyes to see can understand it. The technicalities of scholarship may be out of the ordinary Bible reader's reach, but nonetheless he can, with God's blessing, grasp all the main truths of God's message.[179]

There are several requirements for a proper understanding of Scripture.

The first requirement to accurately interpret Scripture is a careful reading of the literary context of the passage. The literary context is what precedes a passage and what follows it. The immediate context of a passage is the paragraph and chapter in which it occurs. The remote context of a passage is the book and testament in which it occurs.

The second requirement to accurately interpret Scripture is an understanding of the historical context of the passage. The Bible was written by God; therefore it has eternal relevance. The Bible was also written by men; therefore it has historical specificity. Therefore, knowledge of the specific time and place the authors lived and the specific context they wrote in will provide a deeper understanding of a passage.

A major obstacle to understanding the Bible is that we are separated from the historical events by thousands of years. The Bible is a record of the words God spoke through real people in real circumstances in real places at real times. Therefore, every verse has a historical context that determines

---

[179] J. I. Packer, *Fundamentalism and the Word of God* (Eerdmans, 1958), 107.

the meaning of the verse. The more accurately we reconstruct the historical setting, the more accurately we will understand God's Word. The more we understand what God's Word meant to the original hearers, the more we will understand what it means to us.

There are five significant factors in considering the historical context of a passage.

- Who wrote the original document? For example, John Mark was the author of the second Gospel. The Church Father Papias said, "Mark, who became Peter's interpreter, wrote accurately, though not in order, all that he remembered of the things said or done by the Lord. For he had neither heard the Lord nor been one of His followers, but afterwards, he had followed Peter." So Mark's gospel is a presentation of Peter's view of Jesus.
- Why was the original document written? For example, 1 Corinthians was written in response to questions from the Church (7:1, 25; 8:1; 12:1; 16:1) and reports that Paul had received about problems in the Church (1:11).
- When was the original document written? For example, 2 Timothy was written shortly before Paul was beheaded on the Ostian Way outside of Rome. The book contains a record of the things that were uppermost on the mind of the great apostle before his departure from this world.
- Who was the original document written to? For example, the Philippians became Paul's most faithful financial partners. They sent contributions when he was in Thessalonica (Philippians 4:16), a contribution when he was in Corinth (2 Corinthians 11:9), a contribution to his offering for the saints in Jerusalem (2 Corinthians 8:1–5), and an offering during his Roman imprisonment (Philippians 4:18). No wonder Paul could say with such confidence to them, "And my God shall supply all your needs according to his riches in glory in Christ Jesus."
- What were the culture, politics, and geography of the city or region that received the original document?

CULTURE: Corinth was one of the most sinful cities in the Roman Empire. Its main tourist attraction was the Temple to Aphrodite with its one thousand cult prostitutes. The Greek playwright Aristophanes coined the verb "to corinthianize," a slang term for fornication, because of the sensuality of the city. So when Paul said, "It is actually reported that there is sexual immorality among you, and of a kind that does not occur even among pagans," it was a stinging rebuke to a city already known for its sexual excess.

POLITICS: When the Jewish elders caught a woman in adultery, they thought they had discovered the perfect way to trap Jesus. They said, "Teacher, this woman was caught in the act of adultery. In the Law, Moses commanded us to stone such women. Now what do you say?" They were using this question as a trap, in order to have a basis for accusing him. The Romans allowed a measure of self-government in the territories they controlled, but they withheld the right of capital punishment. If Jesus upheld the Law of Moses, he would be in opposition to Rome and would be guilty of treason. If he denied the Law of Moses, he would lose favor with the people. His answer sidestepped both pitfalls and enabled him to extend grace and forgiveness to the adulterous woman.

GEOGRAPHY: Laodicea was one of the most prosperous cities in all of Asia Minor. But it had one major drawback: no local water supply. Its two neighbors, Colossae and Hierapolis, had cold well water and hot springs. But Laodicea was dependent upon water delivered through a system of stone pipes from a spring six miles away. By the time the water arrived it was neither hot (like Hierapolis) nor cold (like Colossae) but lukewarm—mineral-laden and well-suited to induce vomiting. That helps explain Jesus' words in Revelation 3:15–16: "I know your works: you are neither cold nor hot. Would that you were either cold or hot! So, because you are lukewarm, and neither hot nor cold, I will spit [literal translation: vomit] you out of my mouth."

The third requirement to accurately interpret Scripture is an understanding of the different literary styles. To correctly understand a given text's original meaning, knowing its literary form is helpful. You do not read poetry the same way you would read a legal document. Each literary genre has its own unique characteristics.

The fourth requirement to accurately interpret Scripture is an awareness of our prejudices. We come to the text with many of our own ideas. The culture we were raised in shapes our perceptions of many of the issues addressed in the Bible. The religious institutions in which we have participated also shape our views on many topics of the Bible.

Reading the Bible

The first and primary way we ingest the Word is through reading. Reading the Bible gives us a general overview of God's Word. It also gives God a medium to speak to us, either during the reading, or later when the Holy Spirit reminds us of appropriate verses.

The Bible can be read using the fast method or the slow method. Each method has a different purpose and objective. The purpose of the fast method is to gain an overall understanding of the historical development and message of the Bible. The objective is knowledge. The purpose of the slow method is to reflect deeply on smaller sections of the Bible. The objective is understanding.

John Wesley taught several tips for effective Bible reading.[180]

- Set apart time every morning and evening for the purpose of reading.
- Read with a determination to know the whole will of God and with a steady resolution to do it.
- Pray seriously and earnestly before consulting the Word of God, because Scripture can only be understood through the same Spirit whereby it was given. Scripture reading should also end with prayer so that what was read might be written on the heart.
- Pause frequently and examine your heart and life by what you read.
- Whatever light you receive should be used to the uttermost and immediately. Let there be no delay. Whatever you resolve, begin to execute the first moment you can.

Reading the Bible naturally leads to memorization. Jesus obviously memorized Scripture because he was able to defeat the devil in the wilderness (with no scrolls readily available) by quoting the Bible. The following are some tips for memorization.[181]

---

[180] John Wesley, *Wesley's Notes on the Bible* (Grand Rapids, MI: Christian Classics Ethereal Library), Preface.

[181] Modified from *Scripture Memory: Your Key to Success*, Monica Best, http://www.fsbcdc. org (site discontinued).

- Memorize verses that relate to what God is currently saying to you.
- Read the verse aloud and write it out, many times if necessary.
- Write out the verse with the reference on a "flash card."
- Always memorize verses exactly.
- Emphasize key words in the verse when quoting.

Appendix B

Scriptural Confessions

Wisdom and Revelation

(Ephesians 1:17–19; Colossians 1:9; John 16:13, 14:26; Proverbs 2:1–6; Colossians 2:3, 10; Daniel 2:22–23; 1 Corinthians 2:9–12; James 1:5; Mark 4:22; Luke 21:15)

The God of my Lord Jesus Christ—the Father of Glory—has given to me a spirit of wisdom and revelation in the true knowledge of him. The eyes of my heart have been flooded with light, so that I might know what is the hope of his calling, the riches of the glory of his inheritance in the saints, and the surpassing greatness of his power toward us who believe.

I am filled with the knowledge of his will in all spiritual wisdom and understanding. The Spirit of truth has come to guide me into all the truth and to disclose, unveil, divulge, and reveal to me what is to come. He is teaching me all things and bringing all things to my remembrance.

I receive his sayings, I treasure his commands within me, I make my ear attentive to wisdom, I incline my heart to understanding; I cry for discernment, I lift my voice for understanding; I seek her as silver and search for her as hidden treasures; then I will discern the fear of the Lord and discover the knowledge of God. For he gives wisdom; from his mouth come knowledge and understanding.

In Christ are hidden all the treasures of wisdom and knowledge, and in him I have been made complete. It is he who reveals the profound and hidden things; he knows what is in the darkness, and the light dwells with him. To him I give thanks and praise, for he has given me wisdom and power.

Things which eye has not seen and ear has not heard and has not entered the heart of man, all that God has prepared for those who love him. For to me God revealed them through the Spirit, for the Spirit searches all things, even the depths of God. For who among men knows the thoughts of a man but the spirit of the man within him? Even so, no one knows the thoughts of God but the Spirit of God. Now I have received, not the spirit of the world, but the Spirit who is from God, that I might know the things freely given to me by God.

I ask for wisdom and it is given to me generously. For nothing is hidden, except to be revealed; nor has anything been secret, but that it should come to light. He gives me wisdom and utterance which none of my opponents can resist or refute.

Prosperity

(Philippians 4:19; Deuteronomy 28:2, 8; Hebrews 6:13–14; Deuteronomy 8:18; Proverbs 10:22; Psalms 35:27; Malachi 3:10–11; 1 Timothy 6:17; Psalms 37:4, 84:11; 2 Corinthians 9:8)

My God supplies all my needs according to his rich abundance of glory in Christ Jesus. He commands the blessing upon me in all that I put my hand to and blesses me in the land he has given to me. All these blessings will come upon me and overtake me because I obey the voice of the Lord.

For when he made the promise to me, since he could swear by no one greater, he swore by himself, saying, "I will surely bless you, and I will surely multiply you."

He has given me the power to make wealth, that he may confirm his covenant to me. His blessing makes me rich and he adds no sorrow to it. He delights in the prosperity of his servant.

I bring the tithe into the storehouse, so there may be food in his house, and I test him in this, to see if he will not open for me the windows of heaven and pour out such blessing that there will not be room enough to receive it. He will rebuke the devourer for my sake.

He richly supplies me with all things to enjoy. I delight myself in him and he gives me the desires of my heart. No good thing will he withhold from those who walk uprightly. He makes all grace abound to me. I always have everything I need, and I have an abundance for every good deed.

Favor

(Psalm 5:12; Genesis 39:21; Luke 2:52; Psalm 30:5; Psalm 89–17; Proverbs 12:2; Ezra 7:28; Luke 1:28; Proverbs 3–4)

He blesses the righteous and surrounds me with favor like a shield. The Lord is with me. He extends kindness to me and gives me favor. I keep increasing in wisdom and stature, and in favor with God and man.

His favor is for a lifetime; by it I am exalted. A good man will obtain favor from the Lord. I am greatly blessed and highly favored of the Lord.

I do not let kindness and truth leave me; I bind them around my neck, and I write them on the tablet of my heart, so I will find favor and good repute in the eyes of God and man.

Health

(Proverbs 4:20–22; Psalms 103:2–4, 107:20; Proverbs 3:5–8; Isaiah 53:4–5)

I give attention to his words; I incline my ear to his sayings. I do not let them depart from my sight; I keep them in the midst of my heart. For they are life to those who find them, and health to my whole body.

Bless the Lord, O my soul, and forget none of his benefits; who pardons all my iniquities, who heals all my diseases, and who redeems my life from the pit. He sent his word and healed me.

I trust in the Lord with all my heart, and I do not lean on my own understanding. In all my ways I acknowledge him, and he will make my paths straight. I am not wise in my own eyes; I fear the Lord and turn away from evil. It will be healing to my body and health to my bones.

Surely my griefs he himself bore, and my sorrows he carried. He was pierced through for my transgressions, he was crushed for my iniquities; the chastening for my well-being fell upon him, and by his scourging I am healed.

Joy

(Nehemiah 8:10; Psalms 90:14, 30:5, 118:24; Proverbs 15:15; Psalm 21:1–6; Acts 13:52; Romans 15:13–14:17; Psalms 63:7, 36:8, 30:11)

The joy of the Lord is my strength. He satisfies me in the morning with lovingkindness, that I might sing for joy and be glad all my days.

This is the day which the Lord has made; I rejoice and I am glad in it. I shout with joy in the morning. A joyful heart has a continual feast.

I rejoice in his strength. How great is his joy in the victories he gives! He has granted me the desire of my heart, and I have not withheld the request of my lips. He placed a crown of pure gold on my head. He has given me life and length of days. He has granted me eternal blessings and made me glad with the joy of his presence.

I am continually filled with joy and with the Holy Spirit. The God of hope fills me with all joy and peace in believing. For his kingdom is righteousness, peace, and joy in the Holy Spirit.

In the shadow of his wings I sing for joy. I feast on the abundance of his house, and I drink from his river of delights. He has turned my mourning into dancing and clothed me with joy.

Love

(Romans 5:5; Jude 21; 1 Corinthians 16:14; Ephesians 5:1–2; 1 Peter 4:8, 1:22; 1 Corinthians 13:4–8)

The love of God has been poured out in my heart through the Holy Spirit who was given to me. Therefore, I keep myself in the love of God, and all I do is done in love.

I am an imitator of God and I walk in love, just as Christ also loved me. Above all, I keep fervent in my love for others, because love covers a multitude of sins. In obedience to the truth, I purify my soul for a sincere love of the brethren, and I fervently love others from the heart.

Love is patient, love is kind and is not jealous; love does not brag and is not arrogant; it does not act unbecomingly; it does not seek its own and is not provoked; it does not take into account a wrong suffered and does not rejoice in unrighteousness, but rejoices with the truth; love bears all things, believes all things, hopes all things, endures all things. Love never fails.

Victory

(1 John 5:4; 2 Corinthians 2:14; Philippians 4:13; Romans 8:37; 1 John 4:4)

Whatever is born of God overcomes the world; and this is the victory that has overcome the world—my faith. I am born of God, and I overcome the world.

Thanks be to God, who always leads me in his triumph in Christ, and manifests through me the sweet aroma of the knowledge of him in every place I go.

I can do all things through him who makes me strong. In all things I overwhelmingly conquer through him who loved me.

I am from God and have overcome them, because greater is he who is in me than he who is in the world.

Blessing

(Ephesians 1:3; Deuteronomy 28:2–13; James 1:17; Luke 12:32; Psalm 23:6; Numbers 6:24–26; Galatians 3:9, 29)

I am blessed with every spiritual blessing in the heavenly places in Christ.

All these blessings come upon me and overtake me. I am blessed in the city and blessed in the country. I am blessed when I come in and blessed when I go out. I am blessed in my offspring. I abound in blessings. All the works of my hands are blessed. I am the head and not the tail, and I am above and not underneath.

Every good thing and every perfect gift is coming to me from the Father of lights. I am not afraid for my Father has chosen gladly to give me the kingdom. Surely goodness and loving kindness will follow me all the days of my life, and I will dwell in the house of the Lord forever.

The Lord blesses me and keeps me; the Lord makes his face shine on me, and he is gracious to me. The Lord lifts up his countenance on me and gives me peace.

I belong to Christ and I am Abraham's offspring, an heir according to promise. I am blessed with the blessings of Abraham.

Appendix C

Faith Heroes from Church History

The emphasis on the message of faith is not new. It has been a strong emphasis throughout all of Church history. Just as the author of the book of Hebrews could compile a list of the faith heroes of the Old Testament, so too could we compile a list of the faith heroes of the Church. From the writings and example of the Church Fathers, through the medieval saints and great reformers, to the revivalists, missionaries, scholars, church planters, and martyrs, the message of faith has resounded. The following is a brief list of some of these men and women who have declared by their life and their message that "the just shall live by faith."

Polycarp (AD 69–155)

Polycarp was a disciple of the apostle John and the bishop at Smyrna when a local persecution arose.

After twelve Christians were condemned to die, the officials sought to arrest Polycarp. When they arrived to arrest him, he treated them with the utmost courtesy and invited them to eat and drink as his guests. When he was ready, the officials mounted him upon a donkey and led him into the city.

As he was brought to the crowded stadium to be burned alive, he heard a voice from heaven saying, "Be strong, Polycarp, and play the man." He was led before the proconsul who tried to persuade him to recant saying,

"Have respect to your age and swear by Caesar. Curse the Christ and I will release you."

Polycarp responded, "Eighty and six years have I served Him, and He has done me no wrong; how then can I blaspheme my king who saved me?"

The proconsul said, "I have wild beasts; if you do not repent, I will throw you to them." But he said, "Send for them. For repentance from better to worse is not a change permitted to us; but to change from cruelty to righteousness is a noble thing."

Then the proconsul spoke again, "If you despise the wild beasts, I will burn you with fire." Polycarp answered, "You threaten with the fire that burns for an hour and then is quenched, but you do not know about the fire of the judgment to come."

By faith, Polycarp requested not to be nailed in place, believing that "He who grants me to endure the fire will enable me also to remain on the pyre unmoved." As the flames leapt around him, Polycarp looked up to heaven, praising God and thanking him that he was counted worthy to take the cup of Christ.

Cyprian (c. AD 200–258)

Cyprian was born in a wealthy pagan family of Carthage and lived in splendor until his conversion at age forty-six. After conversion, he sold his estates and, by faith, gave all to the poor. Only two years after his baptism, he was made bishop of Carthage and placed at the head of all the North African clergy.

In AD 253, Valerian became the emperor of Rome. Three years later, he began a systematic persecution of the leaders of the Church. Cyprian was brought before the Roman consul in Carthage and ordered to sacrifice to the pagan gods. He refused and firmly professed Christ. The consul forced Cyprian into exile for eleven months. He was then returned to Carthage, tried before the consul, and condemned to be beheaded.

When the sentence was pronounced, by faith Cyprian said, "Thanks be to God." He was immediately taken to be executed. He knelt in prayer, tied the bandage over his eyes with his own hand, gave the executioner twenty-five pieces of gold, and died with the dignity of a hero. He said before his death,

> Only above is true peace and eternal security. There is our dwelling, there is our home. Who would not gladly hasten to reach it? There a great multitude of beloved awaits us; the numerous host of fathers, brethren, and children. There is a glorious choir of apostles; there

the countless multitude of martyrs, crowned with victory after warfare and suffering; there the merciful enjoying their reward. Let us hasten there with longing desire; let us wish to be soon with them, soon with Christ. After the earthly comes the heavenly, after perishableness, eternity.[182]

Augustine (AD 354–430)

Augustine was born in the province of Numidia, North Africa, to a respectable family of modest income. His father was a pagan, but his mother, Monica, was a Christian. At an early age, Augustine followed the faith of his mother, but by sixteen, the influence of a pagan education and his many passions led him to break with Christianity.

For the next seventeen years, he experienced periods of immorality, entanglement in appealing philosophies, and spiritual crisis. During that time, he taught rhetoric and public speaking in Carthage, Rome, and Milan. While in Milan, Augustine would often listen to the preaching of the bishop and church father, Ambrose.

A change slowly took place in Augustine as he listened to the sermons of Ambrose. He eventually reached a turning point and committed his life to Christ. He said about that moment,

> I cast myself down under a certain fig tree, giving full vent to my tears. I said, "O Lord, how long? Will You be angry forever? Why is there not this hour an end to my uncleanness?" While I was speaking, I heard from a neighboring house a voice of a child chanting, "Take up and read, take up and read." I arose, interpreting it to be a command from God to open the book, and read the first chapter I should find. I opened and read, "Let us behave decently, as in the daytime, not in orgies and drunkenness, not in sexual immorality and debauchery, not in dissension and jealousy. Rather, clothe yourselves with the Lord Jesus Christ, and

---

[182] Philip Schaff, *History of the Christian Church, A.D. 1–311* (1859), 524.

do not think about how to gratify the desires of the sinful nature" [Romans 13:13–14]. No further would I read for instantly at the end of this sentence all the darkness of doubt vanished away.[183]

By faith, Augustine was a changed man from that moment on, and he devoted himself heart and soul to the service of the Church. In public debate and through his writings, Augustine defended the teachings of the Church against heretics and schismatics. He molded the theology of the Middle Ages in Europe and greatly influenced the thought and writings of Martin Luther and John Calvin. Luther quoted Augustine over one hundred times in his commentary on Romans alone.

Augustine was a prolific writer and is most famous for his autobiography *Confessions*, and his magnum opus *The City of God*, an unexcelled statement of the biblical view of history and one of the most influential books in history. The literary production of Augustine was so massive that it is difficult to arrive at even an approximation of what he taught on various subjects. Any bibliography on the study of Augustine will list thousands of works in numerous languages.

Next to the Apostle Paul, he did more to shape Christianity than any other person, laying the theological groundwork for the total Christian society. His concept of education, and his administrative energies, produced a system of schools that was the model for the entire Middle Ages—including the university system that began in the twelfth century.

Patrick (c. AD 389–461)

Patrick was born around 389 somewhere in the Roman colony of Britain.[184] At sixteen, pirates captured him and took him to Ireland as a slave. Patrick spent six harsh years working as a shepherd in the mountains. According to his autobiography he was "chastened exceedingly and humbled in truth by hunger and nakedness, and that daily."

Patrick's Christian parents had given him a basic knowledge of the gospel, but he was not a devout believer. His captivity drove him to seek God with all his heart. At the end of his fourth year of captivity, Patrick

---

[183] St. Augustine, *The Confessions of Saint Augustine,* trans. John K. Ryan (Image Books, 1960), 73–74.

[184] Patrick was from either Scotland or southwestern England. Most of the evidence points to the latter.

surrendered his heart completely to Christ. He spent the next two years in constant prayer and communion with God.

> And there the Lord opened my mind to an awareness of my unbelief, in order that, even so late, I might remember my transgressions and turn with all my heart to the Lord my God, who had regard for my insignificance and pitied my youth and ignorance.[185]

The Lord said to him late one night, "Your hungers are over, you are going home. Your ship is here." Although he was two hundred miles from the sea, by faith Patrick walked to it unnoticed by his captors. He found and boarded a ship heading toward his home. But the ship never made it. After several years of wandering (including another brief captivity), he finally arrived home.

Back in England, he had a vision of one of his Irish captors, Victoricus, coming to him with innumerable letters.

> I read the beginning of the letter entitled, "The Voice of the Irish." As I was reading the letter, I heard the voice of those who were beside the forest of Foclut, and they were crying, "We beg you, holy youth, that you shall come and walk again among us."[186]

Ireland was a dangerous and warring culture in the fifth century. The Druids dominated the nation, advocating witchcraft, pagan rituals, and child sacrifice. By faith, Patrick challenged the Druid priests and commanded them to tear down their main idol. They seized Patrick and held him until his friends would return with a child to sacrifice to the idol. As Patrick stood confidently waiting, disease broke out among the Druids. When they commanded Patrick to pray to his God for healing, he refused—saying if they tore down the idol, the plague would stop. They tore the idol down and the power of false religion was shattered in Ireland.

During Patrick's thirty years of ministry, he transformed the Irish from barbarian slavers to Christian free men and women.

---

[185] "Confession of St. Patrick," Christian Classics Ethereal Library, http://www.ccel.org/ccel/patrick/confession.ii.html.

[186] See Note 185.

I came to the Irish people to preach the Gospel and endure the taunts of unbelievers, putting up with reproaches about my pilgrimage, suffering many persecutions, and losing my birthright of freedom for the benefit of others. I am ready also to give up my life, without hesitation and most willingly, for Christ's name. I want to spend myself for that country, even in death, if the Lord should grant me this favor. He makes this promise in the Gospel: "They shall come from the east and west and sit down with Abraham, Isaac, and Jacob." This is our faith: believers are to come from the whole world.[187]

Patrick's faith in Christ won an entire nation and spurred missions throughout the entire Middle Ages.

Columba (c. AD 519–597)

Columba was born in 519 to a royal Irish family. He dedicated his life to God at an early age and joined a monastery. Around 560, he became embroiled in a dispute with another monk over a copy of the book of Psalms. The dispute escalated to the point of a heated battle in which several men were killed.

Columba was deeply grieved by the loss of life and, at the advice of another monk, left Ireland to preach the gospel to a pagan nation and gain as many souls to Christ as lives were lost in battle. By faith he sailed from Ireland in 563 with twelve disciples and settled on the small tidal island of Iona off the coast of western Scotland. From this base, he proceeded to evangelize the nation.

Iona provided a convenient base for missionary labors among the Scots, who were already Christian in name, but needed confirmation, and among the Picts who were unconverted.

He visited the Pictish King Brude in his fortress at Inverness, and won his esteem and cooperation in planting Christianity among his people. He

---

[187] See Note 185.

converted them by example as well as by word. He founded many churches and monasteries in Ireland and Scotland directly or through his disciples.[188]

Aidan (died c. AD 651)

In 634, Oswald the Saxon king of northeastern England requested that Iona send a missionary to convert his kingdom. Oswald had been converted to Christ at Iona as a young man when he sought refuge there after a rival king slew his father in battle.

Some of the leaders at Iona thought the Northumbrians were too stubborn to be converted. When the Irish monk Aidan suggested that their assessment was unreasonably harsh, the other leaders immediately put him forward as the right missionary for the job.

When St. Aidan arrived in 635 with twelve other monks, he was given the tidal island of Lindisfarne to build a monastery and establish a base of operations for the evangelization of the nation.

By faith, Aidan walked through the land, conversing with the people he met and slowly introducing them to Christ. When the king gave him a horse for his travels, Aidan gave it to a beggar seeking alms. This angered the king, and he demanded an account for his actions. Aidan responded, "Is the son of a mare more important to you than a son of God?" The king repented and promised never to interfere with Aidan's missionary work again.

Aidan and the king worked together to establish God's kingdom in Northumbria. The Church historian Bede described their partnership in his biography of Aidan.

> The King applied himself to build and extend the Church of Christ in his kingdom; and when Aidan, who did not perfectly understand the English tongue, preached the Gospel, it was most delightful to see the King himself interpreting the Word of God to his people; for he had perfectly learned the language of the Scots during his long banishment. From that time, many from the region of the Scots came daily into Britain, and with great devotion preached the

---

[188] Columba's biography (written around 704) contains the first reference to the Loch Ness monster. Apparently, Columba came upon the monster as he was about to devour a swimmer. He shouted, "You shall go no further, nor touch the man; go back with all speed." The monster retreated, and the swimmer was saved. The pagan Picts who witnessed this event glorified God and accepted baptism. (You can determine for yourself if the story is valid or not.)

Word of Faith to those provinces of the English over which King Oswald reigned, and many believers received the grace of baptism. Churches were built in several places and the people joyfully flocked together to hear the Word.[189]

Aidan was determined that the evangelistic gains he made during his life would continue after he was gone. So he built a school at Lindisfarne to train the next generation of leaders for the English Church. His efforts were successful and long after his death, Lindisfarne remained a center of learning and a training ground for missionaries.

Boniface (AD 672–754)

Boniface, the apostle of Germany, was born in a noble English family around 675. He felt it was his duty to Christianize those countries from which his Anglo-Saxon ancestors had emigrated. By faith, he sacrificed his prospects at home, crossed the channel, and began his missionary career with a few companions.

Boniface was trained in Benedictine abbeys and ordained a priest around 705. From 716 to 721, he twice attempted to evangelize the German tribes on the continent but was twice rebuffed by their king. He later went on a pilgrimage to Rome, and there Pope Gregory II commissioned him with the task of evangelizing the German pagans.

Boniface returned a third time in 722, and this time met with great success. In the presence of a large assembly, he cut down the sacred oak of Thor at Geismar and used the wood to build the church of St. Peter. This practical sermon became the death and burial of German mythology.

Boniface, a great organizer and educator, profoundly influenced the course of intellectual, political, and ecclesiastical history in Germany and France throughout the Middle Ages. He unified the missionary movement by bringing it under the control of Rome, provided bishops and teachers for many generations, and significantly improved the quality of life in the Frankish kingdom.

In 754, a band of pagan Frisians martyred him while he read the Scriptures to new converts on Pentecost Sunday.

---

[189] The Venerable Bede, *Bede's Ecclesiastical History of England* (London: George Bell & Sons, 1907).

Ramon Llull (c. 1235–1315)

Ramon Llull was born in Palma on the island of Mallorca in 1235. He lived a promiscuous life at the royal court, but at age 31, he had a dramatic conversion.

Shortly after his conversion, he went on pilgrimage to Compostela, and then retired in seclusion to his native island. During that time, Llull developed a burden to reach the unreached Muslims. After his first missionary journey to the Muslim world in 1308, he traveled throughout Europe spreading the vision of reaching the Islamic world.

> The conquest of the Holy Land should be attempted in no other way than as Christ and the Apostles undertook to accomplish it—by prayers, tears, and the offering up of our own lives. Many are the princes and knights that have gone to the Promised Land with a view to conquer it, but if this mode had been pleasing to the Lord, they would assuredly have wrested it from the Saracens before this. Thus it is manifest to pious monks that Thou art daily waiting for them to do for love to Thee what Thou hast done from love to them.[190]

Llull devoted his life to the conversion of Muslims and, by faith, made three missionary tours to Africa. On his third trip in 1315, he was stoned to death for his testimony.

John Wycliffe (c. 1320–1384)

John Wycliffe (1330–1384) produced the first complete translation of the Bible in the English language. He is often called the "Morning Star of the Reformation."

Wycliffe[191] was born in Yorkshire, England, in 1330. He attended Oxford University at thirteen and after graduation was ordained a priest in the Roman Catholic Church. His brilliant mind and academic achievements soon elevated him to prominence among the political leaders in the nation. But his vocal attacks against the doctrines of the established Church would eventually get him in trouble with the ecclesiastical leaders.

---

[190] Philip Schaff, *History of the Christian Church, Vol. 5: Part II, the Middle Ages, From Boniface VIII, 1294, to the Protestant Reformation, 1517 (Classic Reprint)* (Forgotten Books, 2017), 298.

[191] His name is often spelled Wyclif, Wycliff, or Wickliffe.

In 1348, the Black Death ravaged the nation of England. The plague terrified Wycliffe, and he began to seek God in his Word. His study revealed a vast difference between the biblical standards and the ecclesiastical practices of the day. His convictions grew until finally, in 1375, he began to preach against the errors he saw.

By faith, Wycliffe preached that the Bible was the sole authority for faith and practice, and that men had the right before God to interpret Scripture for themselves. He said,

> Believers should ascertain for themselves what are the true matters of their faith by having the Scriptures in a language which all may understand.

When Wycliffe began his translation of the Scriptures into English, he was called a heretic. He replied with the following words:

> You call me a heretic because I have translated the Bible into the common tongue of the people. You say that the Church of God is in danger from this book. How can that be? Is it not from the Bible that we learn who is the Builder and Sovereign of the Church? It is you who place the Church in jeopardy by hiding the Divine warrant, the royal missive of her King.[192]

Martin Luther (1483–1546)

Martin Luther was born on November 10, 1483, to peasant parents. His father was a copper miner who prospered enough to allow his son to attend the University of Erfurt and graduate with a master's degree. Luther then began preparation to become a lawyer. But on July 2, 1505, while returning from a visit to his parents, he was caught in a thunderstorm and cried out in terror, "Help me, St. Anne,[193] and I will become a monk." Luther said, "Not freely or desirously did I become a monk, but walled around with the terror and agony of sudden death, I vowed a constrained and necessary vow."[194]

---

[192] David Fountain, *John Wycliffe: The Dawn of the Reformation* (Revival Literature, 1984), 45–47.

[193] St. Anne was supposed to be the mother of Mary and the grandmother of Jesus. The Medieval Church had fallen so far from the truth that they needed a mediator (Anne) to talk to the mediator (Mary) to talk to Jesus for them.

[194] Leon Stansfield, *Luther On Human Will* (Learning Links Publishers, 2012), 12.

Luther practiced extreme asceticism, but found even the most agonizing attempts to gain assurance of salvation brought him no inward peace. He prayed, fasted, and chastised himself even beyond the strictest monastic rules. After performing his first Mass, he said, "I was utterly stupefied and terror stricken. I thought to myself, 'Who am I that I should lift up mine eyes or raise my hands to the divine majesty? For I am dust and ashes and full of sin, and I am speaking to the living, eternal and true God.'"[195]

He later said of this time,

> For however irreproachably I lived as a monk, I felt myself in the presence of God to be a sinner with a most unquiet conscience, nor could I believe that I pleased him with my satisfactions. I did not love, indeed I hated this just God, if not with open blasphemy, at least with huge murmuring, for I was indignant against him, saying "as if it were really not enough for God that miserable sinners should be eternally lost through original sin, and oppressed with all kind of calamities through the law of the Ten Commandments, but God must add sorrow on sorrow, and even by the gospel bring his wrath to bear." Thus I raged with a fierce and most agitated conscience, and yet I continued to knock away at the Apostle Paul [this refers to Luther's study of Romans] in this place, thirsting ardently to know what he really meant.[196]

In 1510, Luther made a pilgrimage to Rome and was shocked to hear flagrant blasphemies and see gross immorality. He celebrated Mass every day while he was there, sometimes several times a day. He found himself regretting his parents were still alive for, "I would have loved to deliver them from Purgatory with my Masses and other special works and prayers." In an attempt to deliver his grandfather from Purgatory, Luther scaled the steps

---

[195] Roland Herbert Bainton, *Here I Stand: A Life of Martin Luther* (Hendrickson Publishers: 2009), 21.

[196] Martin Luther, *On the Bondage of the Will*, (A Martin Luther Book, 2012).

of the Scala Santa[197] on his knees, saying a prayer on each step. When he reached the top, he looked back and said, "Who knows if it is really true?"

After returning from Rome, he was assigned to Wittenberg, were he took the chair of biblical theology. While studying the New Testament in preparation for his lectures, he came to believe that Christians are not saved by their efforts, but by the gift of God's grace accepted by faith. Luther said of his conversion,

> I was seized with the conviction that I must understand Paul's letter to the Romans [. . .] but to that moment one phrase in chapter one stood in my way. I hated the idea, "in it the righteousness of God is revealed." [. . .] I hated the righteous God who punishes sinners [. . .] At last, meditating day and night and by the mercy of God, I [. . .] began to understand that the righteousness of God is that through which the righteous live by a gift of God, namely by faith [. . .] Here I felt as if I were entirely born again and had entered paradise itself through gates that had been flung open.[198]

About this same time, Johann Tetzel appeared in Germany promoting purgatorial release for a price using every manipulative technique he knew. He was forbidden to sell his indulgences in Wittenberg, but Luther heard of his activities and opposed him with his Ninety-five Theses. Within weeks, copies were circulating throughout Germany, reducing the sale of indulgences to almost nothing. The Pope was angered and ordered Luther to recant. By faith he burned the Pope's sentence in a public bonfire—an act of defiance against the Pope that stirred the whole German nation and initiated the Protestant Reformation.

---

[197] The Scala Santa is twenty-eight wide marble steps that were supposedly the Judgment steps of Pilate that Jesus ascended at his trial. According to legend, they were miraculously transported from Jerusalem to Rome. Pilgrims to this day scale the steps on their knees, kissing and saying multiple prayers on each step. When Charles Spurgeon visited Rome he said about the Santa Scala, "It was a mournful spectacle to look up and see poor human nature so degraded as to be crawling up a staircase with the view of reaching heaven."

[198] Recorded in Luther's preface to his collected works in Latin.

Ulrich Zwingli (1484–1531)

Zwingli received a liberal education at the universities of Vienna and Basel and entered the ministry in 1506. On his thirty-fifth birthday in 1519, he received the pastorate at Zürich, Switzerland.

Prior to his ministry in Zürich, he had read a Latin translation of the Greek New Testament and began to doubt certain teachings of the Roman Church.

When he arrived in Zürich, he began to expound directly from the Scriptures, beginning with the book of Matthew. By faith, he publicly challenged the doctrines of the adoration of saints and relics, promises of miraculous cures, and indulgences. His preaching attracted large crowds, and after someone gave him a printing press, his influence spread to regions far beyond Zürich.

About this time, he read the writings of Martin Luther and was deeply inspired to take a stand against the Roman Church. By faith, images were removed from the church buildings in Zürich and altars, relics, and processions were discarded. Zwingli broke with the Pope and preached openly against celibacy.

When Pope Adrian VI heard the reports from Zürich, he was infuriated. He forbade Zwingli the pulpit and asked the Zürich council to repudiate him as a heretic. Zwingli appeared before the council and defended his position from the Scriptures. The council upheld Zwingli and officially adopted the Reformation.

The Reformation spread from Zürich into other parts of Switzerland. Several of the cantons (democratic states) adopted the Reformation, but several of them remained loyal to Rome. In 1531, five of these cantons attacked an unprepared Zürich, and Zwingli, fighting like a common soldier, died on the battlefield.

Although his ministry was brief, he left a great legacy of commitment to the Scriptures and their application to all of life.

John Wesley (1703–1791)

John Wesley was the fifteenth of nineteen children born to the Reverend Samuel and Susannah Wesley. He was trained for the ministry at Oxford and ordained a priest in 1728. There he became the leader of the "Holy Club," a group of devout students that included his brother Charles and George

Whitefield. The members of this club were derisively nicknamed Methodists because of their methodical Bible study and prayer habits.

The new American colony of Georgia required missionaries, and Wesley and his brother were among those who accepted appointments. En route to Georgia, Wesley's ship sailed into a series of violent Atlantic storms. On board was a company of Moravian Brethren from Herrnhut. This group deeply awed John Wesley. When the sea broke over the deck of the vessel during a storm, the Moravians calmly sang their psalms to God by faith. Wesley realized that, while they were not afraid to die, he was frozen in fear. He later recorded in his journal,

> I went to America to convert the Indians, but, O! who shall convert me? Who is he that will deliver me from this evil heart of unbelief? I have a fair summer religion; I can talk well, nay, and believe myself, while no danger is near; but let death look me in the face, and my spirit is troubled. O who will deliver me from this fear of death? Where shall I fly from it?[199]

When he arrived in America, the Moravian pastor August Spangenberg asked him, "Does the Spirit of God witness with your spirit that you are a child of God?" Wesley did not know what to answer, and the preacher, seeing his hesitation, said, "Do you know Jesus Christ?"

"I know he is the Saviour of the world."

"True, but do you know he has saved you?"

"I do," Wesley said. But later in his journal he wrote, "I fear they were vain words."[200]

After three years of failure and futility in America, Wesley returned to England. He recorded in his journal,

> This, then, have I learned in the ends of the earth, that I am fallen short of the glory of God; that my whole heart is altogether corrupt and abominable; that my own works, my own sufferings, my own righteousness, are so far from reconciling me to an offended God; that, having the sentence of death in my heart I have no hope. But

---

[199] John Wesley, *The Journal of John Wesley: Founder of the Methodist Movement* (F.H. Revell, 1903), Jan. 24, 1738.

[200] John F. Hurst, *John Wesley the Methodist: A Plain Account of His Life and Work* (New York: Eaton & Mains, 1903), 87.

if I seek, I shall find Christ, and be found in him, not having my own righteousness, but that which is through the faith of Christ, the righteousness which is of God by faith. I want that faith which enables every one that has it to cry out, "I live by faith in the Son of God, who loved me, and gave himself for me."[201]

Wesley went to London and met the Moravian preacher Peter Bohler. Bohler taught Wesley many things about faith. When Wesley asked Bohler if he should stop preaching until he had faith, Bohler replied, "Preach faith until you get it. And when you get it, preach faith because you have it." Two months later Wesley attended a Moravian gathering.

In the evening I went very unwillingly to a society in Aldersgate Street, where one was reading Luther's preface to the Epistle to the Romans. About a quarter before nine, while he was describing the change which God works in the heart through faith in Christ, I felt my heart strangely warmed. I felt I did trust in Christ, Christ alone for salvation; and an assurance was given to me that he had taken away my sins, even mine, and saved me from the law of sin and death.[202]

Thus began the preaching ministry of faith that would astound the nation. Eighteen days after Aldersgate, John preached at Oxford University his famous sermon "By Grace Ye Are Saved through Faith" and struck the chord that was to be the theme of his life thereafter.

When the Anglican pulpit was denied him, he took to the open fields, by faith preaching over 40,000 sermons and traveling over 250,000 miles on horseback. He was a prolific author of educational treatises, histories, sermons, and commentaries, publishing 233 books and 5,000 tracts. He edited and compiled an English dictionary, published twenty-three collections of hymns, and recorded his travels in his journal. His medical handbook went through thirty-two editions.

At his death, there were over 500 preachers and 115,000 people who called themselves Methodists.

---

[201] John Wesley, *The Journal of John Wesley: Founder of the Methodist Movement* (F. H. Revell, 1903), Feb. 29, 1738.

[202] John Wesley, *The Journal of John Wesley: Founder of the Methodist Movement* (F. H. Revell, 1903), May 24, 1738.

George Whitefield (1714–1770)

George Whitefield was born in 1714 in the west of England. His parents ran a hotel and a tavern frequented by highway robbers and questionable characters. He was a self-confessed liar, thief, and a gambler, addicted to filthy talk, cursing, foolishness, and fantasy. He had a vivid imagination, a powerful voice, and a talent for mimicking ministers.

He went to Oxford at seventeen, where he began to listen to the dealings of the Holy Spirit and became deadly serious about spiritual things. He read Henry Scougal's book *The Life of God in the Soul of Man* and it so convicted him he said,

> God showed me I must be born again or be damned! I learned a man may go to church, say his prayers, receive the sacrament, and yet not be a Christian. Shall I burn this book? Shall I throw it down? Or shall I search it? I did search it, and holding the book in my hand thus addressed the God of heaven and earth. Lord, if I am not a Christian, or if I am not a real one, for Jesus Christ's sake show me what Christianity is that I may not be damned at last![203]

Then followed a fearfully increased asceticism, with Whitefield wearing patched gowns and dirty shoes, eating the worst food, and spending "whole days and weeks lying prostrate on the ground bidding Satan depart from me in the name of Jesus, begging for freedom from those proud hellish thoughts that used to crowd in upon and distract my soul."

For a year, the fearful pressure ruined his studies and almost drove him mad. But Whitefield had resolved to "die or conquer." Finally, at the end of all human resources, God revealed himself to him. "Oh joy—joy unspeakable—joy full and big with glory was my soul filled when the weight of sin came off, and an abiding sense of the pardoning love of God and a full assurance of faith broke in on my soul!"

Not long after he preached his first sermon, his mother, relatives, Robert Raikes (the founder of the Sunday School), and some three hundred other people crowded impatiently together to hear him. It was a startling introduction. Fifteen people were, said the Bishop, "driven mad." Whitefield was twenty-one years old. Thus began the "preaching that startled the nation."

---

[203] Luke Tyerman, *The Life of the Reverend George Whitefield, Volume 1* (Nabu Press, 2011), 27.

He usually rose at 4:00 a.m. and often spent whole nights in reading and devotion. He preached morning, afternoon, and night on Sundays, 6:00 a.m. every morning and 6:00 p.m. every evening Monday to Thursday, and Saturday night: twelve messages a week, sometimes forty to sixty hours of speaking each week—an estimated eighteen thousand messages.

In the thirty-four years of his ministry, he visited almost every town in England, Scotland, and Wales. By faith he crossed the Atlantic seven times and became America's first celebrity. Record audiences, often exceeding the population of the towns in which he preached, marked every stop along Whitefield's trip. About eighty percent of all American colonists heard him preach at least once,[204] and virtually every American loved and admired him and saw him as their champion.[205]

Charles Finney (1792–1875)

On August 29, 1792, Charles Grandison Finney, the Father of Modern Revivalism, was born in Warren, Connecticut. He was dramatically converted in 1821 and immediately began to preach the gospel, often with astonishing results.

> Finney was tall and handsome, and he had penetrating, hypnotic eyes that riveted his audiences. His eyes were "large and blue, at times mild as an April sky, and at others, cold and penetrating as polished steel." He possessed a majestic voice, which could be immensely persuasive with crowds. In addition, he had studied to be an attorney, and he turned the legal logic he had developed, and his courtroom skills, to the use of the pulpit.[206]

Finney was a vocal and active supporter of the reform movements of his day, especially women's rights and the antislavery movement.

> Finney was convinced that the gospel was meant to do more than just get people saved. It was also to clean up society. Since the late 1820s, Finney had been moving to include social reform in his program for awakening.[207]

---

[204] "Little Known Facts About Whitefield," *Christian History*, Issue 38.

[205] Harry Stout, "Heavenly Comet," *Christian History*, Issue 38.

[206] "Spiritual Awakenings in North America," *Christian History*, Issue 23.

[207] See Note 204.

In 1835, Finney became a professor of theology at Oberlin College. Under Finney and his converts, it became the center of the antislavery movement. Finney said,

> The Church must take right ground in regard to politics. Politics are a part of a religion in such a country as this, and Christians must do their duty to the country as a part of their duty to God.[208]

By faith, over half a million people were converted through Finney's ministry, and it is estimated that 85 percent of them remained true to God all their life. Finney paved the way for later revivalists like D. L. Moody, Billy Sunday, and Billy Graham. Because of that he is called, "The Father of Modern Revivalism."

Adoniram and Ann Judson (1788–1850)

Adoniram and Ann Judson both had dramatic conversion experiences as young people that filled them with a deep desire to be used by God on the mission field. Thirteen days after their wedding, they left for India as missionaries.

The British East India Company opposed the preaching of the gospel to the native population and disallowed the Judsons to stay in India. So by faith, they relocated to Rangoon, the capital of Burma (present-day Myanmar).

They experienced much hardship in this new territory. Ann lost a child and then died of smallpox after a few years. The Burmese imprisoned Adoniram for two years during the First Burmese War with Britain and subjected him to extreme torture. Ann's heroism became a legend during this time. When she died shortly after Adoniram was released from prison, he fell into a deep depression and contemplated suicide. But he survived, married two more times, and outlived all his wives and several of his children.

Judson opened schools and seminaries to train native ministers. He became an accomplished linguist and translated the Bible into Burmese. Through his efforts and the work of his successors, a Baptist community of almost 500,000 people developed in Burma.

---

[208] Mark Beliles & Stephen McDowell, *America's Providential History* (Providence Foundation, 1991), 267.

George Müller (1805–1898)

George Müller was born and raised in Prussia and lived a life of crime even while studying for the ministry of the State Church. But his life was changed when converted at a prayer meeting in a private home. He moved to Bristol, England, and in 1835 opened his first orphanage. By 1870, with no financial assistance, he had built five orphans' homes, and by faith was feeding 2,100 orphans daily. He solicited no one and told only the Lord of daily needs.

> When I first began to allow God to deal with me [. . .] I rested on the simple promises I found in the sixth chapter of Matthew. [. . .] I put my reliance in the God who has promised, and He has acted according to His Word. I've lacked nothing [. . .] while the work has gone on these fifty-one years. [. . .] At first I was able to trust the Lord for ten dollars, then for a hundred dollars, then for a thousand dollars, and now, with the greatest ease, I could trust Him for a million dollars, if there was occasion.[209]

The diary of George Müller chronicles his devotion in prayer: "In November 1844, I began to pray for the conversion of five individuals. I prayed every day without a single intermission, whether sick or in health, on the land, on the sea, and whatever the pressure of my engagements might be. Eighteen months elapsed before the first of the five was converted. I thanked God and prayed on for the others. Five years elapsed, and then the second was converted. I thanked God for the second, and prayed on for the other three. Day by day, I continued to pray for them, and six years passed before the third was converted. I thanked God for the three, and went on praying for the other two. These two remained unconverted." Thirty-six years later he wrote that the other two, sons of one of Müller's friends, were still not converted. He wrote: "But I hope in God, I pray on, and look for the answer. They are not converted yet, but they will be." In 1897, fifty-two years after he began to pray, these two men were finally converted—after Müller died.[210]

---

[209] A. Sims, ed., *George Mueller: Man of Faith* (Wipf and Stock Publishers: 2005), 33–34.

[210] Ben Patterson, *Deepening Your Conversation with God* (Bethany House, 2001), 105–106.

Mary Slessor (1848–1915)

Mary Slessor was born in Aberdeen, Scotland, in 1848 to an alcoholic father and devout mother with a strong interest in missions.

She knew from early childhood that she was called to be a missionary in West Africa, and that missionary zeal was evident early on. When a local gang tormented her by swinging a metal weight on a chain closer and closer to her face, she made a deal with them that if she could endure their torture without flinching, they would all come to Sunday school with her. She stood her ground, won the bet, and they all came with her to church.

By faith, she accepted a teaching position at a new mission in Calabar, Nigeria, in 1875. The average survival rate for Westerners in Nigeria was around two years. When Mary arrived at age twenty-eight with her red hair, blue eyes, and slight frame, most thought she would be lucky to make it through the year.

She arrived in Nigeria during one of its most turbulent times. Witchcraft and superstition abounded in a country decimated by the slave trade. Human sacrifice and ritual murder were common events. Women were considered less valuable than cattle.

Mary thoroughly identified with the people she was called to reach, becoming fluent in their language, culture, and customs. She was so successful in integrating into Nigerian society that the Governor asked her to fill an administrative position as a Member of the Itu Court.

She was constantly urging the Foreign Mission Board in Edinburgh to finance extensions of her work in the interior. The trading markets, which she had enthusiastically encouraged, attracted people from far afield, and her attempts to reach out to them were the natural consequences of these contacts. Gradually the money was forthcoming, and, as new missionaries took over responsibility for the posts vacated by Mary, she could move ever further into the heartland. Her courage in braving the hostility provoked by these incursions is legendary.[211]

Mary Slessor's influence in Nigeria went far beyond the thousands she led to Christ. She attracted foreign markets to trade with local Nigerians. She raised funds for roads into the interior. She set up medical clinics and mission hospitals that provided the first vaccination against smallpox in West

---

[211] Ron Schuler, "Mary Slessor," Ron Schuler's Parlour Tricks. December 2, 2005. http://rsparlourtricks.blogspot.com/2005/12/mary-slessor.html.

Africa. She made a significant difference in the nation in a few, well-lived years of love and dedication.

Often ill with malaria, she finally succumbed to a long battle with fever. She was given a full State funeral at her death in 1915, and then in 1953, she was given a second State funeral when the newly crowned English monarch Elizabeth II made a pilgrimage to her graveside.

William Seymour (1870–1922)

In 1905, William Seymour, a one-eyed preacher of the Holiness movement and the son of former slaves, heard Charles Parham teach on the baptism in the Holy Spirit in Houston, Texas. Parham would not allow Seymour in the classroom because of the Jim Crow laws. But by faith he sat in the hall, heard the Pentecostal doctrine, and embraced it.

In February of 1906, Seymour received an invitation to pastor a small Holiness church in Los Angeles. His first sermon in his new church was from Acts 2:4: "And they were all filled with the Holy Spirit and began to speak with other tongues, as the Spirit was giving them utterance." When he returned that evening for service, the deacons had padlocked the church to keep him out.

However, a few of the members followed Seymour and began a Bible study in their home. On Monday, April 9, several members of the small prayer group were baptized in the Holy Spirit. Soon the crowds were so great they could no longer meet in the home. Seymour brought the piano onto the porch and continued the meetings outdoors. When the front porch collapsed, they rented an abandoned AME church at 312 Azusa Street. For the next three years, they held meetings three times a day at Azusa, attracting people from all over the world and birthing numerous Pentecostal denominations.

The power of God could be felt at Azusa even outside of the building. Scores of people fell to their knees in the streets before they ever reached the mission. By the summer of 1906, crowds had reached staggering numbers, often into the thousands. The scene had become an international gathering. Every day, trains unloaded visitors who came from all over the continent. News accounts of the meetings spread over the nation in both the secular and religious press.

The 35-year-old Seymour was an unlikely ambassador of the Pentecostal message: he was not a gifted speaker, he lacked in social skills, and he had almost no formal education.[212]

But God filled him with power and used him to usher in the century of the Holy Spirit. Church historian Vinson Synan has estimated that over 850 million people were baptized in the Holy Spirit in the twentieth century. We are greatly indebted to the obedience and humility of one man who endured the indignity of racism to follow God's call.

Aimee Semple McPherson (1890–1944)

Aimee Semple McPherson was born in western Canada to Salvation Army parents. As a young girl, she read Darwin and became an atheist, convinced that his theories disproved the Bible. When the Pentecostal evangelist Robert Semple came to her town in 1907, she went to the meetings to mock the preacher and the gullible townsfolk. However, Aimee received Christ that night and was baptized in the Holy Spirit. She also fell deeply in love with the preacher and married him six months later.

After two years of marriage, Robert and Aimee went to China as missionaries. But within two months of their arrival, Robert died of malaria. One month later, Aimee gave birth to her first child, Roberta Star. The new mother and child returned to America, and not long after, Aimee met and married her second husband, Harold McPherson.

A year later in the spring of 1913, Aimee was rushed to the hospital with appendicitis, her life hanging in the balance. She overheard a hospital attendant say, "She's going." At that moment, God said to her, "Now will you go?" She said "Yes" to God, and after fully recovering, was on the road preaching the gospel.

By faith, she purchased the land for Angelus Temple in 1919 and then began a non-stop series of evangelistic crusades to raise money for the project. Within three years, the 5,300-seat Angelus Temple was built and debt-free, constructed at a total cost of $1.5 million.[213]

- By faith, she pioneered the field of religious radio with her station KFSG.

---

[212] Ted Olson, "American Pentecost," *Christian History*. April 1998.

[213] Aimee calculated that the average donation toward the building was two cents.

- By faith, she founded and presided over the International Church of the Foursquare Gospel, today one of the largest Pentecostal denominations in the world.
- By faith, she started the Angelus Temple Commissary, to provide food, clothing, and services to needy people. During the Depression, her dining hall kept thousands alive, serving over eighty thousand meals in the first two months of operation.

Today historians consider her, along with Billy Sunday, the most significant revivalist in the early twentieth century. When she died in 1944, fifty thousand people came to her funeral.

Paul Schneider (1897–1939)

Paul Schneider was a German Reformed minister who became increasingly alarmed at the growing threat of the Nazi party. When the Gestapo told Schneider to stop preaching the exclusive claims of Christ or his six children might become orphans, he replied, "Better that they should be orphans than grow up and know that their father bowed down to the devil instead of the living God."[214]

In 1937, after he disciplined some Nazi members of his parish, they arrested and banished him from his homeland. When he tore up his banishment order and returned to his parish, he was arrested again and taken to Buchenwald.

By faith, he refused to obey an order to salute the swastika. The guards beat him and placed him in the punishment cell, where the director of the camp and infamous sadist, Martin Sommer, tortured him.

The Nazis gave Schneider the freedom to leave Buchenwald at any time. All he had to do was sign an agreement to respect the banishment order. But he chose to stay in the prison to preach to the prisoners and guards.

They put him in solitary confinement, but he preached the gospel from his cell window to everyone who passed by. When Schneider refused to stop preaching, they murdered him by lethal injection.

Vast crowds attended his funeral, including two hundred robed ministers. A Gestapo official who was present said to one of the clergy, "This is like the

---

[214] Arvan E. Gordon, "Between God and the Gestapo," www.anglicansonline.org.

funeral of a king." "Hardly," replied the cleric. "It is a martyr of Jesus Christ who is being carried to his grave."

One of the pastors prayed at Schneider's funeral, "May God grant that the witness of your shepherd, our brother, remain with you and continue to impact on future generations, and that it remain vital and bear fruit in the entire Christian Church."[215]

[215] Benjamin Scott, "Paul Schneider: Martyr of Buchenwald," Family Research Council, updated July 21, 2009, https://www.frcblog.com/2009/07/paul-schneider-martyr-of-buchenwald/.

Appendix D

Healing

General Healing

And he went throughout all Galilee, teaching in their synagogues and proclaiming the gospel of the kingdom and healing every disease and every affliction among the people. So his fame spread throughout all Syria, and they brought him all the sick, those afflicted with various diseases and pains, those oppressed by demons, those having seizures, and paralytics, and he healed them. MATTHEW 4:23–24

The Leper

When he came down from the mountain, great crowds followed him. And behold, a leper came to him and knelt before him, saying, "Lord, if you will, you can make me clean." And Jesus stretched out his hand and touched him, saying, "I will; be clean." And immediately his leprosy was cleansed. MATTHEW 8:1–3

And a leper came to him, imploring him, and kneeling said to him, "If you will, you can make me clean." Moved with pity, he stretched out his hand and touched him and said to him, "I will; be clean." And immediately the leprosy left him, and he was made clean. MARK 1:40–42

While he was in one of the cities, there came a man full of leprosy. And when he saw Jesus, he fell on his face and begged him, "Lord, if you will, you can make me clean." And Jesus stretched out his hand and touched him, saying, "I will; be clean." And immediately the leprosy left him. LUKE 5:12–13

The Centurion's Servant

When he had entered Capernaum, a centurion came forward to him, appealing to him, "Lord, my servant is lying paralyzed at home, suffering terribly." And he said to him, "I will come and heal him." But the centurion replied, "Lord, I am not worthy to have you come under my roof, but only say the word, and my servant will be healed. For I too am a man under authority, with soldiers under me. And I say to one, 'Go,' and he goes, and to another, 'Come' and he comes, and to my servant, 'Do this,' and he does it." [. . .] And to the centurion Jesus said, "Go; let it be done for you as you have believed." And the servant was healed at that very moment. MATTHEW 8:5–13

Now a centurion had a servant who was sick and at the point of death, who was highly valued by him. When the centurion heard about Jesus, he sent to him elders of the Jews, asking him to come and heal his servant. And when they came to Jesus, they pleaded with him earnestly, saying, "He is worthy to have you do this for him, for he loves our nation, and he is the one who built us our synagogue." And Jesus went with them. When he was not far from the house, the centurion sent friends, saying to him, "Lord, do not trouble yourself, for I am not worthy to have you come under my roof. Therefore I did not presume to come to you. But say the word, and let my servant be healed. For I too am a man set under authority, with soldiers under me: and I say to one, 'Go' and he goes; and to another, 'Come,' and he comes; and to my servant, 'Do this,' and he does it." When Jesus heard these things, he marveled at him, and turning to the crowd that followed him, said, "I tell you, not even in Israel have I found such faith." And when those who had been sent returned to the house, they found the servant well. LUKE 7:2–10

Peter's Mother-in-law

And when Jesus entered Peter's house, he saw his mother-in-law lying sick with a fever. He touched her hand, and the fever left her, and she rose and began to serve him. MATTHEW 8:14–15

Now Simon's mother-in-law lay ill with a fever, and immediately they told him about her. And he came and took her by the hand and lifted her up, and the fever left her, and she began to serve them. MARK 1:30–31

And he arose and left the synagogue and entered Simon's house. Now Simon's mother-in-law was ill with a high fever, and they appealed to him on her behalf. And he stood over her and rebuked the fever, and it left her, and immediately she rose and began to serve them. LUKE 4:38–39

The Evening Healing Meeting

That evening they brought to him many who were oppressed by demons, and he cast out the spirits with a word and healed all who were sick. This was to fulfill what was spoken by the prophet Isaiah: "He took our illnesses and bore our diseases." MATTHEW 8:16–17

That evening at sundown they brought to him all who were sick or oppressed by demons. And the whole city was gathered together at the door. And he healed many who were sick with various diseases, and cast out many demons. And he would not permit the demons to speak, because they knew him. MARK 1:32–34

Now when the sun was setting, all those who had any who were sick with various diseases brought them to him, and he laid his hands on every one of them and healed them. LUKE 4:40

The Paralytic and the Roof

And behold, some people brought to him a paralytic, lying on a bed. And when Jesus saw their faith, he said to the paralytic, "Take heart, my son; your sins are forgiven." And behold, some of the scribes said to themselves, "This man is blaspheming." But Jesus, knowing their thoughts, said, "Why do you think evil in your hearts? For which is easier, to say, 'Your sins are forgiven,' or to say, 'Rise and walk'? But that you may know that the Son of Man has authority on earth to forgive sins"—he then said to the paralytic—"Rise, pick up your bed and go home." And he rose and went home. MATTHEW 9:2–7

And many were gathered together, so that there was no more room, not even at the door. And he was preaching the word to them. And they came, bringing to him a paralytic carried by four men. And when they could not get near him because of the crowd, they removed the roof above him, and when they had made an opening, they let down the bed on which the paralytic lay. And when Jesus saw their faith, he said to the paralytic, "Son, your sins are forgiven" [. . .] But that you may know that the Son of Man has authority on earth to forgive sins"—he said to the paralytic—"I say to you, rise, pick up your bed, and go home." And he rose and immediately picked up his bed and went out before them all, so that they were all amazed and glorified God, saying, "We never saw anything like this!" MARK 2:2–12

On one of those days, as he was teaching, Pharisees and teachers of the law were sitting there, who had come from every village of Galilee and Judea and from Jerusalem. And the power of the Lord was with him to heal. And behold, some men were bringing on a bed a man who was paralyzed, and they were seeking to bring him in and lay him before Jesus, but finding no way to bring him in, because of the crowd, they went up on the roof and let him down with his bed through the tiles into the midst before Jesus. And when he saw their faith, he said, "Man, your sins are forgiven you" [. . .] "But that you may know that the Son of Man has authority on earth to forgive sins"—he said to the man who was paralyzed—"I say to you, rise, pick up your bed and go home." And immediately he rose up before them and picked up what he had been lying on and went home, glorifying God. LUKE 5:17–25

Jairus and the Woman

While he was saying these things to them, behold, a ruler came in and knelt before him, saying, "My daughter has just died, but come and lay your hand on her, and she will live." And Jesus rose and followed him, with his disciples. And behold, a woman who had suffered from a discharge of blood for twelve years came up behind him and touched the fringe of his garment, for she said to herself, "If I only touch his garment, I will be made well." Jesus turned, and seeing her he said, "Take heart, daughter; your faith has made you well." And instantly the woman was made well. And when Jesus came to the ruler's house and saw the flute players and the crowd making a commotion, he said, "Go away, for the girl is not dead but sleeping." And they laughed at him. But when the crowd had been put outside, he went in and took her by the hand, and the girl arose. MATTHEW 9:18–25

Then came one of the rulers of the synagogue, Jairus by name, and seeing him, he fell at his feet and implored him earnestly, saying, "My little daughter is at the point of death. Come and lay your hands on her, so that she may be made well and live." And he went with him. And a great crowd followed him and thronged about him. And there was a woman who had had a discharge of blood for twelve years, and who had suffered much under many physicians, and had spent all that she had, and was no better but rather grew worse. She had heard the reports about Jesus and came up behind him in the crowd and touched his garment. For she said, "If I touch even his garments, I will be made well." And immediately the flow of blood dried up, and she felt in her body that she was healed of her disease. And Jesus, perceiving in himself that power had gone out from him, immediately turned about in the crowd and said, "Who touched my garments?" And his disciples said to him, "You see the crowd pressing around you, and yet you say, 'Who touched me?'" And he looked around to see who had done it. But the woman, knowing what had happened to her, came in fear and trembling and fell down before him and told him the whole truth. And he said to her, "Daughter, your faith has made you well; go in peace, and be healed of your disease." While he was still speaking, there came from the ruler's house some who said, "Your daughter is dead. Why trouble the Teacher any further?" But overhearing what they said, Jesus said to the ruler of the synagogue, "Do not fear, only believe." And he allowed no one to follow him except Peter and James and John the brother of James. They came to the house of the ruler of the synagogue, and Jesus saw a commotion, people weeping and wailing loudly. And when he had entered, he said to them, "Why are you making a commotion and weeping? The child is not dead but sleeping." And they laughed at him. But he put them all outside and took the child's father and mother and those who were with him and went in where the child was. Taking her by the hand he said to her, "Talitha cumi," which means, "Little girl, I say to you, arise." And immediately the girl got up and began walking (for she was twelve years of age), and they were immediately overcome with amazement. MARK 5:22–42

And there came a man named Jairus, who was a ruler of the synagogue. And falling at Jesus' feet, he implored him to come to his house, for he had an only daughter, about twelve years of age, and she was dying. As Jesus went, the people pressed around him. And there was a woman who had had a discharge of blood for twelve years, and though she had spent all her living on physicians, she could not be healed by anyone. She came up behind him and touched the fringe of his garment, and immediately her discharge of blood ceased. And Jesus said, "Who was it that touched me?" When all denied it, Peter said, "Master, the crowds surround you and are pressing in on you!" But Jesus said, "Someone touched me, for I perceive that power has gone out from me." And when the woman saw that she was not hidden, she came trembling, and falling down before him declared in the presence of all the people why she had touched him, and how she had been immediately healed. And he said to her, "Daughter, your faith has made you well; go in peace." While he was still speaking, someone from the ruler's house came and said, "Your daughter is dead; do not trouble the Teacher any more." But Jesus on hearing this answered him, "Do not fear; only believe, and she will be well." And when he came to the house, he allowed no one to enter with him, except Peter and John and James, and the father and mother of the child. And all were weeping and mourning for her, but he said, "Do not weep, for she is not dead but sleeping." And they laughed at him, knowing that she was dead. But taking her by the hand he called, saying, "Child, arise." And her spirit returned, and she got up at once. And he directed that something should be given her to eat." LUKE 8:41–55

The Two Blind Men

And as Jesus passed on from there, two blind men followed him, crying aloud, "Have mercy on us, Son of David." When he entered the house, the blind men came to him, and Jesus said to them, "Do you believe that I am able to do this?" They said to him, "Yes, Lord." Then he touched their eyes, saying, "According to your faith be it done to you." MATTHEW 9:27–29

General Healing

And Jesus went throughout all the cities and villages, teaching in their synagogues and proclaiming the gospel of the kingdom and healing every disease and every affliction. MATTHEW 9:35

The Man with the Withered Hand

And a man was there with a withered hand. And they asked him, "Is it lawful to heal on the Sabbath?"—so that they might accuse him. He said to them, "Which one of you who has a sheep, if it falls into a pit on the Sabbath, will not take hold of it and lift it out? Of how much more value is a man than a sheep! So it is lawful to do good on the Sabbath." Then he said to the man, "Stretch out your hand." And the man stretched it out, and it was restored, healthy like the other. MATTHEW 12:10–13

Again he entered the synagogue, and a man was there with a withered hand. And they watched Jesus, to see whether he would heal him on the Sabbath, so that they might accuse him. And he said to the man with the withered hand, "Come here." And he said to them, "Is it lawful on the Sabbath to do good or to do harm, to save life or to kill?" But they were silent. And he looked around at them with anger, grieved at their hardness of heart, and said to the man, "Stretch out your hand." He stretched it out, and his hand was restored. MARK 3:1–5

On another Sabbath, he entered the synagogue and was teaching, and a man was there whose right hand was withered. And the scribes and the Pharisees watched him, to see whether he would heal on the Sabbath, so that they might find a reason to accuse him. But he knew their thoughts, and he said to the man with the withered hand, "Come and stand here." And he rose and stood there. And Jesus said to them, "I ask you, is it lawful on the Sabbath to do good or to do harm, to save life or to destroy it?" And after looking around at them all he said to him, "Stretch out your hand." And he did so, and his hand was restored. LUKE 6:6–10

General Healing

Jesus, aware of this, withdrew from there. And many followed him, and he healed them all. MATTHEW 12:15

The Blind and Dumb Man

Then a demon-oppressed man who was blind and mute was brought to him, and he healed him, so that the man spoke and saw. MATTHEW 12:22

The Fringe of His Garment

And when the men of that place recognized him, they sent around to all that region and brought to him all who were sick and implored him that they might only touch the fringe of his garment. And as many as touched it were made well. MATTHEW 14:35–36

And when they got out of the boat, the people immediately recognized him and ran about the whole region and began to bring the sick people on their beds to wherever they heard he was. And wherever he came, in villages, cities, or countryside, they laid the sick in the marketplaces and implored him that they might touch even the fringe of his garment. And as many as touched it were made well. MARK 6:54–56

And he came down with them and stood on a level place, with a great crowd of his disciples and a great multitude of people from all Judea and Jerusalem and the seacoast of Tyre and Sidon, who came to hear him and to be healed of their diseases. And those who were troubled with unclean spirits were cured. And all the crowd sought to touch him, for power came out from him and healed them all. LUKE 6:17–19

The Syrophoenician Woman

And behold, a Canaanite woman from that region came out and was crying, "Have mercy on me, O Lord, Son of David; my daughter is severely oppressed by a demon." But he did not answer her a word. And his disciples came and begged him, saying, "Send her away, for she is crying out after us." He answered, "I was sent only to the lost sheep of the house of Israel." But she came and knelt before him, saying, "Lord, help me." And he answered, "It is not right to take the children's bread and throw it to the dogs." She said, "Yes, Lord, yet even the dogs eat the crumbs that fall from their masters' table." Then Jesus answered her, "O woman, great is your faith! Be it done for you as you desire." And her daughter was healed instantly. MATTHEW 15:22–28

Now the woman was a Gentile, a Syrophoenician by birth. And she begged him to cast the demon out of her daughter. And he said to her, "Let the children be fed first, for it is not right to take the children's bread and throw it to the dogs." But she answered him, "Yes, Lord; yet even the dogs under the table eat the children's crumbs." And he said to her, "For this statement you may go your way; the demon has left your daughter." And she went home and found the child lying in bed and the demon gone. MARK 7:26–30

•

The Crippled and the Lame

And great crowds came to him, bringing with them the lame, the blind, the crippled, the mute, and many others, and they put them at his feet, and he healed them, so that the crowd wondered, when they saw the mute speaking, the crippled healthy, the lame walking, and the blind seeing. And they glorified the God of Israel.
MATTHEW 15:30–31

Blind Bartimaeus (and Friend)

And as they went out of Jericho, a great crowd followed him. And behold, there were two blind men sitting by the roadside, and when they heard that Jesus was passing by, they cried out, "Lord, have mercy on us, Son of David!" The crowd rebuked them, telling them to be silent, but they cried out all the more, "Lord, have mercy on us, Son of David!" And stopping, Jesus called them and said, "What do you want me to do for you?" They said to him, "Lord, let our eyes be opened." And Jesus in pity touched their eyes, and immediately they recovered their sight and followed him. MATTHEW 20:29–34

And they came to Jericho. And as he was leaving Jericho with his disciples and a great crowd, Bartimaeus, a blind beggar, the son of Timaeus, was sitting by the roadside. And when he heard that it was Jesus of Nazareth, he began to cry out and say, "Jesus, Son of David, have mercy on me!" And many rebuked him, telling him to be silent. But he cried out all the more, "Son of David, have mercy on me!" And Jesus stopped and said, "Call him." And they called the blind man, saying to him, "Take heart. Get up; he is calling you." And throwing off his cloak, he sprang up and came to Jesus. And Jesus said to him, "What do you want me to do for you?" And the blind man said to him, "Rabbi, let me recover my sight." And Jesus said to him, "Go your way; your faith has made you well." And immediately he recovered his sight and followed him on the way. MARK 10:46–52

As he drew near to Jericho, a blind man was sitting by the roadside begging. And hearing a crowd going by, he inquired what this meant. They told him, "Jesus of Nazareth is passing by." And he cried out, "Jesus, Son of David, have mercy on me!" And those who were in front rebuked him, telling him to be silent. But he cried out all the more, "Son of David, have mercy on me!" And Jesus stopped and commanded him to be brought to him. And when he came near, he asked him, "What do you want me to do for you?" He said, "Lord, let me recover my sight." And Jesus said to him, "Recover your sight; your faith has made you well." And immediately he recovered his sight and followed him, glorifying God. And all the people, when they saw it, gave praise to God. LUKE 18:35–43

General Healing

And he told his disciples to have a boat ready for him because of the crowd, lest they crush him, for he had healed many, so that all who had diseases pressed around him to touch him. MARK 3:9–10

The Deaf and Dumb Man

And they brought to him a man who was deaf and had a speech impediment, and they begged him to lay his hand on him. And taking him aside from the crowd privately, he put his fingers into his ears, and after spitting touched his tongue. And looking up to heaven, he sighed and said to him, "Ephphatha," that is, "Be opened." And his ears were opened, his tongue was released, and he spoke plainly. MARK 7:32–35

The Blind Man and the Walking Trees

And they came to Bethsaida. And some people brought to him a blind man and begged him to touch him. And he took the blind man by the hand and led him out of the village, and when he had spit on his eyes and laid his hands on him, he asked him, "Do you see anything?" And he looked up and said, "I see people, but they look like trees, walking." Then Jesus laid his hands on his eyes again; and he opened his eyes, his sight was restored, and he saw everything clearly. MARK 8:22–25

The Dead Man of Nain

Soon afterward he went to a town called Nain, and his disciples and a great crowd went with him. As he drew near to the gate of the town, behold, a man who had died was being carried out, the only son of his mother, and she was a widow, and a considerable crowd from the town was with her. And when the Lord saw her, he had compassion on her and said to her, "Do not weep." Then he came up and touched the bier, and the bearers stood still. And he said, "Young man, I say to you, arise." And the dead man sat up and began to speak, and Jesus gave him to his mother. Fear seized them all, and they glorified God, saying, "A great prophet has arisen among us!" and "God has visited his people!" LUKE 7:11–16

General Healings

In that hour he healed many people of diseases and plagues and evil spirits, and on many who were blind he bestowed sight. And he answered them, "Go and tell John what you have seen and heard: the blind receive their sight, the lame walk, lepers are cleansed, and the deaf hear, the dead are raised up, the poor have good news preached to them." LUKE 7:21–22

General Healings

When the crowds learned it, they followed him, and he welcomed them and spoke to them of the kingdom of God and cured those who had need of healing. LUKE 9:11

The Dumb Man

Now he was casting out a demon that was mute. When the demon had gone out, the mute man spoke, and the people marveled. LUKE 11:14

The Woman with the Spirit of Infirmity

Now he was teaching in one of the synagogues on the Sabbath. And behold, there was a woman who had had a disabling spirit for eighteen years. She was bent over and could not fully straighten herself. When Jesus saw her, he called her over and said to her, "Woman, you are freed from your disability." And he laid his hands on her, and immediately she was made straight, and she glorified God. But the ruler of the synagogue, indignant because Jesus had healed on the Sabbath, said to the people, "There are six days in which work ought to be done. Come on those days and be healed, and not on the Sabbath day." Then the Lord answered him, "You hypocrites! Does not each of you on the Sabbath untie his ox or his donkey from the manger and lead it away to water it? And ought not this woman, a daughter of Abraham whom Satan bound for eighteen years, be loosed from this bond on the Sabbath day?" LUKE 13:10–16

The Man with Dropsy

And behold, there was a man before him who had dropsy. And Jesus responded to the lawyers and Pharisees, saying, "Is it lawful to heal on the Sabbath, or not?" But they remained silent. Then he took him and healed him and sent him away. LUKE 14:2–4

The Ten Lepers

And as he entered a village, he was met by ten lepers, who stood at a distance and lifted up their voices, saying, "Jesus, Master, have mercy on us." When he saw them he said to them, "Go and show yourselves to the priests." And as they went they were cleansed. Then one of them, when he saw that he was healed, turned back, praising God with a loud voice; and he fell on his face at Jesus' feet, giving him thanks. Now he was a Samaritan. Then Jesus answered, "Were not ten cleansed? Where are the nine? Was no one found to return and give praise to God except this foreigner?" And he said to him, "Rise and go your way; your faith has made you well." LUKE 17:12–19

The Slave's Right Ear

And one of them struck the servant of the high priest and cut off his right ear. But Jesus said, "No more of this!" And he touched his ear and healed him. LUKE 22:50–51

The Child of the Royal Official

So he came again to Cana in Galilee, where he had made the water wine. And at Capernaum there was an official whose son was ill. When this man heard that Jesus had come from Judea to Galilee, he went to him and asked him to come down and heal his son, for he was at the point of death. So Jesus said to him, "Unless you see signs and wonders you will not believe." The official said to him, "Sir, come down before my child dies." Jesus said to him, "Go; your son will live." The man believed the word that Jesus spoke to him and went on his way. As he was going down, his servants met him and told him that his son was recovering. So he asked them the hour when he began to get better, and they said to him, "Yesterday at the seventh hour the fever left him." The father knew that was the hour when Jesus had said to him, "Your son will live." And he himself believed, and all his household. JOHN 4:46–53

The Man at the Pool of Bethesda

Now there is in Jerusalem by the Sheep Gate a pool, in Aramaic called Bethesda, which has five roofed colonnades. In these lay a multitude of invalids—blind, lame, and paralyzed. One man was there who had been an invalid for thirty-eight years. When Jesus saw him lying there and knew that he had already been there a long time, he said to him, "Do you want to be healed?" The sick man answered him, "Sir, I have no one to put me into the pool when the water is stirred up, and while I am going another steps down before me." Jesus said to him, "Get up, take up your bed, and walk." And at once the man was healed, and he took up his bed and walked. Now that day was the Sabbath. JOHN 5:2–9

The Man Blind From Birth

As he passed by, he saw a man blind from birth. And his disciples asked him, "Rabbi, who sinned, this man or his parents, that he was born blind?" Jesus answered, "It was not that this man sinned, or his parents, but that the works of God might be displayed in him. We must work the works of him who sent me while it is day; night is coming, when no one can work. As long as I am in the world, I am the light of the world." Having said these things, he spit on the ground and made mud with the saliva. Then he anointed the man's eyes with the mud and said to him, "Go, wash in the pool of Siloam" (which means Sent). So he went and washed and came back seeing. JOHN 9:1–7

The Raising of Lazarus

Now a certain man was ill, Lazarus of Bethany, the village of Mary and her sister Martha. It was Mary who anointed the Lord with ointment and wiped his feet with her hair, whose brother Lazarus was ill. So the sisters sent to him, saying, "Lord, he whom you love is ill." But when Jesus heard it he said, "This illness does not lead to death. It is for the glory of God, so that the Son of God may be glorified through it." Now Jesus loved Martha and her sister and Lazarus. So, when he heard that Lazarus was ill, he stayed two days longer in the place where he was [. . .] he said to them, "Our friend Lazarus has fallen asleep, but I go to awaken him." The disciples said to him, "Lord, if he has fallen asleep, he will recover." Now Jesus had spoken of his death, but they thought that he meant taking rest in sleep. Then Jesus told them plainly, "Lazarus has died, and for your sake I am glad that I was not there, so that you may believe. But let us go to him" [. . .] Then Jesus, deeply moved again, came to the tomb. It was a cave, and a stone lay against it. Jesus said, "Take away the stone." Martha, the sister of the dead man, said to him, "Lord, by this time there will be an odor, for he has been dead four days." Jesus said to her, "Did I not tell you that if you believed you would see the glory of God?" So they took away the stone. And Jesus lifted up his eyes and said, "Father, I thank you that you have heard me. I knew that you always hear me, but I said this on account of the people standing around, that they may believe that you sent me." When he had said these things, he cried out with a loud voice, "Lazarus, come out." The man who had died came out, his hands and feet bound with linen strips, and his face wrapped with a cloth. Jesus said to them, "Unbind him, and let him go." Many of the Jews therefore, who had come with Mary and had seen what he did, believed in him. JOHN 11:1–45

Appendix E

Suffering

There is a good bit of confusion concerning suffering and the life of faith. In this section, we will attempt to answer some of the more prominent questions about this topic.

1. Does a life of faith automatically guarantee the absence of suffering?

    It depends how you define suffering. Suffering is a comprehensive term and, unfortunately, we have a tendency to lump every kind of suffering into one category. There are some types of suffering that a person living the life of faith should not experience. And there are some types of suffering that a person living the life of faith will experience—even to a greater degree than if he or she was not living by faith.

2. Are there extreme views concerning suffering?

    There are two extreme views regarding suffering and both of them should be avoided. The first view is that all suffering is good and should be embraced. Therefore, all suffering is redemptive. In this view, God is the author of the suffering and any attempt to resist the suffering is actually resisting the will of God.

The second view is that all suffering is bad and should be resisted. In this view, the devil and evil men are the authors of all suffering and any passivity toward suffering is disobedience to the will of God.

Both of these extreme views have surfaced throughout the long centuries of Church history, but the first view has been the most prominent.

3. What different kinds of suffering are recorded in the Bible?

    There is suffering that is the result of personal disobedience to God's Word and his will.

    Some sat in darkness and in the shadow of death, prisoners in affliction and in irons, for they had rebelled against the words of God, and spurned the counsel of the Most High. PSALM 107:10–11

    There is suffering that is the result of someone else's disobedience.

    And your children shall be shepherds in the wilderness forty years and shall suffer for your faithlessness, until the last of your dead bodies lies in the wilderness. NUMBERS 14:33

    There is suffering that is demonically inspired.

    Resist him, firm in your faith, knowing that the same kinds of suffering are being experienced by your brotherhood throughout the world. 1 PETER 5:9

    There is suffering that is inflicted upon us by other people.

    And who had suffered much under many physicians, and had spent all that she had, and was no better but rather grew worse. MARK 5:26

    Each of the above categories of suffering should be resisted with God's Word and his promises.

4. Is there a kind of suffering that is according to the will of God?

    Yes. The following is a partial list of Scriptures.

    Therefore let those who suffer according to God's will entrust their souls to a faithful Creator while doing good. 1 PETER 4:19

    Not only that, but we rejoice in our sufferings, knowing that suffering produces endurance. ROMANS 5:3

    Therefore do not be ashamed of the testimony about our Lord, nor of me his prisoner, but share in suffering for the gospel by the power of God. 2 TIMOTHY 1:8

    Yet if anyone suffers as a Christian, let him not be ashamed, but let him glorify God in that name. 1 PETER 4:16

    For it has been granted to you that for the sake of Christ you should not only believe in him but also suffer for his sake. PHILIPPIANS 1:29

    For I will show him how much he must suffer for the sake of my name. ACTS 9:16

    That I may know him and the power of his resurrection, and may share his sufferings, becoming like him in his death. PHILIPPIANS 3:10

    As the above list shows us, there is an abundance of evidence that suffering has a significant place in the life of faith. We should expect this to be true when we look at the life of our Lord.

    For it was fitting that he, for whom and by whom all things exist, in bringing many sons to glory, should make the founder of their salvation perfect through suffering. HEBREWS 2:10

    He was despised and rejected by men, a man of sorrows and acquainted with grief; and as one from whom men hide their faces he was despised, and we esteemed him not. ISAIAH 53:3

    More evidence that suffering fits into a life of faith is seen in Hebrews 11, the great faith chapter. The context of the chapter was the suffering the Hebrew believers were experiencing. The author attempted to encourage them by recounting the example of men and women of faith who had experienced great challenges and suffering in their own lives.

Another example is evident in Paul's defense of his apostolic credentials to the Corinthians. When forced to prove his apostolic credentials, he provided a list of his many sufferings. What an interesting response! Most ministers today would defend their calling with a list of their achievements and accomplishments. But Paul listed his sufferings.

Are they servants of Christ? I am a better one—I am talking like a madman—with far greater labors, far more imprisonments, with countless beatings, and often near death. Five times I received at the hands of the Jews the forty lashes less one. Three times I was beaten with rods. Once I was stoned. Three times I was shipwrecked; a night and a day I was adrift at sea; on frequent journeys, in danger from rivers, danger from robbers, danger from my own people, danger from Gentiles, danger in the city, danger in the wilderness, danger at sea, danger from false brothers; in toil and hardship, through many a sleepless night, in hunger and thirst, often without food, in cold and exposure. And, apart from other things, there is the daily pressure on me of my anxiety for all the churches. 2 CORINTHIANS 11:23–28

George Müller said this about suffering and the life of faith:

I say—and say it deliberately—trials, obstacles, difficulties, and sometimes defeats, are the very food of Faith. I get letters from so many of God's dear children who say: 'Dear Brother Müller, I'm writing this because I am so weak in faith." Just so surely as we ask to have our Faith strengthened, we must feel a willingness to take from God's hand the means for strengthening it. We must allow Him to educate us through trials and bereavements and troubles.

It is through trials that Faith is exercised and developed more and more. God affectionately permits difficulties, that He may develop unceasingly that which He is willing to do for us . . .[216]

5. What are some examples of suffering according to the will of God?

When we are persecuted for our faith.

Then they left the presence of the council, rejoicing that they were counted worthy to suffer dishonor for the name. ACTS 5:41

In October 2000, a nineteen-year-old Christian student was arrested along with over twenty others in China. They were arrested for studying and teaching the Word of God. Each person was beaten and released. The nineteen-year-old was kept and beaten daily as an example to others who might be interested in following the same path. The young man was systematically beaten daily in front of others for twenty-eight days until he died. The police felt this would be a definite blow against Christianity in the region. They were wrong. Over ten thousand letters came into the police station within days of the young man's death stating they, after seeing the courage and strength of the young man, now had greater faith than ever before and they were identifying themselves to the police as Christians.

When we are called upon to take up our cross.

In 2005, I wrote the following article on my website:

I put my nineteen-year-old daughter on a plane to South Africa last month. She is serving in an AIDS orphanage for nine weeks. It was not too emotional for me because I knew she would be home soon. But I wonder how I would feel if she returned with news that God had called her to move to South Africa permanently? At present, it is just an exciting missions adventure; then it would be a major life change. Am I ready for that?

---

[216] A. Sims, ed., *George Mueller: Man of Faith* (Eugene: Wipf and Stock Publishers, 2005), 32.

A few days after contemplating this possibility, I was researching the life of Francis Asbury, the first leader of the Methodist church in America. When Asbury was twenty-six, he responded to John Wesley's call for missionaries to go to America. As he boarded the ship for America, his devout Methodist father wept openly, fearing he would never see his son again.

He never did.

It cut me to the heart when I read that story. I wondered how painful it would be to say goodbye to your son for the last time.

Fortunately, travel has improved since 1771. If my daughter left, I would certainly see her again. But not nearly enough. And what about when she marries and has children? How often would I see my grandchildren?

While reflecting on these things I turned to Jesus' call to discipleship.

Whoever loves father or mother more than me is not worthy of me, and whoever loves son or daughter more than me is not worthy of me. And whoever does not take his cross and follow me is not worthy of me. MATTHEW 10:37-38

I first read these words thirty years ago when I responded to the call to make Jesus the Lord of my life. I was a nineteen-year-old college student with hardly a penny to my name. Sure, I had to surrender everything to him, but there was not much to surrender. But it is different now.

Jesus still wants everything, but it seems there is a lot more to give.

Discipleship gets more costly every year.

On December 13, 2008, my daughter married a South African rugby player, Ernie Kruger. Two weeks later, she boarded a plane to leave for her new life in South Africa. I had no idea when she first left in 2005 that my article would prove to be prophetic.

6.   Is there an answer for human suffering?

Yes. God understands our suffering and is concerned about it.

Then the Lord said, "I have surely seen the affliction of my people who are in Egypt and have heard their cry because of their taskmasters. I know their sufferings." EXODUS 3:7

For he has not despised or abhorred the affliction of the afflicted, and he has not hidden his face from him, but has heard, when he cried to him. PSALM 22:24

Not only is he concerned, but he has an answer: his Word and his promises.

He delivers the afflicted by their affliction and opens their ear by adversity. JOB 36:15

This is my comfort in my affliction, that your promise gives me life. PSALM 119:50

For this light momentary affliction is preparing for us an eternal weight of glory beyond all comparison. 2 CORINTHIANS 4:17

And if children, then heirs—heirs of God and fellow heirs with Christ, provided we suffer with him in order that we may also be glorified with him. ROMANS 8:17